IDIOT'S GUIDES
AS EASY AS IT GETS!

Catholicism

by Julie Young and Fr. Eric Augenstein

ALPHA
A member of Penguin Group (USA) Inc.

To my former teacher and dear friend Mary Helen Eckrich, you were right … my faith is stronger and I learned a lot. —Julie

To my parents, Bernie and Linda Augenstein, who were my first teachers in the ways of faith. —Fr. Eric

ALPHA BOOKS

Published by Penguin Group (USA) Inc.

Penguin Group (USA) Inc., 375 Hudson Street, New York, New York 10014, USA · Penguin Group (Canada), 90 Eglinton Avenue East, Suite 700, Toronto, Ontario M4P 2Y3, Canada (a division of Pearson Penguin Canada Inc.) · Penguin Books Ltd., 80 Strand, London WC2R 0RL, England · Penguin Ireland, 25 St. Stephen's Green, Dublin 2, Ireland (a division of Penguin Books Ltd.) · Penguin Group (Australia), 250 Camberwell Road, Camberwell, Victoria 3124, Australia (a division of Pearson Australia Group Pty. Ltd.) · Penguin Books India Pvt. Ltd., 11 Community Centre, Panchsheel Park, New Delhi—110 017, India · Penguin Group (NZ), 67 Apollo Drive, Rosedale, North Shore, Auckland 1311, New Zealand (a division of Pearson New Zealand Ltd.) · Penguin Books (South Africa) (Pty.) Ltd., 24 Sturdee Avenue, Rosebank, Johannesburg 2196, South Africa · Penguin Books Ltd., Registered Offices: 80 Strand, London WC2R 0RL, England

International Standard Book Number: 978-1-61564-719-4
Library of Congress Catalog Card Number: 2014943320

16 15 14   8 7 6 5 4 3 2 1

Interpretation of the printing code: The rightmost number of the first series of numbers is the year of the book's printing; the rightmost number of the second series of numbers is the number of the book's printing. For example, a printing code of 14-1 shows that the first printing occurred in 2014.

Printed in the United States of America

Note: This publication contains the opinions and ideas of its author. It is intended to provide helpful and informative material on the subject matter covered. It is sold with the understanding that the author and publisher are not engaged in rendering professional services in the book. If the reader requires personal assistance or advice, a competent professional should be consulted. The author and publisher specifically disclaim any responsibility for any liability, loss, or risk, personal or otherwise, which is incurred as a consequence, directly or indirectly, of the use and application of any of the contents of this book.

Most Alpha books are available at special quantity discounts for bulk purchases for sales promotions, premiums, fundraising, or educational use. Special books, or book excerpts, can also be created to fit specific needs. For details, write: Special Markets, Alpha Books, 375 Hudson Street, New York, NY 10014.

Publisher: *Mike Sanders*
Executive Managing Editor: *Billy Fields*
Executive Acquisitions Editor: *Lori Cates Hand*
Development Editor: *John Etchison*
Production Editor: *Jana M. Stefanciosa*

Cover Designer: *Laura Merriman*
Book Designer: *William Thomas*
Indexer: *Heather McNeill*
Layout: *Ayanna Lacey*
Proofreader: *Virginia Vasquez Vought*

Contents

Introduction

The Catholic Church is a 2,000-year-old religious organization instituted by Christ that has a current membership of over 1 billion people worldwide. It measures time by the century rather than the decade. It is known for its ancient rituals, a seemingly exhausting list of rules and regulations, salacious scandals, peculiar practices, and stands on hot-button issues that seem out of touch with the modern world.

"Do you really believe all that stuff?" is a question many Catholics hear throughout their lifetime by well-meaning friends attempting to set them straight. Though there are some differences between Catholicism and other Christian denominations, which we will uncover, at the end of the day "all that stuff" boils down to the same tenets held by Christians everywhere: God is responsible for creation. He sent His only Son Jesus to save humanity from their sins. The Holy Spirit is all around us. And, one day, Christ will come again.

You don't have to break out the Bible or visit the Vatican to learn more about the Catholic faith—although those are both great things to do! These pages offer you a primer on what Catholics believe and how they practice their faith both inside and outside of a church building. If you are already a Catholic, consider this text to be a refresher course. (Especially if you weren't paying attention in class!) If you are not a Catholic, this book will help you better understand the fact behind the fiction and discover what "all that stuff" really is.

How This Book Is Organized

This book is divided into five parts:

Part 1, What Is Catholicism?, will take you on a journey into the universal Church. You will discover what Catholics believe, whom they believe in, and how they profess their faith. You will grasp the concept of the Holy Trinity, find out what's so "different" about the Catholic Bible, and explore the structure of a 2,000-year-old religion that still has much relevance today.

Part 2, The Sacramental Life, requires Catholics to do more than talk the talk, they must also walk the walk—and one of the key ways in which they do that is through the seven sacraments and participation in the Mass. In this part, you will learn how a Catholic is initiated into the faith, which life paths allow them to bring others closer to God, and which sacraments are designed to heal the body, mind, and spirit.

Part 3, Living the Good Life, is about more than going to Mass and participating in the sacraments. Catholics believe they must live their faith by avoiding the near occasion of sin, understanding virtues and vices, and having a working knowledge of Catholic social teaching. We will also look at what Catholics think happens at the end of this life as we explore Heaven, Hell, and whatever may (or may not) come in between.

Part 4, Prayer and Holiness, investigates the importance Catholics place on constant conversation with God. You will find out if Catholics really worship Mary or simply venerate her special role as the mother of Christ. You will learn how Catholics take time out for spiritual growth, and try to understand the Church's unique practice of asking for intercession from an extensive VIP list of deceased souls known as the communion of saints.

Part 5, Catholic Life and Culture, is often a balancing act for members of the faithful. After all, it is an organization that often seems resistant to change but is actually more forward thinking than one might expect. You will see how Catholics live their faith in the information age, where science and religion collide and connect, and how the Church's practices and nuances continue to make a huge impact on the world at large.

We have also included several appendixes, including a conversation with a priest, a glossary of Catholic terms, a quick reference guide to common Catholic prayers, some frequently used abbreviations, and other important facts. In addition, we have provided a list of all the popes throughout the history of the church, as well as a glossary of some of the saints who are shining examples of the faith.

Extras

You will also find several sidebars throughout your reading, which will provide additional context and information you may find helpful. These include:

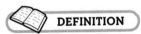 **DEFINITION**

Throughout this book we will use both foreign and familiar terms that have significance in the Catholic Church. We will identify and define these terms according to their canonical meaning.

 CATHOLIC QUOTE

These are direct quotes from famous Catholics (both religious and secular) corresponding to the faith concept discussed within each chapter.

 KEEP IT SIMPLE

Catholicism can be overwhelming, so these sidebars strive to streamline and simplify some of the "big picture" issues being discussed within each chapter.

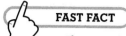

FAST FACT

These quick facts pertaining to the topics covered in each section may dispel misconceptions, clarify key points, and offer interesting insight into the Catholic faith.

Acknowledgments

First and foremost I want to thank Lori Cates Hand for seeking me out for this project, and everyone at Alpha Books. I also want to thank Fr. Eric Augenstein for taking a leap of faith in working with me. Hopefully I didn't try your patience too much! Thank you Sr. Sheila Hackett, OP, for being such a good friend, listening patiently, and offering your wisdom and insight to this project. I must offer a big thank you to my son, Vincent, who offered up his religious materials for my research and did not get mad when I returned them all but destroyed from use. Finally, thank you to every religion teacher I ever had growing up. I know I am responsible for a lot of migraines, but rest assured, I really was paying attention and your efforts were not in vain.
—Julie Young

Throughout my 21 years as a student in Catholic schools, I was blessed with some extraordinary teachers, mentors, and role models who helped me learn about God, the Catholic faith, and how we can live that faith. I am grateful for their example and ministry, particularly the Benedictine monks of Saint Meinrad Archabbey and the De La Salle Christian Brothers. Since being ordained a priest, I have had the opportunity to walk along the journey of life and faith with countless faithful people, who have inspired me to continually grow in wisdom and love. I offer a particular thanks to the people of Our Lady of Perpetual Help Church in New Albany, Indiana—my first pastorate—whose thirst for learning about the Catholic faith inspired me to keep growing myself. Finally, thanks to Fr. Pat Beidelman, Liz Escoffery, and Sr. Eileen Flavin, CSC, some of my current co-workers in ministry, who motivated me throughout this project.
—Fr. Eric Augenstein

Trademarks

All terms mentioned in this book that are known to be or are suspected of being trademarks or service marks have been appropriately capitalized. Alpha Books and Penguin Group (USA) Inc. cannot attest to the accuracy of this information. Use of a term in this book should not be regarded as affecting the validity of any trademark or service mark.

What Is Catholicism?

When you think about the Catholic Church, what images come to mind? Do you picture ornate buildings laden with graphic crucifixes, dripping candles, bowls of holy water, and a few creepy statues? Do you envision over-the-top rituals led by an incense-waving priest bedecked in vestments while a band of genuflecting, guilt-ridden devotees kneel in prayer? Perhaps you've heard whispers that Catholicism is a non-Christian, anti-science religious institution that worships multiple gods, reads from a different Bible, and believes their earthly leader to be infallible in all things.

No matter what your perception and understanding of the universal Church, chances are you know only part of the story—and if you've picked up this book, you have a desire to learn more. In this part, you will discover what the Catholic Church is, what they believe, and more importantly whom they believe in. You will find that in spite of the many misconceptions surrounding the Church, Catholicism is really no different than most other monotheistic Christian denominations around the world.

What Do Catholics Believe?

The heart of Catholicism lies in the belief that our sole purpose on Earth is to know, love, and serve God. It is from Him that we come into this plane of existence, and it is to Him that we hope to return someday. Like many other religions, Catholics believe that God is the alpha and omega of the universe and that He made us out of pure, unselfish love and placed upon our hearts a desire to seek Him.

In order to pursue God, Catholics believe they have to receive the gift of faith—the complete trust in God's existence even if it lacks scientific proof. Faith is the superpower that not only allows us to grasp this abstract idea, but also is essential to enjoying an interactive relationship with God in this lifetime and earning redemption in the hereafter.

It's an awesome concept for the mortal mind, but in this chapter, we will unravel the mysterious nature of faith and help you understand the core tenets and principles Catholics use to lead faith-filled lives.

In This Chapter

- Exploring the mystery of faith
- Understanding why we believe
- Seeking a personal relationship with God
- Examples of faith in action
- Expressing our beliefs in the Creeds

What Is Faith?

Humans have a natural inclination to look for things they cannot see and to understand the things that defy logic. Think about it: when a cool breeze moves through an enclosed room on a winter's day, we immediately search for the source of the draft. After eliminating the obvious explanations for the cold (open door, window, poor weather stripping, and so on …), we do not conclude that the breeze did not exist. We know it was there because we encountered it. We felt the cold air. Our body temperature dropped slightly. Perhaps we saw the curtains rustle or papers flutter in response to the breeze. We bore witness to the effects of the wind's presence and therefore believe in its reality. We take it on *faith*.

Faith is a belief in something when common sense tells you it's not possible. It is the internal knowledge in the probability of a truth no matter how illogical it may sound to others.

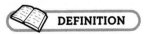 **DEFINITION**

Faith is the complete knowledge and trust in something that lacks empirical proof.

In religious and spiritual matters, faith is the component that enables us to connect to the idea of God and begin a relationship with Him. Faith cannot conclusively prove God's existence beyond our personal satisfaction, but it does give us the ability to open our minds and embrace subjects that are challenging to the human mind. Like our example of the wind, faith begins with an encounter that encourages an individual to seek out the source of the experience and develop a better understanding of what is unknown. As backward as this may sound, faith is not found in the act of inquiry, but rather it is the response to the proposed situation.

Let me make this a little easier for you. Consider for a moment the fact that man cannot fly. We have no wings. We are not lighter than air, and for all intents and purposes, we cannot defy gravity. However, each year millions of us board airplanes that weigh far more than we do. Why? We do this based on a faith in the principles of aeronautical science.

We don't have to understand the mechanics of jet engines to get on a plane: we do it because we have encountered planes in the air, we have talked with people who have flown, and we have absolute confidence that it is a viable form of transportation. Of course we know the risks that come with our decisions, but ultimately it comes down to whether or not we have faith in the applied technology and the belief that this plane can travel through the sky and get us to where we want to go.

 **CATHOLIC QUOTE**

Faith means putting up with God's incomprehensibility for a lifetime.

–Karl Rahner

Faith is the prerequisite to a belief in a Higher Power that challenges everything you think you know. You can't begin a dialogue with someone if you aren't sure they exist, and you can't believe in this unseen presence if you haven't encountered it in some way. However, once you do encounter God, faith becomes the gift that takes the pressure off and allows you to place your confidence in Him. Faith isn't perfect, and neither are we, but it is only through faith that we can experience a being beyond all comprehension and begin to contemplate His plan for us and our lives.

 KEEP IT SIMPLE

Faith is a gift that comes from God. It cannot be forced upon someone who doesn't want it, but it can be given even if someone doesn't ask for it (such as in the case of an infant baptism). In order for our faith to grow, we must respond to this gift and God's help in making it stronger. Faith develops over a lifetime but remains incomplete unless it results in acts of love, and ultimately faith is essential to the development of our personal relationship with God.

An Affirmative Response to God

For most people, mere faith in the existence of God is not enough to sustain and satisfy them, but by reading the Sacred Scriptures they can learn more about the Almighty and what He stands for before believing in Him and investing their faith in His divine plan.

This is a little tricky because it's not as if God is a political candidate canvasing the neighborhood for votes. While He would like to have us on board with His blueprint for the universe and welcomes our collaboration, the truth is He doesn't need us and He's not going to ply us with promises in hopes that we find Him to be the right deity for the job. He's already got the gig and He can't be overthrown, so it's up to the believer to come to the table ready to get behind His existing platform.

In order to begin this spiritual journey, one must desire a personal relationship with God and be ready to accept the validity of what He has to show them. It isn't always easy, but God doesn't promise that it will be. In fact, He assures us that it is quite difficult. Believing in God as a Christian requires one to stake his or her entire life on a 2,000-year-old message told by a 30-something Galilean they believe to be God incarnate.

Believing in God means reconciling perceived contradictions between fact and those things that go beyond natural understanding. It means you must unlearn what you think you know. As a Christian, you will not be told to ignore scientific discovery. In fact, the Catholic Church promotes it. But in doing so, it also promotes the fact that there are some things that are simply beyond our comprehension, and that above all things, there is God. He is in charge, the world cannot continue without Him, and He alone is keeping everything in existence according to His divine plan.

Finally, believing does not mean going at it alone. As a member of the Christian faith, you join billions of others throughout the centuries who have subscribed to the same philosophies as you and on whose faith you can lean when the going gets rough. The Catholic Church believes faith is personal, but it's far from private. Faith is to be shared and celebrated as a community of God who can stand together and say, "We Believe."

Stories of Faith

Church history abounds with tales of those who have encountered God's presence in their lives and put all of their chips, so to speak, on His goodness. They may be confused by God's call at times. They may even question His plan; but once committed, they are all in and they rarely look back. Here are just two stories that serve as models of faith in our own lives.

Abraham

Known as the father of the Hebrew nation, Abraham (formerly Abram) was 75 years old when God called him to leave his father's homeland and embark on a blind journey to the land of Canaan with his aged and barren wife Sarah (formerly Sari). Rather than say he was too old or he was too busy to consider this command, Abraham agreed. Thus begins Abraham's close and interactive relationship with God, who makes a *covenant* with His devoted servant that from him will come a multitude of descendants that will cover the earth like dust.

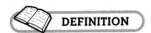 **DEFINITION**

A **covenant** is an agreement between God and His people.

Abraham is intrigued but confused by God's words. How can he be the father of nations when his wife is old and infertile? In an effort to riddle out this divine revelation, Abraham surmises that he will have to name one of his slaves as his heir, but God tells Abraham that it will be a child of his own who will carry on the family name. With his wife's blessing, Abraham impregnates an Egyptian slave named Hagar who gives birth to Ishmael, the son Abraham believes to be his biological successor. Once again, God tells Abraham that he's gotten it wrong and that in spite of her physical condition, it will be Sarah who will conceive and bear a son, that he will be called Isaac, and that it is this child who will be the first in a long line of descendants.

When Sarah hears this, she is skeptical to say the least, but Abraham puts his trust in God, and two seasons later Isaac is born. The couple is thrilled that God has kept His word, but that joy turns to sorrow when God commands Abraham to sacrifice his beloved son's life to Him:

> "Take your son, your only son Isaac, whom you love, and go to the land of Moriah, and offer him there as a burnt offering on one of the mountains that I shall show you." (Genesis 22:2)

It's the kind of request that would cause many parents to become atheists; however, Abraham's faith in God never falters. The following day, he leads Isaac to the designated place and prepares to slaughter the boy. Just before Abraham sinks his knife into Isaac's flesh, an angel calls out from the heavens:

> "Do not lay your hand on the boy or do anything to him; for now I know that you fear God, since you have not withheld your son, your only son, from me." (Genesis 22:12)

It is a bizarre test of loyalty that baffles the human mind. While God never explains His peculiar request, He is so impressed with Abraham's faithfulness that He reaffirms His covenant with him and promises once again that He will make Abraham's offspring as numerous as the stars in the sky. It is the last conversation that is recorded between the two.

However, Abraham isn't the only character in the Old Testament to display an unusual amount of trust in God. There is one man who begrudgingly remains faithful to the Almighty even when his entire world is falling apart around him. His name is Job.

Job

The story of Job is a literary masterpiece that is unlike any other book in the Bible. It reads like a Greek tragedy and is full of beautiful poetry and imagery as it tries to answer the age-old question, "Why do bad things happen to good people?"

In the beginning, Job is a wealthy, benevolent landowner who is also a faithful servant of God. He knows that if he speaks ill of the Father, he will surely die, and God is impressed by Job's level of loyalty. However, in a few short verses, Job becomes the central character in a strange wager between God and *Satan*.

 **DEFINITION**

The word **Satan** comes from a Hebrew term meaning "adversary."

Satan proposes that even the most steadfast servant would curse God if enough misery befell him. God replies that some probably would, but not his servant Job, whose faith is stronger than most. Satan accepts this challenge and with God's approval proceeds to put Job through a battery of tests in an effort to prove his theory.

Job loses everything. His children die. He is rendered bankrupt. His health suffers and he is covered in boils. Still, he never strikes back at God for the cards that have been dealt to him. Rather, he praises Him saying, "The Lord gave and the Lord has taken away; blessed be the name of the Lord." (Job 1:21)

After losing everything he had worked so hard to achieve, three of Job's friends arrive to commiserate with him. During a lengthy visit, they encourage Job to examine his conscience. Surely he has done something to attract the wrath of God. But Job insists that he has always been a righteous man and has done nothing to deserve this.

But Job is bothered by the "why" of it all and in dramatic fashion calls God out on the subject. He suggests that perhaps God has made a mistake and mounts a defense in his case worthy of Atticus Finch.

> "Let me be weighed in a just balance, and let God know my integrity!—if my step has turned aside from the way, and my heart has followed my eyes, and if any spot has clung to my hands; then let me sow, and another eat …" (Job 31:6-8)

It is a bold demand, but even this challenge is not blasphemous. It is merely a question, and after listening to Job's woe-is-me lament, God remarkably answers his cries.

> "Where were you when I laid the foundation of the earth? Tell me if you have understanding. Who determined its measurements?—surely you know! Or who stretched the line upon it? On what were its bases sunk, or who laid its cornerstone when the morning stars sang together and all the heavenly beings shouted for joy?" (Job 38:4-7)

His words are mysterious and they do little to allay Job's concerns, but they do serve to show how little we understand about the mind of God. Job apologizes for his outburst, but God is not angry that he questioned Him. In fact, He is angry with Job's friends for suggesting that Job's fate was a result of his own wickedness as opposed to mere happenstance.

 CATHOLIC QUOTE

The noblest power of man is reason. The highest goal of reason is the knowledge of God.

—St. Albert the Great

God is also impressed that even though Job questions Him, he never rebukes Him, which means that Satan has lost his bet. The book ends happily. God makes up for Job's losses twice over and the story serves as a reminder that faith and belief in God cannot come and go in times of feast and famine, but must remain solid throughout our lives. We must say what we mean and mean what we say every day of our lives.

But how do we profess a belief that is impossible to understand? How can we put these complex principles into words that we can lean on in good times and in bad?

The Creed: The Church's Mission Statement

If you've ever wondered exactly what a Catholic believes, the Apostles' Creed is a good place to start. This *creed* is the bedrock upon which the Church was built and serves as a manifesto for the faithful. Catholics know faith is far more than blind trust in a lot of immaterial concepts. It is the firm conviction in the reality of those intangible theories, and in order to articulate this conviction, the Church developed a faith formula to summarize the essential beliefs held by Christians throughout the world. The Church recognizes two creeds as the central faith formulas from which all other beliefs derive: the Apostles' Creed and the Nicene Creed.

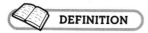 **DEFINITION**

A **creed** is a formal statement of Church beliefs, doctrine, or ideology.

While it is unclear if the apostles of Jesus actually penned their declaration of belief in any kind of formal way, it is generally accepted that the Apostles' Creed was based on the theology found in the Gospels as well as the teachings of the apostles in the latter half of the first century. The earliest version of the Creed was found around the year 215, in the Apostolic Tradition of Hippolytus, but the concept of a faith formula was not developed after the time of Christ. Rather, it was a direct order from Jesus to His followers:

> "Go therefore and make disciples of all nations, baptizing them in the name of the Father and of the Son and of the Holy Spirit." (Matthew 28:19)

For a number of years, this Creed served as the foundation of the Church until the issue of Jesus' divinity threatened to tear Christianity down the middle. There were those who believed Jesus was in fact the incarnation of God on Earth and others who believed Jesus was a human being promoted to God-like status thanks to his perfect devotion to the Father.

In AD 325, Emperor Constantine knew something had to be done. As the first Christian emperor in Rome, he couldn't have any conflict on this crucial principle. He convened the First Council of Nicaea to establish a consensus on what the Christian movement believed and what texts would be included in the official doctrine. It was a heavy topic to be sure, but after much debate the theologians concluded that Jesus was one with God, and they expanded the Creed to establish this conviction once and for all. The result was the Nicene Creed, the most widely used profession of faith in Christianity.

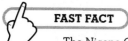 **FAST FACT**

The Nicene Creed is sometimes known as the Niceno-Constantinopolitan Creed because it was finalized at the First Council of Constantinople in 381.

Aside from the Catholic Church, both creeds are used widely and can be found in some form in the Eastern Orthodox Church, the Church of the East, the Oriental Orthodox churches, the Anglican Communion, and most protestant denominations. The Church revised the English translation in 2011 for the third edition of *The Roman Missal,* the book of prayers used at Mass, and there are some variations throughout the Christian denominations, but one word that remains is the word *catholic.* This term (when not capitalized) does not refer to the Church led by the pope, but rather a universal community of God.

DEFINITION

The word **catholic** comes from the Greek word *Katholikos,* meaning "universal" or "concerning the whole."

The Twelve Precepts of the Catholic Creeds

Eight of the twelve articles in the Creeds concern the acknowledgment of a single Supreme Being who is able to hold three distinct forms at the same time: the Father, the Son, and the Holy Spirit.

God the Father is the unseen cloud-dwelling, all-powerful patriarch responsible for the creation of the heavens, the earth, and everything within them. The Son was begotten of the Father before time began, and while the Son is a separate facet of the Trinity, He is also one with the Father. The Creed asserts a belief that God the Father sent His Son down from Heaven to be born through divine intervention into a working-class Jewish family where he was raised by kind, faithful parents and grew up enjoying an existence that was both fully human and fully divine.

Like the Father and the Son, the Holy Spirit has always been in existence, is an equal part of the Trinity, and is not separate from the other two. The Holy Spirit is God's lasting presence in the hearts, minds, and lives of His people on Earth and is what helps keep their faith strong in times of turmoil. The Holy Spirit inspired the Sacred Scriptures as well as other theological texts, and is the energy that calls God's people into service and action. It is through the Holy Spirit that Christians are able to find inner peace and fulfillment in their spiritual lives. The Holy Spirit is the essence of God that not only helps connect his followers but also brings them into a deeper relationship with Him.

CATHOLIC QUOTE

Let the Creed be like a mirror for you. Look for yourself in it to see whether you really believe all that you claim to believe. And rejoice every day in your faith.

—St. Augustine

The last section of the Creed concerns the belief in a universal Church that relies completely on the Holy Trinity to sustain it, a communal body of holy people, both living and deceased, one sacramental baptism for the forgiveness of sins, and Jesus' promise of life after death.

The Apostles' Creed

I believe in God,

the Father almighty,

Creator of heaven and earth,

And in Jesus Christ, his only Son, our Lord,

who was conceived by the Holy spirit,

born of the Virgin Mary,

suffered under Pontius Pilate,

was crucified, died and was buried;

he descended into hell;

on the third day he rose again from the dead;

he ascended into heaven,

and is seated at the right hand of God the Father Almighty;

from there he will come to judge the living and the dead.

I believe in the Holy Spirit,

the holy catholic Church,

the communion of saints,

the forgiveness of sins,

the resurrection of the body,

and life everlasting. Amen.

The Nicene Creed

I believe in one God,

the father almighty,

maker of heaven and earth,

of all things visible and invisible.

I believe in one Lord Jesus Christ,

the only Begotten Son of God,

born of the Father before all ages.

God from God, Light from Light,

true God from true God,

begotten, not made, consubstantial with the Father;

through him all things were made.

For us men and for our salvation

He came down from heaven,

and by the Holy Spirit was incarnate of the Virgin Mary,

and became man.

For our sake he was crucified under Pontius Pilate,

He suffered death and was buried,

and rose again on the third day

in accordance with the Scriptures.

He ascended into heaven

and is seated at the right hand of the Father.

He will come again in glory

to judge the living and the dead

and his kingdom will have no end.

I believe in the Holy Spirit, the Lord, the giver of Life,

who proceeds from the Father and the Son,

who with the father and the Son is adored and glorified,

who has spoken through the prophets.

I believe in one holy catholic and apostolic Church,

I confess one baptism for the forgiveness of sins

and I look forward to the resurrection of the dead

and the life of the world to come. Amen.

The Least You Need to Know

- Faith is the belief in something that common sense tells you is impossible.
- In the Catholic perspective, faith is a gift that comes from God and must be accepted of one's own free will.
- An affirmative response to the offer of faith enables one to believe in the idea of God.
- Faith is developed and nurtured over a lifetime and is often tested.
- Creeds are the faith formulas from which all doctrinal beliefs come.
- The Catholic Church recognizes two creeds as its official faith formulas: the Apostles' Creed and the Nicene Creed.

The Holy Trinity

It is the crux of Christian belief and a divine mystery that cannot be properly comprehended by the human mind. The Holy Trinity is the name Christians give to their belief that God makes himself known in three distinct ways: as Father, Son, and Holy Spirit. It's a theological notion that sounds incredible, requires a tremendous amount of faith, and forces believers to see God in a unique way.

In this chapter, we will go behind the burning bush to meet God the Father. We'll walk in the footsteps of Jesus and learn how a simple carpenter from Galilee was both human and divine. And finally we will encounter the Holy Spirit, the essence of God who has a profound impact on the lives of believers everywhere.

We will answer some questions and raise others as we grapple with an impossible idea within the scope of mortal imagination: the three faces of God.

In This Chapter

- God the Father, maker of Heaven and Earth
- Jesus Christ, fully human and fully divine
- The Holy Spirit: the essence of God within us
- What it means to be three persons but one God

God: The Father Almighty

He is the answer to the question, "Who made us?" and like other Christian faiths, Catholics believe He is the all-powerful source from whom all things come. Infinitely perfect and without beginning or end, He is the Supreme Being in charge of keeping everything in existence according to His divine plan. He is God.

"God" is a small word, but He is hardly a short subject. His reality is largely a matter of faith. His physical location is a mystery and scientific evidence of Him remains elusive, yet an overwhelming number of people believe God is the divine being who transcends all that we know and understand about the universe. They cling fervently to the idea that they have been put on this Earth to serve Him.

Creator of Heaven and Earth

The creation story in the first chapter of the Book of Genesis is one of the first Bible stories we hear as children and one of the first ways we encounter the awesome power of God. (It is also one of the first stories we question, but more about that in Chapter 18.) We are told that the earth was an unformed void of darkness until God flipped the switch and shed light on the situation. After He separated the darkness from the light and the day from the night, we are told that God spent the next 120 hours constructing the heavens, the earth, and everything within them before taking a day off.

The Genesis accounts do more than set the stage for the belief in God's existence. They offered early cultures a basic understanding of the world's sequence of development, and illustrated how everything was called into being as part of a well-organized, well-ordered plan that reflects God's goodness and beauty.

Man: God's Corporeal Creature

The apex of the creation story occurs when God forms the first human beings and breathes life into them. Humans are the only creature made in the image and likeness of God, meaning that we were created with free will and an immortal *soul*, giving us a special connection with God and enabling us to grow in our understanding of Him and in holiness.

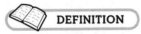 **DEFINITION**

The **soul** is the part of a human being that is immortal and is the presence of God within us. The soul is unique to each individual, has its origin at the moment of each person's conception, and continues to live on after death.

After God created the first humans and settled them in the Garden of Eden where they were expected to live communally with all other life forms, it wasn't long before Adam and Eve disobeyed a rule God had given about not eating from the tree of knowledge of good and evil:

> "So when the woman saw that the tree was good for food, and that it was a delight to the eyes, and that the tree was to be desired to make one wise, she took of its fruit and ate; and she also gave some to her husband, who was with her, and he ate." (Genesis 3:6)

No matter if you have heard that this event involves an apple, nudity, or a talking snake, the point of the story is that man and woman made the conscious choice to reject the will of God and give in to *Original Sin.*

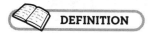 **DEFINITION**

Original Sin refers to people's natural inclination to reject the will of God in favor of their own selfish desires and personal satisfaction.

God knows that the human race is imperfect, and yet He remains faithful to humans even when they turn away from Him or fall into sin. Throughout the Old Testament, He continued to reveal Himself to humanity. He made a covenant with Noah regarding all the living things on Earth. As we saw in Chapter 1, He called Abraham to be the father of many nations, and in the Book of Exodus, he called to Moses from a burning bush on a mountainside and asked the exile in Egypt to be the liberator of the Israelites.

He revealed His mysterious name *Yahweh,* and on the summit of Mt. Sinai, God handed over His Ten Commandments and made a new covenant with His people. This was the same covenant the prophets called the faithful to renew while readying themselves for the promised Savior and Redeemer who would fulfill the Scriptures, establish a new and everlasting covenant with God's people, and take their sins as His own.

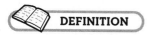 **DEFINITION**

Yahweh is the name God revealed to Moses when asked, "Whom shall I say sent me?" Its translation means "I Am Who I Am."

The Only Begotten Son

Most people associate the second "face" of the Trinity with the life, death, and resurrection of Jesus of Nazareth, but in reality, it's a little more complicated than that. God the Son predates His human form by quite a few years. The Son of God was *begotten* of the Father before time began and while He is a separate facet of the Trinity, He is one with the Father as well. Christians believe that, in the early years of the first century, God sent His divine son to live as a human being among His people and usher in the Kingdom of God on Earth.

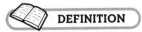 **DEFINITION**

> **Begotten** is a term meaning to give rise to or to create. However, in the matter of the Holy Trinity, it explains the existence of God the Son outside our understanding of creation.

Nearly everything we know and accept about the life of Jesus comes from the Gospels of Matthew, Mark, Luke, and John; however, these books are not biographies. They do not provide a physical description of Jesus. Each Gospel tells different stories from the life of Jesus. They differ from one another on key details. They focus almost exclusively on the last three years of His life and proffer more questions than answers. Still, they offer the primary insight into the life of this incredible individual who changed history during His brief 33 years on Earth.

The Early Years

The prophets foretold the *Messiah's* arrival for hundreds of years before Jesus was born. But for most Christians, the story of Jesus begins when the angel Gabriel appears to a 14-year-old girl named Mary from the town of Nazareth and tells her that she has found favor with God.

> "You will conceive in your womb and bear a son, and you will name him Jesus. He will be great, and will be called the Son of the Most High, and the Lord God will give to him the throne of his ancestor David. He will reign over the house of Jacob forever, and of his kingdom there will be no end." (Luke 1:31-33)

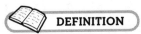 **DEFINITION**

> The word **Messiah** comes from the Hebrew word meaning "anointed one." Christ is the Greek translation of Messiah.

The Gospel of Luke tells us that Mary is confused by this pronouncement and asks how she can become a mother when she is an unmarried virgin. The angel explains to her that she will conceive via the Holy Spirit and that she will remain unspoiled. After hearing this, Mary complies saying, "Here am I, the servant of the Lord; let it be with me according to your word." (Luke 1:38)

Upon hearing the news, Mary pays a visit to her aged cousin Elizabeth, who was surprised to learn via an angel that she, too, is expecting a son. (This son would become known as John the Baptist.) Although the two celebrate, Mary also faces the unpleasant task of having to confide her condition to her fiancé, Joseph. Joseph finds Mary's story more than a little hard to believe, and plans to quietly call off the wedding until an angel appears to him in a dream and tells him that Mary's story is true and it's appropriate for him to take the girl as his wife. From that moment on, Joseph is completely on board and accepts his role in Jesus' life. He and Mary are in Bethlehem when she goes into labor, and from the moment the child is born, Joseph raises Him as his own son.

FAST FACT

A debate rages over the age of Joseph at the time of the birth of Jesus. While some scholars say he could not have been more than 30 years old, others think he may have been an elderly widower with grown children of his own.

Interestingly, only two of the Gospels contain any information about Jesus' early days, and each Gospel contains different details and stories. It is from a combination of the two that we have the "Christmas pageant" version of the story. Luke's Gospel offers the narrative of the angelic visitation, the census, the inn, the shepherds, and the idea that Jesus was born in a stable. He also includes the story of the presentation in the temple when Jesus was a week old, as well as the finding of Jesus in the temple when He was 12. In contrast, Matthew's Gospel includes the Magi, the Star, Herod's slaughter of the innocents, and the Holy Family's flight into Egypt. There is no mention of Jesus' childhood at all.

Cohesion among the Gospels more or less begins with the ministry of John the Baptist, the baptism of Jesus in the Jordan River at the age of 30, and his entry into public life.

God and Man

Although Jesus lived and worked as a human, he was in fact God incarnate. He did not abandon one form for the other, and while God the Son was on Earth, God the Father was still in Heaven. This is a mystery of faith that must be taken at face value. Jesus extends into God and even though He worked with human hands, He allowed His human mind to be developed, and He possessed a human heart, He was keenly aware of His connection to the Father and relied on His Holy Spirit to guide his decisions as a "mortal" man.

KEEP IT SIMPLE

Though it's a bit simplistic, we can think of Jesus' presence as an episode of *Undercover Boss*. Though He looked like one of us and acted like one of us, He was not one of us. He was God experiencing the human condition He had created.

Nazareth's Famous Son

Jesus didn't become a Galilean superstar overnight. In fact, his ministry had a rocky start. After being baptized by John the Baptist, Jesus retreats into the desert for 40 days before returning to Nazareth ready to announce the coming of the Kingdom of God. This does not go over well. When the neighbors hear Mary and Joseph's son make his radical proclamations, they label him insane and plan to throw Him off a cliff. Rather than hang around where He is not wanted, Jesus heads out of town and begins assembling a motley band of apostles ranging from followers of John the Baptist, those who feel inspired by His words, and others who need a little extra convincing. One by one, they leave their families and friends behind in order to follow Jesus and help Him spread His message.

Jesus' first miracle occurs at the Wedding of Cana, during which His mother informs him that the hosts have run out of wine. He demurs, unwilling to draw attention to Himself, but Mary summons the servants over and instructs them to do whatever her son tells them. He calls for some nearby jars and orders them to be filled with water. He then tells the servants to take the water to the chief steward, who discovers that the liquid has turned into wine.

> "The steward called the bridegroom and said to him, 'Everyone serves the good wine first and then the inferior wine after the guests have become drunk, but you have kept the good wine until now.'" (John 2:9-10)

For the next three years, Jesus travels throughout the region preaching to anyone who will listen. His message goes against the grain of conventional thinking. His words focus on tolerance, forgiveness, and love. He tells *parables*, or stories laced with moral lessons, such as the parables of the Mustard Seed, the Prodigal Son, and the Good Samaritan. He offers his followers the Beatitudes. He heals the sick. He feeds the hungry. He consorts with undesirables such as tax collectors and sinners, and it isn't long before His words draw the ire of the local leaders who not only question by whose authority Jesus performs His miraculous works, but also question rumors that this simple Nazarene could be the promised "King of the Jews" sent to usher in the Kingdom of God on Earth.

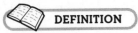 **DEFINITION**

A **parable** is a story with a moral lesson found often in the Gospels.

So You Are the Christ?

When Jesus entered Jerusalem to celebrate Passover with His followers, He was a marked man. Fed up with His walking on water, raising Lazarus from the dead, and whispers that He could be the promised Messiah or "Christ," the authorities are keen to silence Jesus once and for all.

Jesus knows this, but rather than make a quiet entry into the city, He opts to ride on the back of a donkey, fulfilling Zechariah's prophecy that the king of Jerusalem would arrive in such a manner. It's a bold move, and one that says "accept me or reject me; this is it." However, Jesus doesn't stop there. He causes chaos in the temple, providing the high priests with the opening they have been waiting for. There is a concerted effort to trap Jesus in a no-win situation by forcing him to make a heretical statement. However, Jesus sees through this plot and answers their questions in such a way that he avoids the snare.

> "'Teacher, which commandment in the law is the greatest?' He said to him, 'You shall love the Lord your God with all your heart, and with all your soul, and with all your mind.' This is the greatest and first commandment. And a second is like it: 'You shall love your neighbor as yourself.' On these two commandments hang all the law and the prophets." (Matthew 22:36-40)

Unable to muffle the charismatic preacher and fearful of his growing popularity, authorities begin to look for any opportunity to arrest Jesus. They find it when Judas Iscariot, one of Jesus' 12 apostles, offers to help them.

Little is known about Judas Iscariot. He is the only one of the 12 apostles to have been designated with a second name, though it is unclear if the word refers to a surname, the place of his birth, or a nickname given to him by the others. It is believed that he was the treasurer of the group who became disillusioned with Jesus' ministry, and it was he who approached the priests with an offer to betray his friend. Unable to live with what he had done, Judas later committed suicide.

A few days after their arrival in Jerusalem, Jesus and His followers gather in the upper room of a house for their Passover meal. It is during this event that Jesus speaks the words that become central to the celebration of the Eucharist found in the Catholic Mass: "This is my body, which is given for you. Do this in remembrance of me." And he did the same with the cup after supper, saying, "This cup that is poured out for you is the new covenant in my blood ...." (Luke 22:19-20)

After dinner, the assembly moves to the Garden of Gethsemane. When the apostles fall asleep, Jesus ponders what is to come. He offers an impassioned prayer to get out of what is sure to be a messy death, but accepts that it is not His will but the Heavenly Father's will which must be done. He no sooner finishes His prayer than Judas approaches with the soldiers, who promptly arrest Jesus and take Him before the high priest Caiaphas.

What ensues is a tedious back and forth among those eager to do away with Jesus, but unwilling to have His blood on their hands. The high priest misconstrues the answer to "Are you the Messiah?" as an affirmative and sends the blaspheming Jesus off to Pontius Pilate for sentencing. However, Pilate is hesitant to condemn Jesus and, in the Gospel of Luke, passes the case off to Herod. Herod does nothing but mock the Galilean before sending Him back to Pilate, who ultimately signs Jesus' death warrant.

It is a grisly execution. Jesus is flogged, mocked, spat upon, forced to carry a heavy wooden beam to the place of His death, nailed to a cross, and left to hang for three hours until His body succumbs to asphyxiation. His side is pierced to confirm His expiration and under ordinary circumstances, He probably would not have been removed from the beam, but left for the local wildlife to finish off. The Gospels tell us that a wealthy disciple of Jesus named Joseph of Arimathea requested the body from Pilate, and when his request was granted, he covered Jesus' body in a cloth and laid Him in a private tomb.

CATHOLIC QUOTE

Apart from the cross, there is no other ladder by which we get to heaven.

—St. Rose of Lima

The Resurrection

After the burial, Pilate learns that Jesus may be more dangerous dead than alive. The Pharisees warn him of a prophecy in which Jesus claimed He would rise after three days, and they encourage Pilate to place a guard by the sealed tomb lest the apostles try to steal the body in the middle of the night.

He agrees, but 72 hours later, the guards have fallen asleep and the rock used to seal the tomb has been rolled away. Three women who have come to anoint Jesus' body find nothing but an empty tomb and are confused as to what has happened. Accounts of the first Easter differ among the Gospels, but all agree that Jesus rose from the dead, and over the next 40 days appeared throughout Galilee to His apostles and friends before ascending into Heaven and taking His place at the right hand of the Father.

KEEP IT SIMPLE

Through the resurrection, Jesus as God conquered death and illustrates to all of us that death is not the end of our existence but our transcendence into eternal life with God.

The Holy Spirit

Just before His ascension, Jesus tells his apostles that they will "receive power when the Holy Spirit has come upon you; and you will be my witnesses in Jerusalem, in all Judea and Samaria, and to the ends of the earth." (Acts 1:8) When the day of *Pentecost* arrives, the 12 apostles (now joined by Matthias, who was chosen to replace Judas) are hiding in the upper room. They hear a rush of wind and witness tongues of fire descending upon them, giving them the ability to speak the languages they need to take the Christian ministry global.

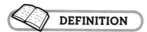 **DEFINITION**

> **Pentecost** is the Jewish Festival of the Weeks celebrated by Christians as the day the Holy Spirit came to the apostles.

The Holy Spirit is the hardest aspect of the Trinity to explain. He does not appear as a person or have a physical form, but is the essence of God who lives and works within the lives of the faithful. Like the other two, the Holy Spirit is not a separate entity but something that is an equal facet of the whole.

In the Catholic Church, the gifts of the Holy Spirit are conferred on a Christian during the Sacrament of Confirmation. However, it is not as though the Holy Spirit has not already been working in our life. It is our knowledge that the third person of the Trinity is there to help us live a Christ-filled life. Confirmation is the completion of one's initiation into the Christian community, the final instructions before we go forth like the apostles did to spread the good news of Jesus.

Saint Patrick and the Shamrock

The idea of three persons in one divine being is hard to understand and even more difficult to profess. The word "trinity" isn't even mentioned in the Bible, although Jesus does allude to it in His commissioning of the apostles, and St. Paul clearly refers to the Father, Son, and Holy Spirit in his letters. The third-century north-African theologian Tertullian was the first person to use the word "Trinity" to explain the relationship between the three persons in one God.

He proposed that the "Father and Son and Spirit are three, however, not in status but in rank, not in substance but in form, not in power but in appearance; they are however of one substance and of one status and of one power, because God is one, from whom these ranks and forms and appearances are designated."

However, it is St. Patrick of Ireland who offered the simplest illustration of what the Trinity is and how it functions using the Emerald Isle's national flower, the shamrock.

There are various theories as to how this fifth-century bishop used the plant to explain the Trinity, but it proved to be a modest visualization tool that creates a comparison between a single plant with three leaves and three persons within a single God. St. Patrick's analogy proved to be a simple method for explaining a deep theological concept and is one of the most widely used to this day.

The Least You Need to Know

- God the Father is responsible for the creation of Heaven and Earth.
- Humans are the only beings made in the image of God.
- God sent His Son to save the world from Original Sin.
- Jesus was conceived by the power of the Holy Spirit. His mortal life lasted for 33 years and ended in execution.
- Jesus sent the Holy Spirit to fill the apostles and enable them to spread the good news.
- The Holy Trinity is a difficult concept to understand, but can be explained by using Saint Patrick's symbol of the shamrock.

The Bible

When it comes to a riveting tale packed with drama, romance, action, controversy, intrigue, and mystery, few books can hold a candle to the Holy Bible. The Bible is truly the greatest story ever compiled, and contrary to a popular misconception, Catholics believe in it, read it frequently, and use it in their various liturgies and rituals.

Like other faith traditions, Catholics believe that through the Sacred Scriptures, God speaks to His people in words they can understand. It is through these words that God reveals His plan of goodness and fulfills it through His Son Jesus Christ.

In this chapter, we will leaf through the best-selling book of all time. We will explore the Old and New Testaments, find out what makes the Catholic Bible "different," meet key contributors, and understand how the Scriptures are interpreted and how they fit into the living tradition of the Church.

In This Chapter

- The assembly of the Bible
- The Old Testament reveals God's plan to humanity
- The New Testament is the fulfillment of God's promises
- What is the apocrypha?
- The Biblical message impacts the apostolic tradition

The Catholic Bible

The Catholic Bible is comprised of the Old and New Testaments found in other Christian faith traditions, and like those other traditions, Catholics believe that the Bible is the divinely inspired word of God. Although the individual books of the Bible were penned by numerous writers over thousands of years, the text was directed by the Holy Spirit and therefore authored by God.

The Bible is not designed to be a record of historic events (though there is some history included within the pages), but rather a conglomeration of cultural tradition, social commentary, philosophy, poetry, prayer, letters, and moral values that was transmitted originally via oral tradition and later in writing.

The Catholic Bible was assembled over several councils and hundreds of years through the wisdom of the Magisterium, or teaching office of the Church. The Magisterium is made up of the pope and the bishops, whose job it is to determine which texts should be included in the official *canon* of the Church and how those texts should be interpreted by the faithful.

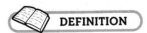

DEFINITION

A **canon** is an official law of the Church or a list that meets certain criteria. It comes from the Greek word *kanon,* meaning "rule" or "measuring stick."

This was not an easy process. After all, it wasn't as if Jesus left behind a list of important points He wanted to include in the final manuscript or who among His disciples possessed the writing talent of C.S. Lewis. As a result, the Magisterium had to cull through and evaluate hundreds of texts floating throughout the Mediterranean in hopes of finding a consensus on Messianic philosophy that they believed was inspired by God.

In order to select the books to be included in the Catholic Bible, theologians:

- Studied the texts in hopes of understanding the intents of the individual authors.
- Studied the culture in which they lived and the message God hoped to reveal in His words.
- Took into consideration the times and conditions under which the texts were written.
- Looked into the entire content of the passage.
- Read the Scripture within the living tradition of the Church.
- Paid special attention to how the text expresses the universal Christian faith in order to determine how the words fit into the whole plan of revelation.

Using both the literal and spiritual senses to interpret the Scripture, the Church believes the study of sacred texts is fundamental in establishing a personal relationship with God and that they are the words that nourish and strengthen the faith of His people.

CATHOLIC QUOTE

To read the scripture is to turn to Christ for advice.

—St. Francis of Assisi

The Old Testament

The Old Testament, or the Hebrew Scriptures, consists of the 46 books through which Catholics contemplate God as the creator of the universe and that tell the story of how the world was made ready for the coming of Christ. Although the books of the Old Testament were recognized as inspired by God since before the days of the apostles, it was only formally set in its current form during the Council of Trent in 1546. It is in these books that God reveals His divine plan, makes Himself known to man, and establishes a covenant that was never revoked. Catholics read these texts in light of the fact that Jesus lived, died, and rose again; however, the Old Testament is more than a prelude to the New Testament. The stories, commandments, and prophecies are an irreplaceable part of the Catholic faith and are used as part of the Church's daily prayer. Without the Old Testament, we cannot understand the message of Christ.

The Old Testament is comprised of the following books:

- The Law (or Torah): Genesis, Exodus, Leviticus, Numbers, and Deuteronomy

- The Historical Books: Joshua, Judges, Ruth, 1 Samuel, 2 Samuel, 1 Kings, 2 Kings, 1 Chronicles, 2 Chronicles, Ezra, Nehemiah, Tobit, Judith, Esther, 1 Maccabees, and 2 Maccabees

- The Wisdom Books: Job, Psalms, Proverbs, Ecclesiastes, Song of Solomon, Wisdom, and Sirach

- The Prophets: Isaiah, Jeremiah, Lamentations, Baruch, Ezekiel, Daniel, Hosea, Joel, Amos, Obadiah, Jonah, Micah, Nahum, Habakkuk, Zephaniah, Haggai, Zechariah, and Malachi

Moses and the Torah

The undisputed star of the Old Testament is Moses, the son of slaves who was adopted into the Egyptian royal family, was later exiled, and became the servant of God who was called to be the liberator of the Israelites. He is credited with writing the *Torah*, which chronicles the history of God's chosen people from creation through the Exodus and into the Promised Land.

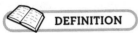

DEFINITION

The **Torah** refers to the first five books of the Bible. They are considered the law of the Jewish people. It is also called the Pentateuch (literally "five books").

The Torah includes the two creation narratives of Genesis, the stories concerning the Great Flood, the call of Abraham, the formation of the people of Israel, and the rise of Joseph as Pharaoh's right-hand man. In Exodus, we learn about the oppression of the Israelites and how God recruited Moses to lead His people out of bondage in Egypt and to receive the Ten Commandments on the summit of Mount Sinai. The last three books offer an exhaustive list of lifestyle rules and regulations to which the Israelites were expected to adhere, the story of Moses' disobedience that prevents him from entering the Promised Land and finally his death and burial in the land of Moab.

The subject of Moses' authorship has been the subject of deep theological debate. Until the 17th Century, both the Jewish and Christian traditions unilaterally believed that Moses was the sole author of the Torah. Eventually, Biblical scholars noted several inconsistencies within the texts that suggest multiple authors and multiple traditions.

Regardless of how many people may have contributed to the Torah, most still point to Moses as the primary source for the books, which hold historic and legal significance for monotheistic religions throughout the world.

FAST FACT

The top ten stories of the Torah:

- The Creation and the fall of Adam and Eve (Genesis 1-3)
- Cain and Abel (Genesis 4)
- The Great Flood (Genesis 6-9)
- The Tower of Babel (Genesis 11)
- The call of Abraham (Genesis 12)
- Jacob's dream (Genesis 28)
- Joseph and the coat of many colors (Genesis 37)
- Moses' birth (Exodus 2)
- The first Passover (Exodus 12)
- The Ten Commandments (Exodus 20)

Other Notable Old Testament Names

Although Moses is a unique figure in Biblical history, there are a number of names beyond the Exodus worth noting. Some were rulers. Some were ordinary people, while others were strange, mystical figures who helped people understand God as not only a fire-and-brimstone kind of deity but also as a transcendent God who is found in the quiet breeze, who loves His people and sympathizes with their trials and tribulations. Here are just a few names worth knowing and where you can find their stories:

- Joshua: Led the Israelites into the Promised Land. Known for fighting the battle of Jericho. (Joshua 6:1-27)

- Samson: One of the judges of Israel and a man of unusual strength, which was tied directly to his hair. (Judges 16)

- Ruth: A Moabite woman who married into an Israelite family and converted to Judaism. She is the great-grandmother of King David and an ancestor of Jesus. (Book of Ruth)

- King Saul: Israel's first King. When he failed to destroy the Amalekites, the Lord withdrew His favor and commanded Samuel to appoint David as King. (1 Samuel 9-31)

- King David: Known as a great king with a strong commitment to God, David was also guilty of serious sins in the Old Testament. (2 Samuel 2-23)

- King Solomon: The son of King David, known primarily for his unorthodox method of settling a custody dispute. He built the Temple in Jerusalem. (1 Kings 1-11)

- Elijah: Known as a healer and miracle worker, Elijah stood up against evil rulers and false prophets during the reign of King Ahab. (1 Kings 17-22, 2 Kings 1-2)

- Isaiah: A prophet who lived in the kingdom of Judah. He is considered the greatest among the prophets, and his works include the recurring theme of salvation. (Book of Isaiah)

- Daniel: A young Hebrew man imprisoned in Babylonia who had the ability to interpret dreams. He is known for surviving overnight in a lion's den due to divine intervention. (Book of Daniel)

CATHOLIC QUOTE

Ignorance of the Scriptures is ignorance of Christ.

—St. Jerome

The New Testament

If the Old Testament exposes humanity to the pedagogy of God's divine plan, then the New Testament is where God's revelation is completed. The New Testament consists of 27 books that focus on the life and ministry of Jesus as well as the early years of the Church:

- The Gospels: Matthew, Mark, Luke, and John

- The Acts of the Apostles

- The Pauline Letters: Romans, 1 Corinthians, 2 Corinthians, Galatians, Ephesians, Philippians, Colossians, 1 Thessalonians, 2 Thessalonians, 1 Timothy, 2 Timothy, Titus, and Philemon

- Hebrews

- The Catholic Letters: James, 1 Peter, 2 Peter, 1 John, 2 John, 3 John, and Jude

- Revelation

The Fab Four: Matthew, Mark, Luke, and John

The Gospels are the centerpiece of Christian Scripture and are the most important documents in the Church. They are our primary source for information concerning the message of Jesus as well as a record of the miraculous events that occurred during His life, through His death and resurrection and until the time of His ascension. The Gospels lead believers everywhere to accept Jesus as the incarnation of God on Earth and apply His words to their daily lives.

The Gospels of Matthew, Mark, and Luke are known as the *Synoptic* Gospels. While they have their differences, they are very similar to one another in terms of the stories they tell and the language they use. Mark's Gospel was written first, around AD 50–67 by a companion of Barnabas, Paul, and Peter named John Mark. It is the shortest of the Gospels and the most action packed. It begins not with the birth of Jesus, but with His baptism in the Jordan River, and moves from one miraculous event to another without a lot of long narrative.

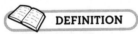 **DEFINITION**

Synoptic means "to look similar." In describing the first three Gospels, it recognizes that they share a similar outline, structure, and stories.

Originally, Biblical scholars believed Mark's Gospel was an abbreviated version of Matthew's texts, but most eventually concluded that Mark's was the original manuscript upon which the

Gospels of Matthew and Luke were built. The Gospels of Matthew and Luke were written before AD 90, but they were written with two very different audiences in mind.

Matthew's Gospel is attributed to a Jewish tax collector and apostle of Jesus, while Luke's Gospel is attributed to a physician who was a traveling companion and student of Paul. Matthew's Gospel was written for a Jewish-Christian audience, quotes the Old Testament more than 60 times, includes the most parables of the four, and includes 600 of Mark's 661 verses. Luke's Gospel is the first volume of a two-volume work that also includes the Acts of the Apostles, both of which are dedicated to Theophilus and designed for a Gentile Christian audience. Resurrection and concern for those on the outskirts of society are key themes throughout the narrative, and Luke alone includes some of the most-loved parables, like the Prodigal Son and the Good Samaritan.

 KEEP IT SIMPLE

The contents of the Synoptic Gospels include:

- The infancy narrative (Matthew and Luke)
- The baptism of Jesus
- The temptation of Christ
- The Sermon on the Mount (Matthew) and the Sermon on the Plain (Luke)
- Parables
- Miracles
- The Last Supper
- Passion narratives
- Resurrection
- Ascension

The Gospel of John is significantly different than the synoptic texts. Written by St. John around AD 90 at Ephesus in Asia, it is not only the last Gospel that appears in the New Testament, but it was also the last one written. It was probably written after the death of Peter as well as the destruction of Jerusalem and the Temple and when John was advanced in age. It is designed to provide supplemental material that is not included in the other three, and like Mark's text, its narrative covers only the last four years of Jesus' life.

John's Gospel does not contain as many stories as Matthew's, Mark's, and Luke's, but the stories that are included are rich in detail and symbolism. John's poetic prologue sets a mystical tone for the work, which uses Christ's dialogue and actions as indicators that Jesus was as much divine as He was human. The first eleven chapters include seven signs that point to Christ's divinity before His death and resurrection, and the Gospel includes seven "I am" quotations that allude to Jesus' status as the Messiah.

The seven signs of Jesus' divinity:

- Turning water into wine at the wedding of Cana (Chapter 2)

- Raising from death the son of a royal official (Chapter 4)

- The healing of the paralyzed man in Bethesda (Chapter 5)

- The multiplication of the loaves and fishes (Chapter 6)

- Jesus walking on water (Chapter 6)

- The healing of the blind man (Chapter 9)

- The raising of Lazarus (Chapter 11)

The seven "I am" statements of Jesus:

- "I am the bread of life …" (6:35)

- "I am the light of the world …" (8:12)

- "I am the gate for the sheep …" (10:7)

- "I am the good shepherd …" (10:11)

- "I am the resurrection and the life …" (11:25)

- "I am the way, the truth and the life …" (14:6)

- "I am the true vine …" (15:1)

John's text does not include any parables, and there are very few tales of healings. John doesn't include the institution of the Sacrament of the Eucharist, but he does offer several long discourses that foretell the importance of this sacrament and hint at the role it will play in the Church.

Despite their similarities and differences, the four Gospels hold a special place in the Church. There is no doctrine more important than the words and actions of Jesus or how those accomplishments affect the lives of Christians everywhere.

 CATHOLIC QUOTE

Most people have no idea what God would make of them if they would only place themselves at His disposal.

—St. Ignatius Loyola

The Acts of the Apostles

The apostles came to the Messianic movement from a variety of backgrounds and for a variety of reasons. They left everything behind to follow Jesus and ultimately were commissioned as the first leaders of the Christian Church. Armed only with the Holy Spirit, they went out into the world to spread the Gospel message and make believers of all nations.

When Jesus called the apostles, He knew their road would be rocky. He knew that they would be persecuted for their beliefs even as they changed the world. In the Acts of the Apostles (the second half of the Luke/Acts compilation) the trials, tribulations, and triumphs of the apostles are outlined as they professed the faith, baptized believers, and continued the work of Christ. The Acts of the Apostles not only showcases the work of the trusted twelve, but also highlights the rise of the Church's foremost evangelists: Peter and Paul.

Peter (formerly Simon) was the leader of the apostles and the one upon whom Christ promised He would build His church. He was a fisherman from the backwaters of Galilee who left his way of life behind when Jesus called him to be a fisher of men. His faith wasn't always perfect, but he grew into his leadership role and is considered the first pope of the Catholic Church.

Paul (formerly Saul) was a learned Jew who actively participated in the persecution of Christians during the early years of the movement. During a trip to Damascus to eradicate more Christians, Paul was struck blind and heard the voice of Jesus calling him to conversion. After his baptism and commission, Paul (along with his companion Barnabas) took the Gospel message throughout Asia Minor and Greece. His ministry failed to win over the Jewish congregations; however, he was a big hit among the Gentiles.

FAST FACT

You may have heard that Paul fell off his horse when he heard the voice of God on the road to Damascus and had his conversion. But in the actual story as recorded in Acts, no horse is mentioned; he just falls to the ground (Acts 9:4).

Acts offers a broad narrative of the Church's development, and while the book ends with Paul's imprisonment, it is accepted that all of the apostles save John were executed for their cause and became martyrs for the faith.

The Epistles

The Epistles are the 21 books of the New Testament written in the form of letters to Christian congregations throughout the ancient world. They are divided between the Pauline letters, written by St. Paul to specific establishments, and the Catholic letters, which are attributed to other apostles and are geared toward a more general audience.

As the most educated and well-traveled of the evangelists, Paul is the author of 13 letters in the New Testament, arranged from longest to shortest as opposed to the order in which they were written. Paul's correspondence follows a traditional format for the time. Each letter contains the name of the sender as well as the addressee, followed by a salutation, a note of thanksgiving, and a prayer. The body of the letter contains dogmatic and moral sections that cover the principles of faith and rules for Christian living before concluding with a sign-off salutation.

Paul wrote his letters to ordinary people facing ordinary problems of the day without any thought to how his words would impact the future Scriptures. Aside from Romans, the Epistles were not deep and theological, but rather pastoral in nature and for a specific body of converts. He paid particular attention to the local difficulties of the particular region in hopes that his words could help these early Christians grow in their faith.

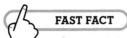

FAST FACT

For years, the letter to the Hebrews was credited to Paul. However, scholars agree that the text was probably written by someone else and it is no longer included in the list of Paul's works.

The Catholic Epistles lack the format that the Pauline letters possess, and are written for a group of churches as opposed to a specific establishment. They have some similarities, but there are some marked differences as well. Some of the letters are addressed to specific people, while others lack a salutation altogether. Some read like correspondence while others (such as 1 John) read like a homily. Ultimately, the Catholic Epistles provide a good overview of early theological teaching. They are considered a body of work all their own due to their distinction from the Pauline letters, rather than having any kind of cohesion among one another.

Revelation

It is the last book of the Bible and one of the most difficult to understand. Written by St. John on the island of Patmos in the Aegean Sea near the end of the first century, the Book of Revelation is a sobering example of *apocalyptic* literature that was popular between 200 BC and AD 200.

Revelation is an account of visions (both symbolic and allegorical) as they pertain to the last days and the second coming of Christ. It is unknown if the visions really occurred or if they were meant to be a literary device, but the book cannot be understood without taking into account the time in which it was written. Revelation came about during a period of brutal oppression by the Roman government. Christians were routinely tortured and killed by the ruling class, and because he was the only apostle to escape martyrdom, it is likely that John thought the end of the world was upon him. Many of the visions use symbolic language to talk about the Roman Empire at the end of the first century; they are not just a prediction of what will happen at the end of time, but a commentary on what was happening when they were written.

Despite the fact that the Book of Revelation was written during a time of crisis, it remains a meaningful text for Catholics and Christians everywhere who believe that it encourages the faithful to trust in Jesus and the promise that he will return someday.

What About the Apocrypha?

If you have heard that there is something "different" about the Catholic Bible, you have heard correctly. Unlike other Christian editions, the Catholic Bible contains an additional seven books (as well as inclusions to two other books) as part of its Old Testament that Catholics believe are divinely inspired but that are not recognized by most Jews and many Protestant Christians: the *deuterocanonical* books or the *apocrypha*.

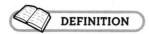 **DEFINITION**

> **Deuterocanonical** means "second canon." These seven books were the second group to be recognized as authentic Scripture by the Catholic Church, after recognizing the rest of the Old Testament books without much controversy or debate. The **apocrypha** refers to the seven books of the Catholic Bible that are not considered official canon by the Jewish tradition or by other Christian denominations.

Typically called the "hidden" or "disputed" books, the apocrypha was rejected by leaders of the Protestant Reformation such as Martin Luther who felt that these texts lacked authenticity and authority. There was also a question of language. All of the other books of the Old Testament were written in Hebrew, while the oldest versions of these seven books are in Greek. There may have been earlier versions written in Hebrew, but they no longer exist.

Over the years a number of Protestant editions of the Bible have included these books as a separate section, but the Catholic Bible continues to combine them with the rest of the Old Testament rather than distinguish them as a separate entity. The Deuterocanonical books include:

- Tobit
- Judith
- Additions to Esther
- Wisdom (or The Wisdom of Solomon)
- Sirach (or Ecclesiasticus)

- Baruch

- Additions to Daniel

- 1 Maccabees

- 2 Maccabees

The Message of the Scriptures

In spite of the fact that the Bible is rooted in events of the past, its message has a timeless and universal appeal. It is more than a compilation of random books, but rather a library that forms the basis for the apostolic tradition and the events upon which the Church was built.

The Bible is not the only way God reveals Himself. Rather, it is through a combination of Scripture and tradition that His words and deeds are handed down through Jesus to the apostles and early disciples, through the structural hierarchy of the Church and into the hearts of the faithful.

The Least You Need to Know

- The Bible is the divinely inspired word of God and was penned by numerous writers over thousands of years.
- The Old Testament is where God reveals His plan of loving goodness to man and where He establishes the Old Covenant, which has never been revoked.
- The New Testament is the fulfillment of God's revelation through the incarnation of His Son, Jesus.
- The Gospels are the centerpiece of the Sacred Scriptures and are the most important documents in the Church.
- The Deuterocanonical texts refer to the seven books of the Catholic Bible that are not typically featured in Protestant editions.
- The Bible is rooted in history but its message has timeless appeal.

The Universal Church

The word *church* comes from the Greek word *kyriake*, which means "belonging to the Lord." The Church is made up of the people throughout the world who, united in baptism, belong to the Body of Christ. The Church is more than an ideology or a building in which people come to pray. It is a living, breathing extension of Christ, sanctified by God, and is where the Holy Spirit flourishes.

In this chapter, we will take a look inside the 2,000-year-old institution known as the Catholic Church and what it stands for. We will examine the structure of the organization, which, under the governance of the pope, boasts a membership of over 1 billion people worldwide.

We will investigate the role of avowed men and women religious who dedicate their lives in consecrated or ordained service, as well as the vast network of the laity who keep the faith and spread Christ's message of love to every corner of the globe.

In This Chapter

- The hierarchical structure of the Church
- The pope's role as the Vicar of Christ
- Various religious vocations for men and women
- The important vocation of the laity

What Is the Church?

The Catholic Church is the religious movement Jesus established during his time on Earth. In the beginning the "Christians" were a subsect of Judaism, geared toward the "next generation" disciple. These believers were no longer awaiting the promised Son of God, but believed He had arrived and brought the Kingdom of God with Him. They believed that, in Jesus, God fulfilled His promises to His people, and through Christ's example these followers were ready to be instruments of God's love in the world.

The first members of this movement were Jesus' apostles. As eyewitnesses to His life, death, resurrection, and ascension, they were commissioned by Jesus to make believers of all nations. He gave them the authority to baptize in His name, forgive the sins of the repentant, and spread the gospel message through their *apostolic* ministry to the ends of the earth.

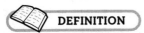

DEFINITION

Apostolic means "of the apostles" or being based on the teachings of the original 12 followers of Jesus Christ.

Catholics believe that there is only one holy, universal, and apostolic Church of Jesus Christ. It is designed to be inclusive of all people, and everyone who is baptized in Him is a member of this organization. Regardless of denomination, all Christians are part of the Body of Christ and are brothers and sisters in the Lord.

This may come as a surprise to you if you are under the impression that Catholics have a "we are better than everyone else" policy regarding interdenominational relations. While there are differences that set Catholics apart from other religions and there have been numerous conflicts over this issue in the past, the Church currently enjoys healthy and respectful relations with its Christian brethren as well as non-Christian religions around the world. We pray together and work alongside each other in charitable ministries. Catholics believe that the freedom of religion is a human right and that everyone who seeks God has the ability to know Him and gain eternal salvation in Heaven.

The Church is comprised of two parts, the laity and the clergy. While both are equal in the eyes of God, they serve two very different kinds of *vocations* within the structure of the organization.

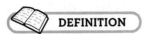

DEFINITION

A **vocation** is a call from God into a field for which one is particularly well suited. In a spiritual sense, it is not a career or a profession, but can overlap with these areas as well.

The vocation of the laity is to promote the Kingdom of God throughout the world and live the gospel in their daily lives. Every member of the Catholic Church is born into the laity; however, there are some who are called to serve God as members of the clergy or as consecrated religious. These men and women dedicate their lives in an avowed public profession of obedience to God and the good of all His Church.

No matter what their role, all Catholics who commit their lives to God through the Sacrament of Baptism (and later Confirmation) offer themselves up in service to the Church, knowing that God will give them the gifts and tools they need to live out their vocation according to His will.

The Structure of the Catholic Church

When most people think of the Catholic Church, the Roman or Latin *rite* is the celebration that typically comes to mind. Though that is the focus of this book, it bears mentioning that there are several families of rites that comprise the Catholic faith. All of them fall under the jurisdiction of the pope and the Holy See in Rome, although each of them has its own style of worship and particular customs of how they live the Catholic faith. The Eastern Rites of the Catholic Church are not to be confused with Orthodox Churches, which often have similar names but are not in union with the pope.

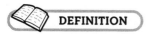 **DEFINITION**

> A **rite** is a tradition that regulates the liturgy, discipline, and governance of particular churches.

The Rites of the Catholic Church include:

The Western Rites

- The Roman Catholic or Latin Family of Liturgical Rites

The Eastern Rites

- Antiochian Rite: Maronite Catholics, Syrian Catholics, Syro-Malankara Catholics

- Chaldean/East Syrian Rite: Chaldean Catholics, Syro-Malabar Catholics

- Byzantine Rite: Albanian Catholics, Belarusian Catholics, Bulgarian Catholics, Krizevci Catholics, Greek Catholics, Hungarian Catholics, Italo-Albanian Catholics, Melkite Catholics, Romanian Catholics, Russian Catholics, Ruthenian Catholics, Slovakian Catholics, and Ukranian Catholics

- Alexandrian Rite: Coptic Catholics and Ethiopian Catholics
- Armenian Rite: Armenian Catholics

The Church is not a democracy. Its power comes not from its people but from Christ, and is filtered through a chain of command known as a hierarchical structure. At the top of this structure is the supreme pontiff or pope, Christ's representative (vicar) on Earth. The pope is the successor of St. Peter and lives in Vatican City—an autonomous 108-acre city-state located in the heart of Rome, Italy. From his offices in the papal palace, he oversees all of the worldwide Catholic community.

The Pope: The Vicar of Christ

The pope is not only the supreme pastor of over one billion souls, but he is also the Bishop of Rome, the head of the worldwide College of Bishops, and the leader of the Magisterium or teaching authority of the Church. His primary responsibility, however, is to watch over the transmission of the faith throughout the world and to be a visible sign of unity among followers of Christ. Needless to say, it's a god's burden to bear, but the papacy is borne by a man—a human man with a human character.

How Is the Pope Elected?

The pope is elected in a sacred process known as *conclave.* When a pontiff dies, or resigns his position, the College of Cardinals convenes at the Vatican to meet in the Sistine Chapel where they discern whom among them God has chosen to lead His people. There is no politicking or campaigning for votes, and while the proceedings are secretive, each man in attendance is expected to pray and put forward of his own free will the name he believes God is calling to the post.

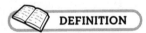
DEFINITION

A **conclave** is a secret meeting during which the College of Cardinals elects a new pope. It comes from the Latin term meaning "with a key."

When conclave begins, a benchmark vote is taken, and if no one receives the required two-thirds majority to assume the office, subsequent votes occur four times each day for three consecutive days, followed by a one-day break after which voting resumes. If several rounds of unsuccessful balloting occur, the cardinals can opt to elect the pope based on a simple 50-percent-plus-one majority.

During conclave all eyes turn to a small chimney atop the Sistine Chapel. It is the chimney connected to the furnace in which each round of votes is burned in order to announce the result of the vote to the masses. If a pope has not been elected, the ballots are burned in such a way to ensure the smoke appears black. If a pope has been elected (and accepts the position) chemicals are added to the ballots to make the resulting smoke appear white.

When the white smoke emerges from the chimney, the bells of St. Peter's Basilica peal and the new pope is taken into the Room of Tears—so-called because of the tears often shed by the new pontiff as he realizes the weight of the responsibilities now given to him. There he is dressed in the white papal garments before returning to the chapel to greet the cardinals and tell what name he will use as pontiff. He is then led to the balcony of St. Peter's Basilica where he is formally announced to the public and speaks his first words as the leader of the universal Church.

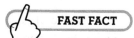

FAST FACT

The traditional way a high-ranking cardinal announces the election of a new pope is by appearing on the balcony of St. Peter's and saying, "Habemus Papam" which means "We have a pope."

What Does the Pope Do?

The pope's duties are wide and varied. They are both religious and political in nature. He is the "face" of the Catholic Church and the eyes of the world are upon him. He spends his days in prayer, celebrating the liturgy, and composing both formal and informal communications. He studies issues that may require his theological scholarship and ministers directly to his congregation through Mass and in his weekly general audiences. He travels the globe to meet with his people. He appoints bishops and cardinals. He creates dioceses and he has the authority to canonize saints. The pope is the unifier of the faith and the primary witness to the gospel. He is responsible for the proper transmission of the faith to Catholics all over the world, and he has the responsibility to revoke the commissions of those who have failed in their ministerial or moral duties.

As the head of the sovereign city-state of Vatican City, the pope meets with other heads of state and maintains diplomatic relations with more than 100 countries. He is well versed in current events around the globe and regularly offers his thoughts on how these issues affect the Church.

However, the pope is not a micromanager. He tends to offer a broad overview of the universal Church rather than get involved in the daily inner workings of regional parishes. He appoints bishops to that task and trusts that they will offer him regular reports or consult with him on issues needing his intervention.

The Infallibility Issue

The issue of the pope's infallibility is one of the most misunderstood aspects of the Catholic faith. Many people are puzzled by any religious organization that believes their earthly leader is perfect in thought, word, and deed, so let's clear this one up: Is the pope perfect? No. Can he speak infallibly? Yes, but only under certain conditions.

As the leader of a major religious organization, the pope is expected to speak out on a variety of social, moral, and political issues and offer an opinion as to how these issues fit within the teachings of the Church. However, this is not the same as making an infallible statement. The pope can only speak infallibly when defining dogma or other moral issues in a solemn act known as *ex cathedra*.

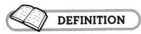

DEFINITION

Ex cathedra comes from the Latin, meaning "from the chair." It is used as a technical term when referring to a special case in which the pope exercises his authority to speak infallibly on a matter of faith or morals.

Make no mistake about it. The ability to speak ex cathedra has nothing to do with the pope's reliability or astuteness and does not make the man flawless. He is a sinner and makes mistakes like everyone else. What is flawless in these cases is the Church's teaching. It is not something that happens every day, but when the pope speaks infallibly after much study, prayer, and counsel, the result is the first, last, and only word on the subject where the Church is concerned.

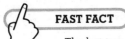

FAST FACT

The last two times a pope spoke ex cathedra concerning a matter of faith were in 1854 defining the doctrine of the Immaculate Conception of Mary and in 1950 defining the doctrine of the Assumption of Mary's body into Heaven.

Bishops and Cardinals

As the successors of the apostles, the bishops (some of whom have the title Archbishop, Major Archbishop, or Patriarch) are responsible for overseeing several parishes in a territory known as a diocese (or archdiocese). Each diocese has one bishop who is its chief pastor or leader, though auxiliary bishops can assist him. His three main responsibilities are to teach, govern, and sanctify.

- **Teach.** A bishop is the primary teacher of his diocese and is charged with conveying the word of God to his people as well as ensuring that others entrusted to teach in his stead are teaching the truth.

- **Govern.** A bishop oversees the administrative duties of the diocese, meets the needs of the congregations, visits the various parishes, attends meetings, and sends reports to Rome.

- **Sanctify.** A bishop must ensure that the sacraments are administered and celebrated correctly, that Mass is said each week, and that priests and deacons are ordained.

There are also a number of symbols associated with bishops that have special significance to his role in the Church. These symbols include:

- Crosier: A staff that looks like a shepherd's crook and is used at liturgical celebrations.

- Mitre: The triangular hat worn at liturgical celebrations that is also used by the pope.

- Pectoral cross: An ornamental cross worn around the neck.

- Ring: A symbol of a bishop's mystical marriage to the Church and being a spiritual father to the faithful.

- Zucchetto: A skullcap associated with the upper echelon of the clergy. Bishops wear purple. Cardinals wear red and the pope wears white.

- Coat of Arms: A bishop may use a personal one as well as one to represent his diocese.

- Motto: Usually a quote from Scripture, it speaks to the bishop's vision for ministry.

Cardinals are a unique part of the Catholic clergy, and their primary responsibility is to elect the pope from among their members under the age of 80. They are typically bishops from around the world who are chosen by the pope and given this special title. While some cardinals hold cabinet-like posts in Rome, for the most part their duties remain the same as every other bishop. The bishops and cardinals do not speak out against the pope, nor do they contradict his teachings. By the same token, the pope relies on the bishops and the cardinals for counsel in order to make the best decisions for the good of the overall Church.

Men and Women Religious

At the local level of the Catholic Church, there are a number of ordained or consecrated men and women religious who respond to God's call and train for a career in Christian service. Once they take their vows, their lives are subject to the will of God through their superiors. These include priests, deacons, nuns, sisters, monks, and brothers.

Priests and Deacons

Priests serve as the front line administrators of the sacraments in parishes throughout the world. While they may be men associated with a religious order (such as the Jesuits), others, called diocesan priests, serve the parishes of a particular diocese in union with the bishop.

Roman Catholic priests are unmarried men who receive the Sacrament of Holy Orders and dedicate their lives in service to God. On a diocesan level, they celebrate Mass, administer the sacraments, pray daily, and preach the gospel. They work in parishes. They teach in Catholic schools. They visit the sick, the homebound, and the dying. They educate and counsel their congregants, report to the bishop, and may divide their time between parish duties and administrative positions within the diocesan Church.

A Catholic priest is a disciple of Jesus who has a vocation to serve his Church at the altar. A priest, like the apostles, is a witness to the reality that Jesus Christ suffered, died, and was raised up, and that God loves the world and wants humanity to live forever. Priests, although human and weakened by sin, are given the grace to tell the good news of Jesus.

A deacon is an ordained member of the clergy who can preside over the ministry of the Word, assist at the liturgy, and coordinate charitable works. He holds the authority not only to baptize (which any Catholic can do in an emergency, but more on that in Chapter 6), but also to preach the homily at Mass and to preside over the sacrament of matrimony. Some men are ordained a deacon on their way to becoming a priest, while others choose to be part of the diaconate on a permanent basis. The men in the permanent diaconate are the only members of the Roman Catholic clergy allowed to remain married if they are wed prior to being ordained. However, they do take a vow promising not to remarry should they ever be widowed.

The steps to becoming a priest in the Catholic Church are …

- Internal discernment: determining on a personal level if they have a call from God to be a priest.

- Application process: psychological and medical screening and extensive conversations with the diocesan vocations office to determine if one is a good candidate for the priesthood.

- Seminary formation: formal training in philosophy and theology during college and/or after college both in practical and academic matters concerning the priesthood.

- Transitional diaconate: a position that a seminarian is ordained into roughly after his third year of studying theology.

- Priestly ordination: the final step to becoming a priest in the Catholic Church.

Ordained or consecrated? All bishops, priests, and deacons are ordained—meaning that they receive the Sacrament of Holy Orders and can celebrate the sacraments for the faithful. Nuns, sisters, monks, and brothers—members of religious orders—are often referred to as consecrated religious because they set their lives aside to serve God and the Church. Some monks and brothers are also ordained, but not all.

Nuns and Sisters

For some, they are a painful reminder of a strict Catholic school education. For others, they are the closest things to angels on Earth. Studies show that they are the longest-living demographic on the planet, as well as the most educated one. They are the brides of Christ: Catholic nuns and sisters.

While the term "nuns" and "sisters" are used interchangeably to refer to consecrated women religious, there is a distinct difference between the two. Both are unmarried women who are members of a religious order. Both are called "sister." Both take vows of poverty, chastity, and obedience and both live communally (whenever possible) with others in convents whose symbols, ministry, and fashion vary from order to order, but that is where the similarity ends.

A Catholic nun is an unmarried woman who relinquishes all of her worldly goods and professes solemn vows to live a contemplative life of prayer "behind the walls," so to speak. She makes her home in a cloistered or semi-cloistered monastery and her work is situated within this environment for the good of the world beyond.

By contrast, a Catholic sister is an unmarried woman who lives, ministers, and prays in the world at large. Her vocation is often referred to as "active" or "apostolic" because she is engaged in works of mercy and ministries that spread the good news of Jesus Christ to others. She is expected to live a simple life in accord with the gospel.

Delores Hart was a successful Hollywood actress who gave up her film career (and fiancé) to enter a Benedictine convent at the age of 24. Her film credits include 1957's *Loving You* with Elvis Presley (which featured Presley's first on-screen kiss) and 1960's *Where the Boys Are*. Hart maintains a Screen Actor's Guild membership and each year the Academy of Motion Picture Sciences sends her copies of the Oscar-nominated films so she can vote on them. She was the focus of the documentary *God Is the Bigger Elvis*.

Monks and Brothers

Like nuns and sisters, the distinction between a Catholic monk and brother has to do with the life they lead. These men are consecrated members of the Church who dedicate their lives to service, but not all of them are ordained priests or deacons. A monk is the male equivalent to a nun and lives a quiet life of contemplation in a monastery. Some monks are ordained priests, but not all. A brother enjoys a more active and secular ministry and lives among his colleagues in community.

Brothers and monks are members of a religious order, but like the varied roles of the sisters, brothers can be found in all walks of life. He may be a doctor, writer, or teacher, or engage in another profession, but he commits to live his life serving as a "brother" to others.

Some of the most well-known religious orders include …

- Benedictines (men and women): a monastic order founded by St. Benedict in the fifth century, centered on a balance of prayer and work (*ora et labora*).

- Franciscans (men and women): a community of friars and sisters founded by St. Francis of Assisi in the thirteenth century with a particular connection to the poor.

- Dominicans (men and women): a preaching order founded by St. Dominic in the thirteenth century.

- Jesuits (men): an active, apostolic community founded by St. Ignatius of Loyola in the sixteenth century with an emphasis on missionary zeal and education.

- Missionaries of Charity (women): founded by Blessed Teresa of Calcutta in the twentieth century in India with a mission of loving and serving the poorest of the poor.

- Sisters of Charity (women): founded by St. Elizabeth Ann Seton in the nineteenth century in the United States with a mission of education in Catholic schools.

- Congregation of the Holy Cross (men and women): founded by Blessed Basil Moreau in the nineteenth century in France as an active community focused on education.

- Redemptorists (men): founded by St. Alphonsus Liguori in the eighteenth century in Italy to preach the good news of Jesus Christ the Redeemer to the poor.

- Carmelites (men and women): Monastic and apostolic communities founded on Mt. Carmel in the Holy Land in the twelfth century.

 CATHOLIC QUOTE

Many people mistake our work for our vocation. Our vocation is the love of Jesus.

—Blessed Teresa of Calcutta

The Laity

Although they are neither ordained nor consecrated members of the Church, the importance of the laity's role in the structure of the Catholic community cannot be overstated. The laity is not a bunch of second-class Christians, but a vital part of the Church's mission.

As mentioned earlier in the chapter, the laity is comprised of non-ordained baptized Catholics and is the largest group within the Church's structure. They are men, women, young, and young at heart who are active members of their parishes and live out their vocations in a variety of ways. They have a right to preach the gospel and they are expected to live out its message. They engage in works, prayer, and ministries that are considered spiritual sacrifices that help promote the message of the Church.

Those with the required qualities can hold permanent ministerial positions, while others perform auxiliary roles. Members of the laity can be teachers, catechists, ministers, servers, lectors, and more. They visit the sick. They distribute communion. They go on missions and they volunteer in Catholic agencies all over the world. For the vast majority of laity who do not work in a parish or Church agency, they are called to be a witness to gospel values in their own workplaces and to evangelize the people they encounter on a daily basis. No matter what part they play, the laity is just as important in the eyes of God as the most venerated member of the clergy.

The Least You Need to Know

- The Church is a living, breathing extension of Christ and is not a democracy. Its power comes from Christ and is sifted through a hierarchal structure.
- The pope is Christ's representative on Earth with a variety of political and religious responsibilities worldwide.
- Cardinals and bishops are appointed by the pope and generally have similar responsibilities. However, cardinals are the only ones who can elect the pope.
- There are a number of men and women religious, either consecrated or ordained, who serve the Church and its mission.
- The laity is just as important as the most venerated member of the clergy.

PART 2

The Sacramental Life

As modern-day disciples of Jesus, Christians are called to bear witness to the gospel in every-thing they say and do. This requires more than participation in a weekly religious service—it's a total life commitment. In order to help us with this endeavor, Jesus provided His people with the avenues by which God's grace comes into the soul—the Celebration of the Christian Mystery (the liturgy) and the seven sacraments of the Catholic Church.

In this part, we will uncover what it means to live a sacramental life. It's not just a lot of hocus pocus and holy water, but an opportunity to encounter the living presence of Christ at every stage of our human existence. By immersing ourselves in the sacred mysteries and liturgical celebrations of the Church, we not only receive gifts through the Holy Spirit, we deepen our relationship with Jesus and connect more fully to God.

Sacraments: Outward and Visible Signs

The sacraments are Christ's legacy to His Church—seven gifts that come to us at key moments in our lives and are designed to help us transcend our human existence, become more like Jesus, and by His example, grow closer to God.

Sacraments are visible signs that connect to an invisible reality. They are experiences in which one can feel the healing, forgiving, and energizing presence of Christ within. The sacraments allow us to share in the mysteries of His life, death, and resurrection, feel God's love, and share that love with the world around us.

In this chapter, we will help you understand what the sacraments are, where they come from, and why Jesus established them in the first place. You will learn that they are not symbolic super powers, but symbols that have the power to nourish our bodies, heal our souls, and raise us to a supernatural state.

In This Chapter

* The sacraments are our inheritance from Christ
* Understanding the gift of grace
* Sacraments can be found in the Scriptures
* Finding strength and healing in the sacraments

Sacramental Celebrations

Have you ever experienced the loss of someone to whom you were particularly close? If so, then you no doubt have those moments when you still feel their presence in your life. Perhaps it happens when you hear your loved one's favorite song on the radio or wear a cherished piece of their jewelry. Maybe it's when you make a special meal using their signature recipes or find yourself repeating a familiar phrase they used. In those moments, the memory of their life and all it stood for is tangible as you symbolically connect to their spirit even after their body and soul are gone.

A *sacrament* works in a very similar way. Sacraments are our inheritance from Christ—the part of Him that He left behind and entrusted to the apostles and their successors to be conferred at various points in our lives.

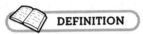 **DEFINITION**

The word **sacrament** comes from the Latin word *sacramentum,* which refers to a military oath of allegiance. In Catholicism a sacrament is a holy and visible sign that represents the intangible in order to refine one's faith.

The official public worship of the Catholic Church is called the liturgy. Although the word literally means "the work of the people," it is more than a gathering of like-minded souls in a Sunday service. In fact, the Catholic Mass is only one of many liturgical celebrations in the Church that incorporate the sacraments.

The Mass is comprised of two parts: the Liturgy of the Word and the Liturgy of the Eucharist. Together they form a single act of worship that has followed the same basic format since St. Justin Martyr first recorded the order of Mass in AD 155. When we celebrate Mass and the sacraments, we are drawn into the loving presence of God where we are consoled, healed, and transformed by His grace.

Grace: Why Jesus Instituted the Sacraments

As we learned in Chapter 1, God is not the kind of deity who wants to remain at arm's length from His people. He sent Jesus to us as the fulfillment of His divine revelation and to illustrate how deep His merciful love goes; and by instituting the sacraments, Jesus gives us entry into the inner circle of the Holy Trinity through the gift of God's *grace.*

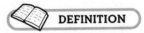 **DEFINITION**

Grace is God's free and unmerited help. It is a gift from God to help us follow Him and live holy lives.

In plain English, grace is like chicken soup for the Christian soul. It is comfort food that you can't hold in your hand; shows up when you need it the most; and when it's received has the ability to satisfy, nourish, and strengthen. It is the kind of thing you didn't know you wanted or needed until you finally ask for it and feel it act like a soothing balm in your heart.

Grace is something God freely bestows upon a person that enables him or her to connect and respond to Him in a very solid way. By instituting the sacraments, Christ connected us to the events in His life that people around Him experienced on a sensory level. They saw His miracles. They listened to His teachings. They felt His physical presence. They tasted the bread He provided. They smelled His death and rejoiced in His resurrection.

When we take part in the rituals of the sacraments, we, too, experience something on a physical level that enables us to believe that through baptism we become children of God. We share the mystery of the Last Supper. We have acknowledgment that our sins are forgiven, and even though a priest or bishop confers God's grace upon us, it actually comes from the Holy Spirit, which means that it comes from Christ.

However, merely receiving grace is not enough. Grace is not a present that arrives by mail never to be opened and used. It summons us to react to it, though it does not demand. God doesn't work that way. His grace is given freely and He hopes that we will respond in kind.

 KEEP IT SIMPLE

Grace is not something that only comes through the rituals of the sacraments, but can be found in any moment or action that connects us with Christ. The sacraments are merely proscribed events in which we know for certain that Christ is physically present in the moment to give us grace.

What Are the Seven Sacraments?

There are seven sacraments in the Catholic Church, divided into three categories based on their overall purpose. All of them have special rituals associated with them, along with specific prayers, blessings, and symbols unique to them.

- The Sacraments of Initiation: Baptism, Confirmation, and Eucharist (Holy Communion)
- The Sacraments of Healing: Penance and Reconciliation and Anointing of the Sick
- The Sacraments of Service: Holy Matrimony and Holy Orders

The Sacraments of Initiation introduce and install new members in the faith community, while the Sacraments of Healing seek to repair our relationship with God and find comfort in his presence at critical times in our lives. Finally, the Sacraments of Service pertain to one's life direction in which people answer the call to become servants of love as either a married couple or (if a single male) a deacon, priest, or bishop.

Three of the sacraments can be received only once in a lifetime: Baptism, Confirmation, and Holy Orders. It is believed that these sacraments leave an indelible imprint on the soul that cannot be removed, reworked, repeated, or replaced. The rest can be administered whenever appropriate to the situation, and some, such as the Eucharist, can be dispensed on a daily basis.

 CATHOLIC QUOTE

What was visible in our Savior has passed over into his mysteries.

—St. Leo the Great

So what are the visible signs and inner graces associated with the sacraments? We will talk more in depth about these over the next few chapters, but the basics include:

Baptism

Visible sign: Water

Grace: Forgiveness of all sins and entrance into the Christian community as a child of God

Confirmation

Visible sign: Anointing of the forehead with Chrism Oil

Grace: The gifts of the Holy Spirit and the responsibility to profess faith publicly

Eucharist

Visible sign: Wheat bread and grape wine

Grace: Unity as the Body of Christ, strength and nourishment, and forgiveness of lesser sins

Penance and Reconciliation

Visible sign: The confession of the penitent

Grace: Forgiveness of all sins, reconciliation with God and the Church along with the grace to resist sin

Anointing of the Sick

Visible sign: Anointing the person with oil

Grace: Spiritual (and physical) healing, forgiveness of all sins, and union with the Passion of Christ

Holy Matrimony

Visible sign: The mutual exchange of vows with full consent

Grace: Man and woman become one flesh with the possibility of having children

Holy Orders

Visible sign: The bishop imposing his hands on the head of the candidate

Grace: The grace of the Holy Spirit to stand in the place of Christ (as head or servant)

Is It a Kind of Magic?

The short answer is no. The issue of magic within the Church comes up from time to time, especially where the sacraments and other liturgical celebrations are concerned. However, let me make it perfectly clear: sacraments are not super powers, magic spells, secret formulas, potions, or tricks of the mind.

There are a few big distinctions where sacraments and magic are concerned. Magic is an act of power. Even when we watch an illusionist on stage, he or she is in a controlled situation. They have set up the environment where, if the elements come together in just the right way, there is only one possible outcome. In magic, the ritual leads to an eventual end.

In sacramental celebrations, a relationship is established, strengthened, and renewed. What will come from it, who knows? There is no formula involved. The graces received certainly have the power to transform the life of the receiver, but they cannot compel the receiver to behave or act in a certain way. Sacraments do not control us or have power over our lives. They have power within our lives. If we choose not to use the graces God bestows on us, they can certainly be lost (with the exception of Baptism, Confirmation, and Holy Orders), but sacraments are divine acts that are designed to liberate us and make the most of our lives through the mysteries of Jesus.

 CATHOLIC QUOTE

He became what we are so that he might make us who He is.

—St. Athanasius the Great

Sacraments in the Scripture

While sacramental celebrations are not uncommon in Christianity, the names and numbers vary depending on denomination. For example, Baptists refer to the sacraments as "ordinances" and recognize only two. Most Lutherans acknowledge three official sacraments, but have four less formal, nonsacramental rites as well. Various denominations also have different understandings of what exactly the sacraments do in the lives of those who receive them. For some, they are just symbols that bring up a memory of what happened in the life of Jesus; for others, they give strength and grace. The reason for the discrepancy stems from the belief by some churches that some of the sacraments were manmade rituals rather than institutions of Christ. Make no mistake, however—the seven sacraments of the Catholic Church are rooted in Scripture and can be traced directly to events in the life of Jesus.

The Sacrament of Baptism can be found in Matthew 28:19 when Jesus commissions his disciples to "Go therefore and make disciples of all nations, baptizing them in the name of the Father and of the Son and of the Holy Spirit." The Church celebrates this event with *sacramental* holy water either by pouring it on the candidate's head or by immersing them in water as Jesus was in the Jordan River. As the bishop, priest, or deacon blesses them, they die to sin and are reborn again in Christ.

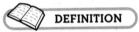 **DEFINITION**

A **sacramental** is a sacred sign or action featured in a blessing. The Church uses a number of these symbols in their sacraments and liturgies, including but not limited to holy water, candles, incense, and oil.

The concept of confirmation comes from the Gospel of John (and later in the Acts of the Apostles) but concerns the moment in which the disciples of Jesus came in contact with the Holy Spirit through the resurrected Christ when He says, "Receive the Holy Spirit. If you forgive the sins of any, they are forgiven them; if you retain the sins of any, they are retained." (John 20:22) In the modern day ritual, the candidate's forehead is anointed with Chrism Oil as the bishop (or priest in some cases) seals them with the same Spirit that the apostles received.

There are numerous references to the celebration of the Eucharist throughout the New Testament, including the gospels of Matthew, Mark, and Luke, along with 1 Corinthians. The story that is recounted during every Mass concerns the last meal Jesus celebrated with His friends prior to His execution. It is during this event that he takes the bread and wine, blesses it, breaks it and hands it to His apostles, and equates it to His body and blood. When Catholics receive the Holy Eucharist, they are united with Christ each and every time they celebrate the sacrament.

Once upon a time, the Sacrament of Penance and Reconciliation was called confession, and while some still call it this today, the sacrament is more like mediation between friends than a punishment from on high. There are a number of examples of Christ forgiving the sins of the repentant, but one of the most famous concerns a sinful woman who entered the house of a Pharisee to anoint Jesus with ointment. When he is admonished for not rebuking her affections, he says to His host:

> "Do you see this woman? I entered your house; you gave me no water for my feet, but she has bathed my feet with her tears and dried them with her hair. You gave me no kiss, but from the time I came in she has not stopped kissing my feet. You did not anoint my head with oil, but she has anointed my feet with ointment. Therefore, I tell you, her sins, which were many, have been forgiven; hence she has shown great love." (Luke 7:44-47)

In the Sacrament of Reconciliation, the penitent recounts their sins, and asks for absolution from the priest or bishop, which cleanses the soul of both the serious and less serious types of sin.

FAST FACT

Many people think the sinful woman who washed Jesus' feet and anointed them with ointment—or any other sinful woman who appears in the Gospels—was Mary Magdalene. In actuality, this sinful woman is never named and there is no reason to suspect that Mary Magdalene was particularly sinful. Luke 8:1–3 says she was possessed by seven demons, but it is unclear if that is a reference to literal demonic spirits or the "demons" of sin.

The Anointing of the Sick can be a comforting sacrament to those who are critically ill. While the prayers, symbols, and blessings cannot guarantee a cure, it does offer the soothing presence of Christ to get them through that difficult time. In the Gospel of Mark, a paralyzed man is presented to Jesus in hopes that He might be able to heal the man of his disability. Jesus bends to the man and tells him that his sins are forgiven, but when challenged by the authorities as to who authorized this Nazarene to forgive sins, Jesus responds, "Which is easier, to say to the paralytic, 'Your sins are forgiven,' or to say, 'Stand up and take your mat and walk'?" (Mark 2:9) He opts to do the latter and the man stands and walks, to the amazement of all who witnessed the event.

Though Christ Himself was never married, we do know that he attended at least one wedding (and was kind enough to provide refreshments when the host ran out) and had a great deal of respect for the marital union between husband and wife and the mutual vows exchanged between them. When questioned by the Pharisees as to whether or not it was lawful for a man to divorce his wife, Jesus said to them:

"Have you not read that the one who made them at the beginning 'made them male and female,' and said, 'For this reason a man shall leave his father and mother and be joined to his wife, and the two shall become one flesh'? So they are no longer two, but one flesh. Therefore what God has joined together, let no one separate." (Matthew 19:4-6)

> **FAST FACT**
>
> Holy Matrimony is the one sacrament that actually predates the life of Christ. By quoting the Old Testament, Jesus alludes to the fact that God sanctified the institution of marriage long before He came to Earth.

Like the institution of the Last Supper, Christ's commissioning His apostles is referenced numerous times in the New Testament. In the Acts of the Apostles, we read about the apostles "laying hands" on new ministers similar to the ordination ceremony that installs new priests, deacons, and bishops today. Through Holy Orders, a candidate answers in the affirmative to follow the call of God and to feed the Lord's sheep.

Saints and Sacraments

The sacraments have been known to have a profound impact on the lives they touch. No matter if one is a "cradle Catholic" or a convert to the faith, the sacraments have a way of renewing the spirit, soothing the soul, and enabling one to see the presence of Christ in the gifts He left behind. Following are just two stories of how the sacraments changed the lives of future saints in the Church.

St. Elizabeth Ann Seton

Elizabeth Ann Seton was born on August 28, 1774, to a non-Catholic New York society couple. She was a child of keen intellect and was a voracious reader with particular interest in the subjects of history and religion. She was raised in the Anglican faith and was a very religious young lady, reading her Bible frequently and genuinely enjoying the words of comfort the Book of Psalms provided her.

In 1794, at the age of 20, Elizabeth married the love of her life, William Seton. They had five children together. For a few short years her life seemed almost impossibly perfect, but then her father-in-law died and left her and William to care for several siblings as well as the family business. Things went from bad to worse when William contracted tuberculosis and had to declare bankruptcy.

As a last-ditch effort to save her husband's life, the family set sail for Italy, where William had business friends who promised to help take care of him. William died in Pisa, Italy, on December 27, 1803. For a period of time after her husband's death, Elizabeth remained in Italy, where she was introduced to the Catholic faith and began to contemplate a religious vocation. She said she became consumed with a desire for the Bread of Life, and after returning to America, she joined the Church in 1805, making her First Communion a few days later. She was so fervent about the Eucharistic celebration that she would visit two churches each Sunday in order to partake in the sacrament twice. It was the sacraments—especially the Eucharist—that sustained her during these years and the rest of her life.

With the little money she had left after her husband's death, Elizabeth purchased a building in Baltimore with plans to start a religious community and the first free Catholic school in America. Though she still had children of her own to raise, when the community adopted their Rule (based on the Rule of St. Vincent de Paul for his Daughters of Charity), a provision was made to allow her to continue parenting. She took her vows with the Sisters of Charity on March 25, 1809, and has been called Mother Seton ever since. By that time, she had contracted tuberculosis, the same illness that killed her husband, and she suspected that God would call her to Him in the near future. The Rule of the Sisters of Charity was formally ratified in 1812, and by 1819, the community established two orphanages and another school in addition to the first. Today, six groups of sisters can trace themselves to Mother Seton's initial foundation.

Mother Seton died in 1821 at the age of 46 and was formally canonized on September 14, 1975. She was the first canonized saint to be born in America and is known as the Mother of Catholic Education in the United States. Her feast day is January 4.

St. Damien of Molokai

Born on January 3, 1840, in Tremelo, Belgium, Joseph de Veuster was the seventh child of a farmer. At a very young age, he felt called to be a Catholic missionary and on October 7, 1860, he entered the congregation of the Sacred Heart of Jesus and Mary. He took the religious name Damien. In 1864, he replaced his ill brother on an assignment to the Kingdom of Hawaii, and it was on the islands that he was ordained a priest later that year.

Nine years later, Father Damien answered his bishop's call to attend to the residents of the leper colony on the island of Molokai. Despite the idyllic setting, it was a human wasteland that would have horrified even the strongest priest. But Father Damien accepted the task and resolved to be an instrument of God's love to the diseased, disfigured, and debilitated.

For 16 years, Father Damien treated the afflicted as God's children meeting more than their spiritual and sacramental needs. He not only built their homes, but he also dug their graves. He served in a medical capacity and served them food when they were too weak to eat.

A priest of tremendous faith, Father Damien found strength in Holy Communion. "Without the constant presence of our Divine Master upon the altar in my poor chapels, I never could have persevered casting my lot with the lepers of Molokai. Holy Communion being the daily bread of a priest, I feel myself happy, well pleased, and resigned in the rather exceptional circumstances in which it has pleased Divine Providence to put me," he wrote.

In 1873, Father Damien had the opportunity to leave the colony, but he requested permission to stay. It was granted. Of all the hardships he faced while serving the lepers on Molokai, he said the greatest was that he was the only priest on the island, and thus unable himself to regularly receive the Sacrament of Reconciliation. When ships would pass by the island to drop supplies into the water, he would ask from shore if there was a priest on board the ship. If so, he would shout his confession from the island to the priest, who typically wasn't willing to get any closer for fear of contracting leprosy. That's how important the Sacrament of Reconciliation was to Father Damien as a penitent.

Not surprisingly, in time, Father Damien succumbed to the conditions he ensconced himself in. In December of 1884, he lost feeling in his leg. It was the first sign that he had contracted leprosy. He continued to serve and work alongside his people, but the final years of his life were difficult. He struggled psychologically, had disagreements with his superiors, and was accused of deviant behavior by those who thought leprosy was a sexually transmitted disease.

In the spring of 1889, Father Damien predicted that he would spend Easter in Heaven rather than on Molokai with his people and that prediction proved to be correct. He died on April 15, 1889, at the age of 49. He was originally buried in Hawaii, but his body was eventually moved to his home in Belgium. He was beatified in 1995 and was canonized by Pope Benedict XVI in 2009. His feast day is May 10.

The Least You Need to Know

- Christ instituted the sacraments as outward and visible signs of the graces he bestows on His people. They are our inheritance from Him given to us at certain milestones in our lives.
- There are three categories of sacraments: the Sacraments of Initiation, the Sacraments of Healing, and the Sacraments of Service.
- The sacraments can be found in Sacred Scripture and are not manmade rituals.
- The sacraments are not symbolic super powers or magic, but they are symbols that have the power to transform lives depending on how people allow Christ's graces to affect them.

The Sacraments of Initiation

Have you ever wondered what it takes to be a card-carrying member of the Catholic faith? Are you ready to wash away your sins, be filled with the Spirit, and eat the Bread of Life? Then the Sacraments of Initiation are the place to start!

The Sacraments of Initiation are the orientation package of the Catholic Church. Though they often occur before one is old enough to vote, they familiarize new members with the faith, lay the groundwork for Christian living, sustain folks in good times and in bad, and enable one to stand strong as a soldier of Christ. Best of all, they are absolutely free!

In this chapter, we will explore the sacraments that connect us in turn to the Father (Baptism), the Son (Eucharist), and the Holy Spirit (Confirmation). These developmental milestones have a powerful impact on the soul, offer an increasing measure of God's grace, and help form one's commitment to the Catholic Church.

In This Chapter

- Washing away your sins in Baptism
- Receiving the Holy Spirit in Confirmation
- Partaking of the Body and Blood of Christ
- Converting to the faith through RCIA

Baptism: Welcome to the Club

Baptism is the doorway to the Christian faith. Though its origins in ritual washings date back to the time of the Torah, most people associate pre–Christian-era baptism with one man: John.

John the Baptist was Jesus' cousin and earned a reputation as an eccentric and outspoken preacher who lived in the desert wearing clothes made of camel's hair and surviving on a daily diet of locusts and wild honey. He spent his time calling his followers to repent in preparation for the Kingdom of God and symbolically cleansing them of their sins in the Jordan River. As his ministry grew, people began to wonder if John was in fact the Messiah the prophets promised, but John was quick to let them know that he was the one sent ahead to ready the world for His arrival.

> "I baptize you with water for repentance, but one who is more powerful than I is coming after me; I am not worthy to carry his sandals. He will baptize you with the Holy Spirit and with fire." (Matthew 3:11)

While John is credited with baptizing Jesus when he was about 30 years old, it is important to note that it was not the sacramental act we celebrate today. It was an act of repentance. Baptism did not become a sacrament until Jesus instituted it after the resurrection when He commissioned His apostles to "make disciples of all nations baptizing them in the name of the Father and of the Son and of the Holy Spirit." (Matthew 28:19)

Christians consider baptism the sacrament in which one is connected to God through Christ and claimed for His Kingdom. It is the primary way to salvation, and without it, one cannot gain access to the other sacraments and share in all of the graces God has in store for them. In John 14:6, Jesus said, "I am the way, and the truth, and the life. No one comes to the Father except through me." It is a permanent mark on the soul that joins an individual to Christ's sacrificial death on the cross, frees the person from Original Sin, and guarantees this person an eternal life in Heaven upon death, provided he or she continually says yes to it.

 FAST FACT

Although baptism is critical, it is important to note that because Jesus sacrificed Himself for all humanity, even those who did not have the opportunity to learn about Jesus or the faith during their lifetime, but live a moral life in which they consistently seek God, have the opportunity to find salvation after death.

How Does Baptism Work?

Baptism is the first Sacrament of Initiation in the Catholic Church, and it is generally bestowed upon an infant during the first few weeks of life; however, anyone who has not received the Sacrament of Baptism and wishes to do so is eligible. The only requirement is that he or she must possess faith in God and must be able to profess it publicly, unless the person is an infant, in which case the parents profess their faith on the child's behalf.

This raises the question of why Catholics baptize babies instead of holding a christening or dedication ceremony as many other Christian churches do. Baptizing infants who cannot speak for themselves emphasizes that God takes the first initiative in offering us grace, calling us to be His children, and incorporating us into the Church. We spend our lives continually living out the commitment made at baptism—either by ourselves or by our parents—but baptizing infants recognizes that it all starts with God, that grace is God's gift, and that God wants us for Himself.

Baptism can occur within a Mass or in a separate service, and is usually administered by a bishop, priest, or deacon. (Though in an emergency, anyone has the authority to baptize.) When the day arrives, the minister, candidate, parents (if applicable), and sponsors (or *godparents*) gather at the baptismal font or immersion pool for the ceremony. The priest asks for the person's name and what he or she is seeking. He confirms that the person or parents understand the sacrament and what it entails, and after several blessings, prayers, and readings, the priest anoints the candidate with the Oil of Catechumens in preparation for the formal baptism.

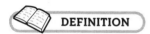 **DEFINITION**

A **godparent** is one who promises to assist the parents of a newly baptized child in raising the child according to the laws of the Catholic Church.

The critical element of the baptismal process is, of course, the action with water accompanied by the words: "I baptize you in the name of the Father, and of the Son, and of the Holy Spirit." The water may be poured three times over the head of the person being baptized, or the person may be fully or partially immersed in water. Once the water has been poured or the person immersed and the words proclaimed, the newly baptized person is now and forever a child of God, guaranteed a place at His side in the heavenly kingdom and presented with the light of Christ (a baptismal candle) and a white garment in commemoration of the event.

There are two different anointings that occur during baptism and two oils that are used. The first anointing uses the Oil of the Catechumens and occurs before the baptism. The second one uses the Sacred Chrism Oil, which is also used in the Sacraments of Confirmation and Holy Orders. Chrism is a perfumed oil that is consecrated by each local bishop on Holy Thursday. Anointing one with Chrism signifies the call of the baptized to the threefold ministry of priest, prophet, and king.

What's in a Name?

One of the most common questions to arise around the Sacrament of Baptism is whether or not Catholics have to name their child after a saint. This is not exactly a requirement, but the Church believes that names should not be given lightly and that it is important for children to be named after a person of exemplary moral virtue. The purpose of a saintly name reaffirms one's belief in the communion of saints and gives the child a patron in heaven that they can turn to as an example of Christian living. Put simply, naming a child after a saint is like giving them a friend who lives with God.

Confirmation: Catch the Spirit

Christian churches that have dedication ceremonies or christenings hold off on baptism until the person can decide for himself or herself if they are ready to commit to Christ. Because the Church feels it is also important for one to make the personal commitment to the faith at a time when he or she feels ready, there is a sacrament that enables one to reaffirm the baptismal promises made on their behalf. It is called confirmation and most often is conferred in the junior high or high school years.

Despite the similarities and the fact that the two sacraments are interconnected, confirmation is not Baptism Part II. This sacrament seals Catholics' baptismal vows, fills them with the Holy Spirit, and prepares them to serve as adult witnesses of Christ. It is technically the second Sacrament of Initiation, but typically, it is the third one received (after First Holy Communion).

Like baptism, Christ bestowed the gift of the Holy Spirit on his apostles after His resurrection; however, the Holy Spirit's biblical history is deep and varied. In the Old Testament, it spoke through the prophets. It played a major role in the birth of Jesus and descended upon Him during His baptism, but the story in which the Holy Spirit takes center stage occurs in the Acts of the Apostles during the feast of Pentecost.

"And suddenly from heaven there came a sound like the rush of a violent wind, and it filled the entire house where they were sitting. Divided tongues, as of fire, appeared among them, and a tongue rested on each of them. All of them were filled with the Holy Spirit and began to speak in other languages, as the Spirit gave them ability." (Acts 2:2-4)

When Christ sent the Holy Spirit, He fulfilled His promise to be with His followers even after He ascended to the Father. The Holy Spirit gave the apostles the strength they needed to profess the faith, face their fears, and keep the early Christian Church alive. Those who seek this sacrament from the Church want to deepen their relationship with God in hopes of serving him through the gifts the Holy Spirit promises.

"If you love me, you will keep my commandments. And I will ask the Father, and he will give you another advocate, to be with you forever. This is the Spirit of truth, whom the world cannot receive, because it neither sees him nor knows him. You will know him, because he abides with you and he will be in you." (John 14:15-17)

The seven gifts of the Holy Spirit are:

1. Wisdom

2. Understanding

3. Counsel

4. Fortitude

5. Knowledge

6. Piety

7. Fear of the Lord

Fueling the Fire

In order to prepare for the sacrament, candidates spend several months learning more about their faith, praying, participating in the liturgy, and discerning the direction of their lives. They do this in order to make an informed decision about their Christian journey and then take that next step with confidence.

To help in this endeavor, the candidate chooses a sponsor who serves as a support person throughout the process and who will present the candidate to the bishop during the ceremony. This is similar to the role their godparents played during their baptism, and while it is permissible to choose one of their godparents to stand beside them once more, they are allowed to select anyone who meets the following criteria:

1. Is a fully initiated practicing Catholic age 16 or older

2. Serves as an exemplary model of Christian living

3. Is willing to pray with and for the candidate

Prior to the ceremony, a candidate also chooses a confirmation name. This is not a requirement, particularly if the candidate has already been named for a saint, but it is a lot of fun and many take the opportunity to select a heavenly role model to whom they can turn throughout their lives.

FAST FACT

Some of the most popular saint names chosen for confirmation include:

St. Francis of Assisi

St. Michael the Archangel

St. Patrick

St. Therese of the Little Flower

St. Lucy

St. Catherine of Siena

How Does Confirmation Work?

The Sacrament of Confirmation is conferred during a liturgy that is presided over by a bishop. (In some cases permission can be given to a priest to confer the sacrament, but the ordinary minister of confirmation is a bishop.) It is typically a larger ceremony than a baptism because it usually includes several Catholic parishes from around the diocese and hundreds of candidates. Anyone who has been baptized and is in a state of grace (meaning that they do not have a mortal sin on their soul) is eligible for the sacrament.

Together with their sponsors the candidates gather at the Mass, and after the Scripture readings, everyone renews their baptismal promises. Those to be confirmed approach the bishop where the sponsor presents the candidate using their new saint name. The bishop anoints them with Sacred Chrism Oil and lays his hands on their head to bless them with Holy Spirit and all of the gifts that come with it. As the bishop imparts the final blessing on the newly confirmed, they become full-fledged, responsible adult members of the Catholic community.

The Eucharist: Sharing in the Supper of the Lord

The Holy Eucharist is the third Sacrament of Initiation and the sacrament at the center of Catholic belief. When Jesus made His famous "I am the bread of life" sermon to the Jewish people at Capernaum in the Gospel of John, it was more than a symbolic metaphor. It was a literal claim. He promised the spiritual anorexics of the world that if they believed in Him, He would fill their bellies and keep their spirit alive for all time.

> "Those who eat my flesh and drink my blood have eternal life, and I will raise them up on the last day; for my flesh is true food and my blood is true drink. Those who eat my flesh and drink my blood abide in me and I in them." (John 6:54-56)

Jesus knew that when He made His triumphant entry into the city of Jerusalem at the start of Passover, He would be dead by the end of the week. As He gathered with His friends for that final time in the Upper Room for the feast, He knew that before the night was over He would be arrested and that nearly all of His followers would be in hiding. During the meal, He utters the monologue that is the core of the Eucharistic celebration and is accounted for in the three Synoptic Gospels:

> "'I have greatly desired to eat this Passover with you before I suffer; for I tell you, I will not eat it until it is fulfilled in the kingdom of God.' Then he took a cup, and after giving thanks he said, 'take this and divide it among yourselves; for I tell you that from now on, I will not drink of the fruit of the vine until the kingdom of God comes.' Then he took a loaf of bread, and when he had given thanks, he broke it and gave it to them saying, 'this is my body which is given up for you. Do this in memory of me.'" (Luke 22:15-19)

The Eucharist is the sacred mystery of the Church and the most precious gift Jesus gave us. Through it, we celebrate the Passion, death, and resurrection of Jesus and all that it means for us. From that first Easter Sunday on, the Christians met on the day of His resurrection to break bread together and proclaim his *Paschal Mystery*.

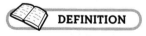 **DEFINITION**

> The **Paschal Mystery** is a phrase used to refer to all of the events surrounding the suffering, death, and resurrection of Jesus and their meaning for humanity.

Preparing for Catholic Communion

While a full explanation of the Eucharistic Liturgy will be covered in Chapter 9, there are a few things you may want to know about who is eligible to receive the sacrament.

First, in Catholicism, Holy Communion is a closed event, meaning that one must be a Catholic in order to participate. (Though non-Catholics may approach the altar and receive a blessing from the priest, if they wish.) There is a reason for this. Unlike other Christian traditions that use bread and wine (or grape juice) as a symbolic representation of Christ's body and blood, Catholics believe that Christ Himself is present in the appearance of bread and wine. This is known as *transubstantiation* and refers to the unexplainable change that occurs on the altar, which turns the ordinary into something extraordinary. Sharing the Eucharist is a statement of belief and a sign of unity. Everyone who receives the Eucharist should believe it truly is the Body and Blood of Christ and be in union with the community that is celebrating it, both at a particular church and in union with all others who believe the same thing throughout the world.

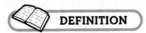 **DEFINITION**

Transubstantiation is a theological term used to explain the presence of Christ in the bread and wine during a Catholic communion service. Although everything about the bread and wine that can be experienced by the senses remains the same—the look, taste, and smell—the substance or identity is transformed through the grace of the Holy Spirit to become the Body and Blood of Christ.

Second, Catholics wishing to receive communion must be free of sin before they approach the altar. There is a prayer prior to the communion service that asks for absolution from sin, but in the event someone has a serious sin on his or her soul, it is vital that they go to the Sacrament of Reconciliation before taking the sacrament in order to reconcile their soul with God and the community. They must also fast from food and drink for at least one hour prior to receiving the Eucharist, with the exception of water and medicine.

Prior to communion, Catholics are encouraged to spend some time in quiet reflection on the importance of the sacrament they are about to receive and to prepare themselves mentally for receiving Christ.

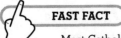 **FAST FACT**

Most Catholics who were baptized as infants receive the Eucharist for the first time around the age of seven, while in second grade. After a period of prayer, study, and preparation, they participate in a Mass with family and friends for their First Holy Communion.

The Steps to Catholic Communion

When it is time, Catholics approach the altar where the priest or Eucharistic minister holds up the host and makes a slight bow of reverence to the presence of Christ.

The priest or Eucharistic minister says, "The Body of Christ." The proper response is "Amen."

You may receive the host in one of two ways: in your hand (one on top of the other) or on your outstretched tongue. You allow the host to dissolve in your mouth and reflect on the sacrament's significance.

After receiving the consecrated host, you may then approach the chalice of consecrated wine. (This is not required, but is considered a more complete celebration.)

The minister says, "The Blood of Christ." Again, the proper response is "Amen." The communicant then sips a small amount from the chalice.

After receiving communion, it's appropriate to spend time conversing with the Lord. After all, it's the closest you will ever be to Him on this Earth, so it's a good time to chat. And as Jesus said in Matthew 7:7, "Ask, and it will be given you; search, and you will find; knock, and the door will be opened for you."

The Eucharistic Sacrament is unlike the other two Sacraments of Initiation because it can be received more than once. In fact, it can be received daily. Although Catholics are certainly encouraged to participate in the Mass as often as possible, they are only required to attend a weekly service (which might occur on Saturday evening or Sunday) as well as the Holy Days of Obligation throughout the year (more on those in Chapter 24). The Holy Mass is a memorial of the Paschal Mystery made on our behalf and the promise that one day we, too, will sit at His heavenly table and dine in communion with Him.

CATHOLIC QUOTE

God would have given us something greater if he had something greater than Himself.

—St. John Vianney

The Rite of Christian Initiation for Adults (RCIA)

If you are an adult who is unbaptized, baptized but not catechized, or a baptized non-Catholic Christian looking to make the move to the faith, then you need to check out the Rite of Christian Initiation for Adults (RCIA). The RCIA is the spot for immersion conversion!

The RCIA is not in and of itself a Sacrament of Initiation, but it is the process by which adult converts join the Catholic faith. When an unbaptized individual feels called to the Catholic faith, he or she meets with a priest, deacon, or RCIA director in a parish to discuss their intentions and options. This period of inquiry is called the precatechumenate. The length of this stage varies depending on the individual's discernment as to whether or not God is calling him or her to the Catholic faith.

When the person is ready to continue the process, they profess their intention during a Mass and once the assembly affirms their desire, they are accepted into the order of *catechumens* during the Rite of Acceptance, denoting the beginning of one's catechumenate stage. It is typically at least one full year but can be longer or shorter depending on individual circumstance. It is a period of faith formation, study, questioning, and discernment as the individual learns how to live as a Catholic.

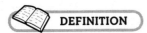 **DEFINITION**

> A **catechumen** is an unbaptized adult who is studying the Catholic faith with the intention of joining it.

When the individual, priest, and parish team feel that they are ready to be installed, they express a desire to receive the sacraments. This begins the third stage of the process—the period of purification and enlightenment. It coincides with the first Sunday of Lent and is called the Rite of Election. During this event, the catechumens gather at the local cathedral in which they publicly ask the bishop to receive the sacraments. Their names are recorded in a book and from that moment forward, they are known as the "elect."

Lent is a time of intense study and prayer as the catechumens prepare for the Easter Vigil Mass in which they receive the Sacraments of Initiation.

 CATHOLIC QUOTE

> The most important thing is to begin decisively.
>
> —St. Teresa of Avila

The Easter Vigil, which takes place on Holy Saturday (the night before Easter), is a very special event in the Church calendar that will be discussed in detail in Chapter 22. It is during this celebration that the catechumens stand with their sponsors (just like in other celebrations of baptism and confirmation) and are presented to their new parish, who pray for them and recite the Litany of the Saints. The priest blesses water and prepares it for the baptismal rite in which the candidates renounce sin, profess their faith in God, and are baptized in turn.

Afterward, the candidates are changed into white robes to signify that their sins have been washed away and are handed their baptismal candle, which is lit from the church's Easter candle. They then receive the Sacrament of Confirmation and are anointed with the Sacred Chrism. As the Mass continues, they receive Holy Communion for the first time.

After they are received into the faith, the new members spend the next 40 days reflecting on their experiences in a period known as *mystagogy,* which enables them to continue their faith formation, study Catholic scripture and teachings, and look for the ways in which they can actively participate in their new parish.

 **DEFINITION**

Mystagogy is the ongoing study of the mysteries of the Catholic faith.

Through the Sacraments of Initiation, Catholics are freed from the darkness of sin, learn to be strong against all evil, and become one with the Lord. They enable individuals to stand as a community of God's people, and when combined, help the people of Christ carry out the mission of Christ in our homes, in our parishes, in our diocese and throughout the world.

 KEEP IT SIMPLE

The RCIA process works differently for those who have already been baptized or who want to return to the faith. They are called a Candidate for Full Communion. They sometimes go through the full RCIA process in preparation for being received into the Church and celebrating Confirmation and Eucharist at the Easter Vigil, or—depending on their level of knowledge and participation—they could make a profession of faith and receive Confirmation and Eucharist at any Mass during the year, whenever they are ready.

The Least You Need to Know

- The Sacraments of Initiation include Baptism, Confirmation, and the Holy Eucharist.
- Baptism is the doorway to Christianity and the primary method of salvation.
- In the Sacrament of Confirmation, a Catholic's baptismal vows are sealed and they are filled with the gifts of the Holy Spirit.
- In the celebration of the Holy Eucharist, Catholics commemorate the sacrifice of Jesus and unite with His living presence in the bread and wine.
- The RCIA program is for adults who wish to convert to the Catholic faith.

The Sacraments of Healing

They are the sacraments that offer us comfort and consolation at those times when we need it most. When we are troubled, scared, overwhelmed, exhausted, or full of grief and anger, the Sacraments of Healing help us make it through the tough times and find new life in Christ.

The Sacraments of Penance and Reconciliation and the Anointing of the Sick strengthen the spirit and restore the soul. They patch up wounds, erase our errors, and give us a chance to reconnect with God. He's no stranger to our pain and rejection and in those moments when we feel lost and afraid, that's when He wants us to lean on Him the most.

In this chapter, we will examine the sacraments that soothe what ails us. No matter if we have hurt those around us, turned away from God, or simply feel out of sorts, we know that we will be made clean by God's grace and be able to face the world again.

In This Chapter

- Confession is good for the soul
- Do you need a priest to be forgiven?
- How anointing can heal the body and the soul
- Whatever happened to the Last Rites?

Restoring the Soul

We all have those times when we don't feel 100 percent. Perhaps we quarreled with a friend and now feel guilty over the things we said. Maybe we made a poor decision and are suffering the consequences of our actions. Perhaps we've been diagnosed with a serious illness and are now fighting an uphill battle. It's in those moments that we want someone to forgive and forget. We want someone to love us when we find it hard to love ourselves, and we want someone to hold us close and tell us that everything is going to be alright.

Jesus wasn't one to shy away from suffering. Scripture tells us that "the Son of Man came to seek and to save the lost" (Luke 19:10) and the Gospels are full of stories in which Jesus reached out to heal those who were both physically and spiritually ill. He embraced them, comforted them, and helped them feel whole again. He forgave their mistakes. He cured their afflictions and he consoled them with stories about compassion and caring. He encouraged reconciliation rather than retaliation, told His followers to turn the other cheek, and commanded them to "love one another just as I have loved you …." (John 13:34)

Even today, Jesus knows how heavy one's emotional and physical baggage can be, and he is ready to lighten the load. Through the Sacraments of Healing, we are offered the opportunity to tell Him our troubles, make our apologies, turn over to Him the things we can't handle, and know that things will turn out according to His will.

Make no mistake about it: the Sacraments of Healing are not miracle medicines that can make all of life's difficulties go away. They cannot fix financial problems. They cannot cure all cancer, and they cannot prevent us from making mistakes. They are graces that, with God's help, enable us to change what we can, cope with those things we cannot change, and learn to know the difference.

The Sacrament of Penance and Reconciliation

There is a lot of confusion as to why Catholics have the Sacrament of Penance and Reconciliation in the first place. Many Christian traditions say it is unnecessary for someone to acknowledge their sins to anyone other than God, but in this section, I will show you that the sacrament is based in Scripture, that it was instituted by Christ, and that He alone has the power to forgive sins.

The Sacrament of Penance and Reconciliation goes by a lot of different names. However, most people know it by one: Confession. Though the term conjures images of foreboding phone booths in which Catholics bare their souls to a priest in the hope that he will forgive them of their sins and dole out an appropriate punishment for their deed, the reality is not so archaic. In actuality, confession is a place where Catholics disclose their struggles, reconnect with God, ask His pardon for their failings, and receive His grace to become holy.

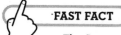

FAST FACT

The Sacrament of Penance and Reconciliation is also known as:

- The Sacrament of Penance: Where one makes amends and repairs what has been broken.
- The Sacrament of Reconciliation: Where one reunites with God.
- The Sacrament of Conversion: Where one turns away from sin and returns to the Father's love.
- The Sacrament of Forgiveness: Where one receives God's pardon and peace.
- The Sacrament of Confession: Where one discloses his or her sins to a priest in order to receive absolution for them.

But why do we need a sacrament to forgive sins? After all, isn't that what Baptism is for? Well, yes and no. While baptism turns us toward God and makes a union with God possible in this life as well as the next, we are still human and we are still inclined to make sinful choices from time to time. Baptism is not a free pass to do whatever we want without consequence. When we turn away from God, we have to be accountable for our behavior and make reparation.

We also need God's help. If you're a parent, have you tried to always be patient and loving with your children? On your own, it's sometimes impossible—but God's grace can help. If you're a teenager, have you tried to treat your peers and parents with love and respect? On your own, it's often impossible—but God's grace can help. No matter what our sins and failings—anger, lust, gossip, jealousy, judging others—we need help in order to overcome them and grow in holiness. All the sacraments give us God's grace, but the Sacrament of Penance and Reconciliation gives us the particular grace and strength to overcome the very specific failings we bring to God in the confessional.

As we learned in Chapter 5, Jesus instituted the Sacrament of Reconciliation after his resurrection when he appeared to the apostles on the evening of the first day of the week and gave them the ability to forgive sins in His name. He said, "Receive the Holy Spirit. If you forgive the sins of any, they are forgiven; if you retain the sins of any, they are retained." (John 21:22b-23) However, He spent a lot of his time on Earth emphasizing the importance of repentance and forgiving the sins of the penitent.

In the parable of the Prodigal Son, He tells the story of a young man who convinces his father to divide the family estate between himself and his brother. After squandering his inheritance on riotous living, the boy finds himself flat broke and having to take any job that will enable him to survive. Lost, frightened, and ashamed of his behavior, he makes the difficult decision to return to his father's home and face the music rather than continue to live in squalor among strangers. To his surprise, when his father hears he is en route, he races to meet him, thrilled that he has returned to the fold.

The Sacrament of Reconciliation, which has been passed down from the apostles and their successors throughout the ages, is similar in the fact that it is an opportunity to come clean with someone you have hurt, who has already put the past behind them, is happy to see you again, and is ready to move on.

 CATHOLIC QUOTE

> The good Lord knows everything. Even before you confess, he already knows that you will sin again, yet he still forgives you. How great is the love of our God: he even forces himself to forget the future, so that he can grant us his forgiveness.

—St. John Vianney

Why Does God Need a Middleman?

He doesn't. God can forgive sins anytime, anywhere, and without the assistance of a priest. However, there is an adage that says you can't change what you can't acknowledge, and when we merely think about our faults and failings in private it is very easy to do nothing about them. We can rationalize the behavior, justify our choices, and convince ourselves that we have done nothing wrong. By meeting with someone who has been given the authority to forgive sins in Jesus' name, it lends weight to the encounter and forces us to own up to the truth in a personal way.

Think about it this way: Why do people sign up for diet programs in which their weight will be recorded and announced for everyone to hear? Why do they join gyms or find friends to work out with? We all know it is possible to lose weight privately, so why get another person involved? The simple truth is that when we have to look another person in the eye, we are more heavily invested and more inclined to make a change for the better.

In the Sacrament of Reconciliation, a priest is present not only as a representative of God, but also as a representative of humanity, whom we have wronged. Our sins are not always against only God, but often are against other people as well. His presence denotes a sign of reconciliation between the entire community and us.

The priest is also there standing in the place of Jesus Christ to make sure we know God forgives our sins. If we sit down and really reflect on our failings, it often is the case that we have a hard time believing anyone—let alone God—would actually forgive us. We also sometimes have a hard time forgiving ourselves. It is the responsibility of the priest not only to proclaim God's forgiveness, but to make sure we are reminded how much God loves us, that no sin is too great for God to forgive, and that God wants to help us with His grace to be good and holy in the future.

CATHOLIC QUOTE

What is repentance? A great sorrow over the fact that we are the way we are.

—Marie Von Ebner-Eschenbach

Contrition, Absolution, and Penance

Catholics who have reached the age of reason are obligated to confess their sins. They may receive the Sacrament of Reconciliation any time a priest is available, but they are expected to confess serious sins at least once a year and are strongly encouraged to take advantage of this sacrament during the Advent and Lenten seasons (see Chapter 22) or before receiving another sacrament such as Confirmation, Eucharist, Matrimony, or Holy Orders.

There are three things Catholics must do in order to make a good confession:

1. They must tell all of their sins.

2. They must be truly sorry for their sins.

3. They must have a firm intention not to sin again.

In order to take responsibility for our actions and settle our account with God in the Sacrament of Reconciliation, we need to examine our conscience and determine where our actions take a detour from God's will. This is called *contrition*. We have to know what we are truly sorry for and why we are truly sorry for it in order to disclose it with the proper intention.

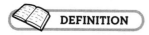

DEFINITION

Contrition is the longing inside one's self to turn away from sin and improve one's life for the better.

Under ordinary circumstances, one must reveal all serious sins that can be recalled (and that have not been previously confessed) in confession. This is not easy, and sometimes it can feel quite embarrassing, but remember even the pope goes to confession to reconcile his relationship with God. If he can do it, so can you!

You also have to be willing to make amends for your actions through penance. It's one thing to say you are sorry for something inside your head or to pay "lip service" to the event, but usually an apology carries a bit more weight when you are willing to make up for it in some way. This can be through prayer, fasting, charity, and other acts of reparation. Above all, the contrite must have the firm intention not to sin again. God can spot a "piecrust promise" all the way from Heaven, so if you repent it, don't plan to repeat it!

Lest you think only the penitent has rules to follow in the confessional, the truth is that the priest has rules he must follow as well. For example, there are some serious sins that even the average priest cannot forgive. Sins that result in *excommunication* from the Church may require special absolution from a bishop or a priest delegated by a bishop, or in some cases by the pope. Of course, in extreme emergencies such as immediate death, a priest has the authority to absolve one of all sins and of excommunication.

 **DEFINITION**

Excommunication is the exclusion of a Catholic from the sacraments of the Church.

Also, what happens in the confessional stays in the confessional. A priest is not allowed to divulge anything he has learned through a confession—no matter what. This principle is called the Seal of Confession. To violate this rule would result in excommunication of the priest.

While they do not take pleasure in hearing everyone's dark deeds, priests do welcome the opportunity to let people open up about what is troubling them in order to lead them into a better relationship with God. Priests understand that merely talking about an issue encourages one to confront it and make a move to rectify it. Although the issue may not go away overnight, getting it off your chest can feel as though a huge weight has been lifted from your soul, or like a refreshing shower after a hard day at work.

When it comes down to it, priests know that the Sacrament of Reconciliation is not really about sin, it is about love—how God loves each of us so much that He will forgive us whenever we come to Him. And that's a beautiful thing. No one is defined by his or her sins, and priests don't think of a person's sins when they see the person outside of the confessional. Through formation in seminary and especially through the grace of God given in the Sacrament of Holy Orders, priests are able to see and remember God's great love given in the Sacrament of Reconciliation, not the details of the sins.

Steps to Making the Sacrament of Reconciliation

The Sacrament of Reconciliation can happen anonymously (behind a screen) or face to face, depending on personal preference.

- The Priest may begin with a short blessing or a Scripture reading.
- Begin by saying "Forgive me, Father for I have sinned; it has been (however long) since my last confession."
- Confess the sins you have identified through your examination of conscience. Try not to feel embarrassed, and answer any questions the priest has openly and honestly.

- End by expressing sorrow not only for the sins you mentioned, but also any you might have forgotten.

- Listen as the priest offers you counsel as well as a penance for your confession.

- Say an Act of Contrition expressing your sorrow and bow your head while the priest offers you absolution in Jesus' name.

The Act of Contrition

An Act of Contrition is any prayer that expresses sorrow for sin, asks for God's forgiveness, and includes an intention to avoid sin in the future. Some people offer a prayer in their own words, but here is one common version of an Act of Contrition that is often memorized and used in the Sacrament of Reconciliation:

> Oh my God, I am heartily sorry for having offended Thee, and I detest all of my sins because of Thy just punishments, but most of all because they offend Thee, my God, Who are all-good and deserving of all my love. I firmly resolve with the help of Thy grace, to sin no more and to avoid the near occasion of sin. Amen.

The Sacrament of the Anointing of the Sick

The Anointing of the Sick is a sacrament designed to heal the body and soul while reuniting an individual with God. Its scriptural roots date back to Christ's miraculous healings, both physical and spiritual, during His public ministry. In the Gospel of Matthew, Jesus saw some people carrying a paralyzed man over to see Him. Moved by their faith in Him and touched by the man's condition, Jesus tells the paralytic that his sins are forgiven, which draws the scorn of the nearby scribes who question his authority to do such a thing. He examines the man's poor quality of life and asks, "For which is easier to say, 'Your sins are forgiven'? or to say, 'Stand and walk'?" (Matthew 9:5)

In the Gospel of Mark, after His resurrection, Christ institutes the sacrament when He tells His apostles to cast out demons in His name and that if they lay their hands on those who are ill, "they will recover." (Mark 16:18) However, the basic format for the sacrament that is celebrated today by the Church is based on the Letter of James, which says:

> "Are any among you sick? They should call for the elders of the church and have them pray over them, anointing them with oil in the name of the Lord. The prayer of faith will save the sick, and the Lord will raise them up; and anyone who has committed sins will be forgiven." (James 5:14-15)

Any Catholic experiencing serious illness (either physical or psychological) or the effects of old age, regardless of perceived proximity to death, is eligible to receive the sacrament. It is a sacrament that can be received repeatedly if one's health deteriorates or if the condition has changed. The Anointing of the Sick is one of the most powerful of the sacraments because those who receive it do so at a very vulnerable time in their lives and are seeking to be united to God. The Anointing of the Sick often brings great comfort and strength in challenging times.

As James writes, during the Anointing of the Sick, a priest prays over a sick person, lays hands on the individual's head, and anoints his or her forehead and palms with sacred oil while saying these words: "Through this holy anointing, may the Lord in His love and mercy help you with the grace of the Holy Spirit. May the Lord who frees you from sin save you and raise you up. Amen." The oil used is the third holy oil that is blessed during Holy Week: the Oil of the Sick. Through this sacrament, the person receives a twofold grace: that they will be saved and that their sins will be forgiven.

Because the Anointing of the Sick includes forgiveness of sins, only a priest or bishop can administer the sacrament. Often it is celebrated in hospitals, in long-term care facilities, or in people's homes when a priest visits someone who is sick. However, many parishes offer a communal celebration of the Anointing of the Sick in the church once a year, when the entire local community can gather to pray for those who are ill. This can be done either during a Mass or at a separate liturgical celebration.

KEEP IT SIMPLE

Notice that this sacrament does not guarantee a healing will take place. The Anointing of the Sick is not a miracle cure—all for what ails you. The term "saved" in this context can mean several things depending on the will of God. While some people have been healed after an anointing, others are given the strength they need to persevere in their struggles. Regardless, they are united with Jesus Christ in his suffering, death, and resurrection and all sins are forgiven.

Is This the Same as the "Last Rites"?

Technically, there is no such sacrament as the "Last Rites," despite what you may have heard or read. Though it is true that historically Catholics were not anointed unless it was believed that they were very near death, there were sensible reasons for this practice:

1. The person was critically ill.

2. Death was the most likely outcome.

3. The medical community was not able to cure many serious illnesses.

As a result, the Anointing of the Sick came to be called Extreme Unction, or Last Rites. Unction means anointing, and it was called extreme because it happened at the final extremity of life. It was the last of the anointings a Catholic received: Baptism, Confirmation, Ordination (for clergy), and then the final anointing, the "last rite" immediately before death.

With the Second Vatican Council in the 1960s, the Anointing of the Sick was restored to its original (scriptural) purpose of being administered at any time of serious illness, and not just immediately before death. So it happens in much broader circumstances now. In the ideal circumstances, the Anointing of the Sick would happen earlier in a person's illness or in the immediate aftermath of a tragic incident, such as a car accident. As death approaches, the person would continue receiving the Eucharist as often as possible until they are no longer physically able to consume a host, at which point prayers continue.

FAST FACT

Former U.S. President John F. Kennedy suffered from so many health issues that he received the sacramental "Last Rites" several times before he took office. This included once on a 1947 trip to England, once when returning to America aboard the Queen Mary, once while suffering from a high fever while in Asia in 1951, and again in 1954 when he developed an infection and slipped into a coma after back surgery.

The Sacraments of the Dying

When a person is nearing death, there are three sacraments that are proper during this time: the Eucharist, Reconciliation, and the Anointing of the Sick. As you might expect, the most important of these is the Eucharist, a final receiving of the Body and Blood of Christ. In these circumstances, it has a special name: Eucharist as *Viaticum*, which means "food for the journey." There are additional prayers that accompany giving the Eucharist as Viaticum that pray for the person's journey from this life to eternity. In addition, if the person is capable of speaking, they should celebrate the Sacrament of Reconciliation, and they should also be anointed. There are rituals that combine all three of these sacraments into a single celebration.

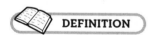

DEFINITION

Viaticum is a Latin word meaning "food for the journey." It refers to the last Eucharist one receives before death.

Unfortunately, in a lot of cases people do not call a priest to visit someone who is near death until after the person is beyond the point of being able to receive communion. Very often they are already in a coma or their bodily systems have rendered them unable to consume a consecrated host, which is why the sacrament celebrated most often in these cases is the Anointing of the Sick. Though a priest is necessary for this sacrament, as well as the Sacrament of Reconciliation, any Eucharistic minister using a host that has been consecrated at Mass can administer the Eucharist, even as Viaticum.

The Least You Need to Know

- The Sacraments of Healing restore the soul and reconnect one with God.
- The Sacrament of Reconciliation is completely confidential and nonjudgmental.
- The Sacrament of Reconciliation is not about sin, but about love and forgiveness.
- The Sacrament of Anointing of the Sick is not the "Last Rites." It can be administered to any Catholic who suffers from serious illness.
- When a person is near death, the sacraments of Anointing, Eucharist, and Reconciliation are appropriate; however, the person's condition may not allow for all of these to occur.

The Sacraments of Service

As we learned in Chapter 4, every member of the Catholic Church is called to holiness and to live the gospel message in every aspect of his or her life. This call, known as a vocation, is something that is rooted in baptism and sets them on a path of service to God.

There are four types of vocations in the Church: the single life, the consecrated life, and the two Sacraments of Service: Holy Orders and Matrimony. Although they seem to be on opposite ends of the spectrum, these sacraments have a deep common denominator—to build up the people of God.

In this chapter, we will explore the Sacraments of Service and learn how these vocations, though geared toward the salvation of others, aid in one's individual salvation as well. We will say "I do" to God's call and discover two of the channels by which God's love is infused into the world.

In This Chapter

- Listening for God's call
- How can we discern a vocation?
- Understanding the three degrees of Holy Orders
- Enjoying a Christ-centered marriage

Discerning the Vocation

Before anyone can follow God's plan for their life, they have to know what that plan is. Does God want them to remain single forever, or to take vows as a consecrated religious? Marry and have children, or serve in the ordained ministry? Whatever the call, all vocations begin with *discernment*, a period of time during which an individual contemplates his or her suitability for a particular life. No path is without benefits and sacrifices, and it is important to weigh all of the pros and cons in order to find out what might be the right fit. But the most important part of discernment is discovering the vocation that God calls you to live.

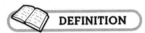 **DEFINITION**

Discernment is the process by which people discover how God is calling them to follow Him.

In the professional world, this might include participating in internships, job shadow programs, or classes in a field of interest. However, when discerning God's call, Catholics typically ...

- Listen for God's voice through meditation and prayer.

- Participate in Mass and in the sacraments in order to ask for the strength to respond to God's call.

- Read spiritual material to help nourish their faith and inspire them to live a Christ-centered life.

- Develop a relationship with the Virgin Mary, and entrust their vocation to her maternal instinct.

- Seek spiritual counsel with a priest or spiritual director.

Those called to the single life or the consecrated life use their freedom to be at the service of others through their work and prayer. They can be either men or women, and although those in the consecrated life are bound by vows of poverty, chastity, and obedience while those in the single life are not, each in their own way strives to model and follow Christ in their everyday life. Those who choose one of the Sacraments of Service are given the additional graces necessary to feed the faithful through ordained ministry or to fortify their spouse (and children) by bringing them closer to God through marriage.

No matter which path one chooses, vocations challenge Catholics to live their faith more deeply and to follow Christ's example as closely as possible. It's not always fun and games. While a vocation can result in rewarding and happy experiences, there will be times of pain and suffering as well. One is not better than the other, but each has its own purpose. It is important for Catholics to follow the vocation that is right for them.

> **CATHOLIC QUOTE**
>
> I am created to do or to be something for which no one else is created: I have a place in God's counsels, in God's world, which no one else has.
>
> —Bl. John Henry Newman

Holy Orders

The Sacrament of Holy Orders is conferred on a baptized Catholic man who has a call to serve the Church as a member of the clergy. It is called holy because it is a vocation that is sanctified by God and it is an order because it serves to guide and direct people on the pathway toward God. There are three orders in this Sacrament: the diaconate (deacons), the presbyterate (priests), and the episcopate (bishops).

When Jesus commanded His apostles to carry on His mission, it was not a request. It was a directive by the commander-in-chief and one that these men felt compelled to respond to. The apostolic ministry that Jesus instituted was to be in direct contrast to the priesthood of the Old Testament, in which men held exalted positions of power and acted as intermediaries between God and His people.

Jesus transformed this idea during His time on Earth and gave us a vocation in which the ordained minister holds no power of his own. He may receive the healing, saving, and transformative power of Christ through his ordination, but he is to be first and foremost a servant and must use these gifts for God's will alone.

Who Qualifies for the Sacrament?

To put it bluntly, not women. Holy Orders is reserved exclusively for baptized Catholic men. As you might expect, this distinction is a hot-button topic for some within the Catholic community, but the Church insists that this rule is not intended to be a slight. In God's eyes, of course, men and women are created equal, and Jesus was not at all shy about including women in his public ministry. However, because Jesus chose only His male companions to be present at the Last Supper for the institution of the priesthood, the Church feels there is no Biblical precedent for including women in the sacrament, and therefore the hierarchy's hands are tied.

It is not meant to hold women back or to demean them in some way, and while there are no signs of anything changing in this area any time soon, there are some members of the hierarchy willing to explore more prominent Church roles for women in the future that do not require ordination.

CATHOLIC QUOTE

It is necessary to broaden the opportunities for a strong presence of women in the Church … we have to work harder to develop a profound theology of women. Only by making this step will it be possible to better reflect on their function within the Church. The feminine genius is needed whenever we make important decisions.

—Pope Francis, 2013 (*La Civiltà Cattolica* interview)

Two Types of Deacons

The first of the three orders of clergy is the diaconate, a ministry of service and charity. After studying philosophy for two to four years and theology for three years, if a man is planning to become a priest, he is first ordained as a transitional deacon. Then, after one more year of studying theology, he is ordained a priest. He spends that year as a deacon as part of his preparation for the priesthood.

A permanent deacon goes through a similar formation process, but with no intention of being ordained a priest. He can be married, if that marriage takes place before being ordained a deacon, and he often has a job outside of the Church, with his ministry as a deacon occupying only part of his time.

Both "types" of deacons receive the Sacrament of Holy Orders and enjoy a special relationship within the hierarchy of the Church. As ordained servants of God, deacons assist in the ministry of the Word, the ministry of the Liturgy, and the ministry of charity in cooperation with priests and bishops. The resurgence of the permanent diaconate in recent years has been a welcome presence in dioceses throughout the world. Both transitional and permanent deacons can baptize, witness marriages, preach at liturgical services, and preside at funeral rites.

FAST FACT

The concept of the deacon was modeled after St. Stephen, who was called as one of seven men to relieve the demands placed on the apostles in the early days of the Church. In Acts 6:5 he is described as "a man of faith and the Holy Spirit" and after the apostles laid hands on him (ordained him) he became a very passionate servant, especially among the poor. The graces he received enabled him to remain strong after his arrest and to forgive those who stoned him as he became the first Christian martyr.

The order of clergy that people are most familiar with is the priesthood. When a priest is ordained, he receives the gifts from the Holy Spirit that enable him to teach as Christ would teach; minister as Christ would minister; heal as Christ would heal, and to forgive as Christ would forgive. A priest represents Christ to the people of God and serves as the living embodiment of Christ's continued presence with His people.

A priest's vocation is wide and varied, as one can imagine. Although some are assigned to a specific ministry outside of parishes, most priests in a diocese work in parish ministry. Through this role they are close co-workers of the bishop and have the responsibility of overseeing the Church's mission at the parish level. In addition to the sacraments and duties of deacons, priests also preside over the celebrations of the Sacraments of the Eucharist, Reconciliation, and Anointing of the Sick. On any given day, a priest may have to …

- Celebrate Mass.

- Counsel an engaged or married couple.

- Visit the sick at hospitals and nursing homes.

- Hear confessions.

- Preside at a funeral or burial service.

- Spend time in personal prayer and study.

- Teach classes to adults, youth, and children.

- Oversee the administrative functions of a parish.

- Perform works of charity.

It sounds overwhelming, and it is definitely a full life, but priests are able to take time off for vacations and relaxation and to spend time with family and friends. But the needs of the Church always come first. You won't hear him complain when he is appointed to a new parish or called upon for a special ministry. It's what he signed up for and he wouldn't trade it for anything in the world. This vocation is one that is focused solidly on Christ and the mission of His Church.

In the Latin or Roman Rite of the Catholic Church, most priests lead celibate lives, in imitation of Jesus who did so to demonstrate his undivided love for the Father and the Church. Yes, they forego romance, marriage, and children of their own, but these men genuinely do not feel as if they have "given up" anything. Their lives are not devoid of love, but rather are full of it. To hear them tell it, they are most definitely in a relationship. They are madly and passionately in love with the Church in the way that a husband loves his wife. And they have the privilege of being part of many families through the parishes and ministries they serve.

Becoming a Bishop

At the highest level of the Sacrament of Holy Orders, a bishop is a man who has been ordained with the fullness of the sacrament and is considered a successor to the apostles. He is admitted into the College of Bishops where, along with the other bishops, cardinals, and the pope, he bears the responsibility for the entire church, but specifically the diocese that he is assigned to.

No one campaigns to be a bishop, and there aren't job interviews. Bishops are chosen and appointed only by the pope, who seeks counsel from his official representative in each country (called the Papal Nuncio) and other bishops in the region. The greatest qualifications to be a bishop are not great managerial or administrative skills, but the heart of a servant and a closeness to the people, especially those on the margins.

Bishops ensure that all parishes and Catholic agencies in a local area have the spiritual and material resources they need to carry out the Lord's work, closely collaborating with priests, deacons, religious, and laity in the process. They are the chief teachers and shepherds of all the churches in their diocese and can preside over the celebrations of all seven sacraments. Only a bishop can ordain someone else a deacon, priest, or bishop for service in the Church.

The Rite of Ordination

Most people have been to a wedding, but not many people have been to an ordination. If you ever have a chance to witness an ordination, go: it is one of the most powerful and meaningful liturgies in the Catholic Church. The Rite of Ordination for each of the three orders of clergy differs slightly, but the basic structure is the same for all three.

A bishop presides at an ordination, with many of the priests, deacons, and lay leaders of the diocese present. After the Scripture readings, the candidates are presented to the bishop, who asks for confirmation that they have been found worthy to undertake this vocation. The diocesan Vocation Director or the Rector of the Seminary confirms that they have been found worthy. The bishop then delivers the homily, after which the candidates make their promises of obedience, of celibate chastity, and to conform their lives to the life of Jesus Christ.

The most moving part of the ceremony comes as the candidates lie prostrate on the floor while the congregation sings the Litany of the Saints, asking all of the holy men and women of the Church to pray for these men as they undertake their new office. The candidates then kneel before the bishop, who lays his hands on their heads. This is the actual moment of ordination, which comes from the practice of the apostles themselves. If it is a priesthood ordination, all of the priests present also lay hands on the heads of the candidates (or if it is a bishop being ordained, all the other bishops present lay hands on the candidate). The bishop then prays a Prayer of Consecration, presents the candidates with symbols of their office, and offers them a sign of peace.

Once a man is ordained a deacon, priest, or bishop, they are always a member of the clergy because of an indelible mark placed on their soul. Even if they leave active ministry, that mark of ordination remains, and while someone who has left the ministry can no longer function in the role of the clergy, he can still be available in times of grave emergency to celebrate the Sacraments of Reconciliation and the Anointing of the Sick for someone who is dying.

The Sacrament of Matrimony

The Sacrament of Matrimony is unique among all of the sacraments because it is not only a holy union sanctified by God, but a lawful one as well. It is also the only sacrament that predates the public ministry of Jesus, and yet is not a human invention. God himself authored the sacrament of matrimony at the dawn of creation. "It is not good that the man should be alone; I will make him a helper as his partner." (Genesis 2:18)

Though God made humanity male and female, and called them to love one another and to be fruitful and multiply, Jesus sanctioned the sacrament as well—and not only by his presence at the wedding of Cana. He validated marriage further when he told the Pharisees, "What God has joined together, let no one separate." (Matthew 19:6)

When couples enter the state of Holy Matrimony, they stand before God and promise to love one another no matter what circumstances befall their lives. They are charged with bringing one another closer to God, and also indulge in a sexual union that will (God willing) result in children who will be called to a vocation of their own.

 CATHOLIC QUOTE

How can I ever express the happiness of a marriage joined by the Church ...? How wonderful the bond between two believers, now one in hope, one in desire, one in discipline, one in the same service, ... undivided in spirit and flesh, truly two in one flesh. Where the flesh is one, so is the spirit.

—Tertullian

When a couple is ready to enter into the sacrament, they make an appointment to talk with a priest or deacon, set their wedding date, and sign up for marriage preparation classes. Over the years, there has been a big misconception about what these classes are and what they do. They are not a test in which the Church decides if a particular couple is suitable for the sacrament, but are a series of classes designed to help a starry-eyed couple prepare for the reality of married life rather than merely the excitement of the wedding itself. It's very easy to get so caught up in the details of saying "yes to the dress" that important issues such as money management, household responsibilities, and the desire for children can be overlooked.

This is not to say that once marriage preparation classes are over, a couple can look forward to a happy, trouble-free life. On the contrary, no marriage is perfect and there will be struggles along the way. There may even be times when the marriage is on the brink of collapse, but hopefully, when sin threatens the marriage, the couple can find it in their hearts to forgive one another and to reconcile, trusting that God's presence will help them get through the rough patches.

KEEP IT SIMPLE

Although we may think of infidelity as the only "sin" that can tear apart a marriage, in actuality there are lots of them. Some marriages can be threatened due to poor communication, economic difficulties, greed, envy, power struggles, and quarreling for the sake of quarreling. For this reason, forgiveness between one another as well as participation in the Sacrament of Reconciliation is an important component of any marriage.

Who Can Be Married in the Catholic Church?

The Church is clear about what matrimony is and who qualifies for it. Despite the growing movement approving same-sex unions, in 2003 the United States Council of Catholic Bishops reaffirmed the Church's stance that the sacrament of marriage was instituted by God and is to be between one man and one woman.

There are reasons that the Church does not view a same-sex union as an equivalent to a traditional marriage, primarily because a union of this sort cannot enter into a traditional conjugal relationship and cannot cooperate with God to produce life. The Church also feels that the traditional marital union provides the best environment for raising children and while the Church feels justified in denying the sacrament to same-sex couples, it is not meant to offend the dignity of homosexual persons. (We will talk more about this issue in Chapter 12.)

CATHOLIC QUOTE

Someone who loves a neighbor allows him to be as he is, as he was and as he will be.

—Michel Quoist

That being said, the Sacrament of Matrimony can take place between two Catholics, a Catholic and a baptized non-Catholic Christian or a Catholic and someone of another religion. Obviously the first scenario is the easiest coupling while the other two require special permission before the sacrament can take place. There is real concern that a "mixed" (interdenominational) marriage can lead a Catholic to give up the faith or become inactive in the Church. While this is not an insurmountable problem, it does mean that everyone's cards must be on the table. The Catholic person has to make it known that they intend to remain active in the Church and to baptize and raise any children accordingly.

A Catholic Wedding

The ceremony itself takes place in a church and can happen within the Mass to connect it to the Paschal Mystery or independent of the Mass, depending on a couple's preference. Regardless of the format, the ceremony consists of three questions of intention and an exchange of consent.

When a couple enters a marriage, they must give themselves freely and without reservation to the union. No one can marry if they are already encumbered by another relationship, and neither the Church nor the state can force someone into a marriage that they do not want. It is also unlawful for a marriage to take place if someone knows of a serious reason why a couple should not be wed.

The couple must also affirm that it is their intention to remain in this exclusive relationship for the rest of their lives. Lastly, a couple must be willing to be fruitful, to multiply and accept the number of children God has planned for them. Of course, not every couple will be blessed with a houseful of kids, and some may be infertile, but the point of this element is that the couple will allow God's will rather than their own to direct their family.

CATHOLIC QUOTE

To love someone means to be the only one to see a miracle that is invisible to others.

—François Mauriac

After the bride and groom affirm their intention to marry one another, they exchange their vows, promising to love one another "for better or worse, richer or poorer, in sickness and in health until death do they part." They then exchange rings that are blessed by the priest or deacon as a sign that they are now joined together. The celebrant then validates the wedding for the Church and the state and administers the wedding blessing.

The Issue of Divorce

The marriage vows are not designed to be easily made and easily broken. They are an irrevocable commitment and are indissoluble. In other words, there is no divorce in the Catholic Church. Even if the civil law allows for the dissolution of a marriage, in the Church's eyes the couple are still joined by the sacrament. There are three reasons for this:

- It was a love given freely and without reservation.

- Marriage is a living image of the love that exists between God and all of creation.

- It represents the devotion that Christ had to His Church even when He died on the cross.

The Church believes that it is important for couple to do everything in their power to keep the promise they made before God. Couples can pray for strength, seek counseling, and communicate in an effort to get beyond whatever struggle is threatening their union. However, the Church acknowledges that there are some issues that cannot be overcome (i.e., physical violence). While the individual may seek a divorce and notify the Church of the separation, the sacrament remains valid even if the legal marriage has ended.

Of course, there are those instances in which the marital crisis reverts to the fact that someone in the union was not quite eligible for the sacrament from the beginning or did not fully consent to the vows they made. In that case the couple can seek an *annulment* through a diocesan tribunal, a Church court.

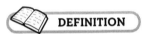 **DEFINITION**

An **annulment** is a decree recognizing a marriage that was previously sanctified by the Catholic Church is now invalid.

While the Church welcomes divorced Catholics lovingly and wants them to find eventual happiness, there are consequences for any Catholic who divorces their spouse and then remarries while the original spouse is still alive. If there has been no annulment to negate the marriage and the person marries in another church or civil service, they are cutting themselves off from the Eucharist. This new union is in direct contrast to Jesus' command in the Gospel of Matthew as well as what the Eucharist stands for (total love, commitment, and sacrifice), and therefore someone in such a contradictory state cannot participate in Holy Communion.

However, to be clear, getting a civil divorce on its own does not prevent a Catholic from being able to receive the Eucharist in good conscience. Only a remarriage after a civil divorce without an annulment would lead to a Catholic not being able to receive communion until the issue is resolved, because the first marriage is still considered valid and lawful in the eyes of the Church.

Pathways to Heaven

The end goal of both Sacraments of Service—Holy Orders and Matrimony—is to get someone else to heaven. Bishops, priests, and deacons are called to spend their lives leading the members of their flocks to Heaven and going beyond their own congregations to spread the good news of salvation to all people. Husbands and wives are called to do everything they can in their marriage to get each other to Heaven, and together to lead their children to Heaven by introducing them to Jesus Christ and the life of the Church. In this way, both sacraments are outward focused—they're not about the individual who receives the sacrament, but about serving and loving others. Bishops, priests, deacons, and married couples are called to be selfless.

The Least You Need to Know

- A vocation is a call from God.
- There are four specific vocational paths in the Catholic Church.
- There are three degrees of Holy Orders: deacons, priests, and bishops.
- A Catholic marriage must be entered into freely and with the intent of the relationship lasting for life.
- A Catholic union must be willing to accept the children God has planned for them.

The Catholic Mass

The Catholic Mass is a ritual that has been celebrated in more or less the same format for 1,800 years. Although Catholics believe that Christ instituted the Eucharistic Liturgy central to the Mass, He did not provide His disciples with a weekly program to follow or specific elements to include.

However, there is evidence to suggest that the structure of the Mass as we know it was already in place by AD 155. When St. Justin Martyr wrote to the pagan emperor Antoninus Pius (AD 134–161) around that same year, he outlined a second-century Christian practice that bears uncanny resemblance to the same Mass we celebrate today.

Though it has been tweaked, streamlined, and modified in terms of language, it is essentially the same event, and in this chapter, we will examine the structure of the Catholic Mass in an effort to discover why this 1,800-year-old practice continues to be relevant in the twenty-first century.

In This Chapter

- The Mass is a universal celebration of Christ
- Understanding the Roman Missal
- A step-by-step walk-through of the Mass
- Go in peace to love and to serve

What Is the Mass?

The Second Vatican Council describes the Mass as the "source and summit" of the life of the Church. It is the most important thing Catholics do, and all other ministries and activities of the Church flow from the celebration of the Eucharist, which leads us to be the presence of Christ to others.

It is a ritual that is celebrated using signs and symbols, words and actions, and songs and music. It is officiated by a priest or bishop and includes elements that change depending on the Church calendar. It is the same at every Catholic church, everywhere in the world. The language used in the celebration may be different, the music might be unique to a particular culture, but the prayers and Scripture readings of the Catholic Mass on any particular day are the same at every church in every land.

FAST FACT

Nearly all of the prayers and song lyrics featured in the Mass are based on Scripture, often weaving together different verses from Scripture that have connected meanings. Many of the prayers are hundreds of years old, having been composed by such people as Pope St. Leo the Great and St. Hippolytus, who in the third century wrote the oldest Eucharistic Prayer that is still in use today.

As we learned in Chapter 6, the Catholic Mass is comprised of two liturgies: the Liturgy of the Word and the Liturgy of the Eucharist, with introductory and concluding rites surrounding them. The basic structure of the Mass comes from a combination of the two major types of Jewish prayer, the Sabbath meal on Friday evenings when bread and wine is blessed and shared, and the synagogue service on Saturday mornings when the Scriptures are read and reflected upon. Jesus gave new meaning to each of these types of prayer by fulfilling the Scriptures and by giving us the Eucharist to replace the Sabbath meal. By combining these two forms, we have the basic structure of the Catholic Mass.

The first example of the united structure of the Mass occurs after the resurrection in Luke's Gospel when Jesus joins two people walking along the road to Emmaus. The two are unaware of who has joined them and proceed to tell stories about the Messiah and what has happened to Him. Jesus proceeds to interpret the Scripture for them (Liturgy of the Word) and when they arrive at Emmaus, they sit at a table where Jesus takes bread and blesses and shares it (Liturgy of the Eucharist).

Although St. Justin Martyr is credited for being the first to record the basic format of the Catholic Mass, he did not come up with it himself. No one knows for sure how long the structure had been in place when he wrote the emperor in AD 155. He was merely outlining what was in practice at that time.

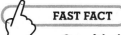

FAST FACT

One of the key elements that St. Justin Martyr discusses in his outline of the Christian service is the fact that it happened on Sunday. This was in direct contrast to Jesus and the Jewish people whose day of prayer (Sabbath) occurred on Saturday. Because the resurrection occurred on a Sunday, Christians from the earliest years began to gather on that day of the week for their communal celebration.

The Development of the Roman Missal

In the early days of the Church, the prayers and practices used during the Mass were memorized and handed down orally from one generation to the next. After all, the Gospels had not been written and copies of the epistles were limited. Eventually scribes were able to record these elements into books including sacramentaries (for prayers), lectionaries (for Scriptures), and evangelaries (for the Gospels). However, it became tedious to have that many volumes in use during a service and there was a need to streamline them into one body of work: the Roman *Missal*.

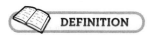

DEFINITION

A **missal** is a book that contains the texts and directions for celebrating Mass in the Catholic Church.

The Roman Missal is a collection of the readings, prayers, chants, and instructions used for celebrating Mass in the Roman or Latin Rite of the Catholic Church. It is not a Bible, though it is often mistaken for one, and it is not a "cheat sheet" for the clergy and congregation. It originally contained not only the scriptural readings that correspond to the Church calendar, but also the Order of Mass and other liturgical procedures to help everyone follow along.

FAST FACT

When Lyndon B. Johnson took the oath of office following the assassination of President John F. Kennedy, he did so on a Catholic Missal, which was mistaken for a Bible by a Kennedy aide.

With the invention of moveable type in the mid-1400s, it was possible to standardize and publish the complete Missal universally. The first edition to take advantage of the printing press was introduced in 1570 and would remain more or less in place for the next 500 years. This version (in Latin, of course) is called the Missal of the Council of Trent.

During the Second Vatican Council (1962–1965) there were a number of changes in how the Church celebrated the Mass, one of which concerned a completely new version of the Roman

Missal and the inclusion of three cycles of readings to be rotated through the Church calendar. Due to the size of included texts, the Missal was divided into the Lectionary for Mass (which contains the scriptural readings) and the Roman Missal (which contains prayers, chants, and procedures used in the service). This version is called the Missal of the Second Vatican Council.

FAST FACT

Mass can still be celebrated today using the Missal of the Council of Trent (also called the Tridentine Missal). It is officially called the Extraordinary Form of the Roman Rite and is celebrated in Latin using the version of the Roman Missal published in 1962, prior to the Second Vatican Council.

These texts were published first in Latin (and revised over the next few years) and then translated into the language of the region to correspond with the new directive that the Mass could be celebrated in languages other than Latin. Due to the push for rapid implementation, the first translations of the Missal into various languages in the 1960s were completed quickly and aimed for an "essence" of the words rather than a more literal interpretation of the texts.

Today's Roman Missal

Although this version of the Missal was revised and edited in the 1970s, in 2001 the liturgical commission in Rome examined the Missal and recommended a more literal translation of the original Latin. They gathered a group of scholars, poets, and theologians to provide the Church with a third edition of the Missal, first in Latin and then translated into other languages, which went into effect in English in the United States on November 27, 2011.

This twenty-first century translation was enough of an update that many longtime Catholics who recited their part of the service by rote now had to invest in personal Missals or refer to a card placed in the pews in order to follow along. After a few weeks most people adjusted to the change, but if you listen carefully you'll still hear the occasional slip-up or two.

Getting the Lay of the Land

The Catholic Mass takes place in a church that may seem a bit overwhelming if you are not used to it. While there is a lot to see, there are a few elements of note that play an important part in the service, including:

- Holy water fonts: Catholics dip their fingers into the vessels and make the Sign of the Cross upon entering the sanctuary.

- Crucifix: A large cross with an image of the dying Christ affixed to it. This is always found near the altar.

- Altar: Where the Eucharistic meal is consecrated. It is a fixed structure that represents Jesus Christ, the cornerstone of the Church.

- Tabernacle: The place where the consecrated hosts are kept for prayer and to take to the sick and dying.

- Presider's chair: Where the priest sits.

- Lectern/ambo: Where the Scripture is read during the service and the homily is delivered.

- Sanctuary lamp: A candle next to the Tabernacle that is continually lit to denote the presence of Christ in the Blessed Sacrament.

- Pew Missals: These are more condensed versions of the Roman Missals that enable the congregation to follow the songs, readings, and Order of Mass. They often also contain the music used for the Mass.

Other things you might see that are not directly related to the Mass itself:

- Statues: The number and style of these sculptures vary depending on the church, but they are designed to offer images of important religious figures to the faithful.

- Stations of the Cross: Fourteen sculptures or paintings on the walls of the church building that represent the path Jesus took to the crucifixion.

- Candles: Small votive-size candles are usually placed before statues to encourage the faithful to light one in honor of a particular prayer intention.

- Reconciliation room: A small space in which congregants can take advantage of the Sacrament of Reconciliation prior to Mass or whenever the priest is available.

- Sacristy: The "backstage" area of the church where supplies and vestments are kept for the celebration. It's not overly obvious, but you will see people coming in and out of it.

Prior to Mass, Catholics enter the building, dip their fingers in the holy water font, and make the Sign of the Cross as a reminder of their baptism. As they approach their seat, they genuflect (take a knee) in the direction of the Tabernacle and then enter the pew. If the Tabernacle is in a chapel separate from the main part of the church, they make a deep bow toward the altar. Then they spend a few moments kneeling in silent prayer in order to mentally prepare for the service.

The Introductory Rites

The first portion of the Mass is the Introductory Rites, which begin when the priest (possibly with a deacon) dressed in sacred vestments, along with the other ministers and altar *servers* process to the altar while the congregation or musicians sing the entrance song or chant. Music, both sung and instrumental, plays a vital role in the Catholic Mass. It adds both solemnity and joy to the celebration and can serve as a way to unite everyone together in one voice of praise to God. Everyone is encouraged to join in the singing, even if you don't think you have a good voice. All the voices blended together make a beautiful sound to God!

The deacon or a lector carries the Book of the Gospels in the procession and places it on the altar. When the party reaches the altar, they all genuflect or bow and proceed to their stations. The priest and deacon approach the altar and honor it with a kiss.

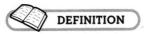

DEFINITION

A **server** is most often a young person (boy or girl) who assists the priest at Mass. They carry candles, hold the Missal, prepare the altar, and perform other duties as needed.

When the entrance song is completed, the priest and the congregation open the celebration with the Sign of the Cross. The priest then greets the people using one of three prescribed greetings, which all convey an acknowledgment that the Lord is present within them. The congregants reply, "And with your spirit."

In order to prepare themselves for the sacrament that lies ahead, the Penitential Act asks the faithful to recall and repent of any sins they have committed. There are three forms of this rite, which includes the Confiteor (I confess) and one of three versions of call and response phrases between the clergy and the congregation that end in "Lord have mercy" and "Christ have mercy." You may know these as the *Kyrie*.

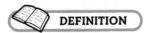

DEFINITION

Kyrie means "Lord" in Greek. In the Mass, the Kyrie is a chanted call asking for mercy from Christ.

On occasion the Rite for the Blessing and Sprinkling of Water may preempt the Penitential Act and Kyrie (especially during the Easter season) as a remembrance of the promises made in the Sacrament of Baptism.

Following the Penitential Act, the Gloria is sung, except during Advent and Lent. It is a song of praise derived from Luke 2:14-15 when the angels came to the shepherds in the field to announce the birth of the Christ Child saying, "Glory to God in the highest heaven, and on earth, peace among those whom he favors." The introductory prayer (called the Collect, pronounced with the stress on the second syllable) follows it and closes out the Introductory Rites.

FAST FACT

Catholics are able to attend Mass every day of the week if they wish. However, Masses during the week are a bit simpler than Sunday (or Lord's Day) Masses. There is no Gloria or Nicene Creed on weekdays, there is one less reading from Scripture, and often there is no music. However, when a major feast day falls during the week—such as All Saints Day or the Solemnity of St. Joseph—it is celebrated like Sunday Mass.

The Liturgy of the Word

At the conclusion of the Introductory Rites, the congregation sits while the reader (or lector) approaches the ambo to read the first reading. The first reading comes from the Old Testament, except during the Easter Season, when it is from the Acts of the Apostles. It is generally chosen to correspond with the Gospel reading of the day. When the lector completes the text, he or she concludes by confirming that this is the Word of the Lord—to which those in the pews respond, "Thanks be to God."

After a few moments of silence, the psalmist or cantor begins a short reading from the Book of Psalms (this is often sung, but can be recited as well) followed by the second reading, which comes from one of the epistles or the Book of Revelation. Once again, at the conclusion of the reading, the psalmist acknowledges that this is the Word of the Lord and the congregation responds, "Thanks be to God."

FAST FACT

Silence is an important part of the Mass. There are brief moments of silence after the introduction to the Penitential Act and after each of the Scripture readings, then longer periods of silence after the homily and after the distribution of communion. The silence is a time for everyone present to spend a few moments speaking to God in prayer, reflecting on the words and experiences of the Mass, and listening for God's voice.

The congregation then stands to sing the Gospel Acclamation as the priest or deacon takes the Book of Gospels from the altar, holds it aloft, and carries it to the ambo. Depending on what year's cycle the Church is on, the reading comes from one of the Gospels:

> Year A: The Gospel of Matthew
>
> Year B: The Gospel of Mark
>
> Year C: The Gospel of Luke

The Gospel of John is used on major feast days, during Lent and Easter, and during the summers of Year B (because the Gospel of Mark is shorter than the other Synoptic Gospels).

When the Gospel is read, the servers sometimes carry candles and stand on either side of the ambo while the priest or deacon reads the Scripture. After the name of the Gospel is announced, the congregants respond by saying, "Glory to you, O Lord," and making a small Sign of the Cross on their foreheads, lips, and chests in order to signify that the words of Christ should always be on one's mind, on one's lips, and in one's heart. When the Gospel is over, the priest acknowledges that this is the Gospel of the Lord, to which the congregants respond, "Praise to you Lord Jesus Christ."

The homily follows the Gospel. This is the portion of the Mass in which the priest or deacon offers some insight and reflection into the readings and the Gospel. When he is finished, the congregation enjoys a few moments of silent reflection and then stands to recite the Creed. The Apostle's Creed and the Nicene Creed both are proper, but typically the Nicene Creed is used.

The priest invites the faithful into a universal prayer and then the lector or deacon approaches the ambo to read the prayers of intention while the congregation replies to each with a variation of, "Lord, hear our prayer." When the prayers of petition are finished, the priest concludes the Liturgy of the Word with a concluding prayer.

 KEEP IT SIMPLE

Is it a homily or a sermon? In the Catholic Church, the reflection given by the priest or deacon is most often a homily, which is based on the assigned Scripture readings for a particular day. A sermon is based on a topic chosen by the preacher, who then selects Scripture passages that apply to the chosen topic.

The Liturgy of the Eucharist

Once again everyone takes their seats as the offertory song or chant is sung. During this time, the altar is set up for the preparation of the bread and wine for the Eucharist while the collection is taken and presented to the priest (along with the bread and wine) by a designated individual or family. Just before the song or chant is completed, the priest says a prayer of blessing over the bread and wine and then calls the congregation to stand for prayer.

FAST FACT

The word *Eucharist* literally means "Thanksgiving."

This leads into the preface to the Eucharistic Prayer, which varies depending on the Church calendar. There are also variations on the Eucharistic Prayer depending on the Mass. There are nine different versions of the Eucharistic Prayer that come from the whole history of the Church. The Eucharistic Prayer begins in a similar way as the Introductory Rites, with another acknowledgment that Christ is present in the assembly. This is followed by a prayer appropriate to the day and the *Sanctus*.

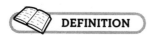

DEFINITION

Sanctus is a Latin word that means "holy." In the Mass, it is the name of the chant praising God as the people did when He made His entry into Jerusalem, "Blessed is the king who comes in the name of the Lord! Peace in heaven and glory in the highest heaven!" (Luke 19:38)

The congregation kneels as the prayer continues. The priest asks the Holy Spirit's blessing to come upon the bread and wine and change them into His body and blood. The words that follow are a retelling of the Last Supper using a combination of words from the Gospels of Matthew and Luke. At the end of each portion of the Last Supper narrative, the priest genuflects at the altar while the congregation bows toward the consecrated host and the chalice. This is the moment in which it is believed that transubstantiation occurs, and the bread and wine truly become the Body and Blood of Christ.

The bread used for the Eucharist must be made from wheat and the wine from grapes, because those are the elements Jesus used at the Last Supper. (For those who are gluten intolerant, there are low-gluten hosts available in many parishes.)

FAST FACT

The phrase "Hocus Pocus" actually comes from the Latin words said in the Mass when consecrating the bread (*Hoc est enim corpus*). People who didn't understand what the Eucharist was about, or the language in which it was celebrated, thought it was magic, and thus used a modified version of the Latin words of consecration in magic acts.

Following the consecration, the congregation offers an acclamation of the mystery of faith which means that even though it's beyond comprehension, there is a firm belief in Christ's death, resurrection, and eventual return. The priest concludes the Eucharistic Prayer with the doxology, to which the congregation assents with an "Amen."

The Communion Rite

The Communion Rite is part of the Liturgy of the Eucharist and begins when the priest invites the congregation to join him in the Lord's Prayer.

The way Catholics pray the Lord's Prayer is different than the way most Protestant Christians pray it. In the early years of the Church, every prayer ended with a statement of praise to God (doxology). The doxology for the Lord's Prayer was, "For the kingdom, the power, and the glory are yours, now and forever." It is not part of the prayer itself, and it won't be found in Scripture, but including it was a common practice, even during the Mass, and most Protestants always include it today. When barbarians were threatening the city of Rome, the pope added a prayer for peace in between the Lord's Prayer and the doxology. Catholics got used to saying the Lord's Prayer on its own, separate from the doxology, and that is still the most common practice for Catholics today. Regardless, the doxology is Church tradition, not from the lips of Jesus himself.

The priest then invites the congregation to share a sign of peace with one another and for a few moments, everyone in the pews exchanges handshakes and greetings with those around them. As the priest breaks the host over the paten (or small dish) and places a small amount of the consecrated host in the chalice, the congregation sings the Lamb of God chant before kneeling again.

After quietly saying a prayer to prepare himself to receive communion, the priest holds up a portion of the host he has broken and acknowledges that this is in fact the Body and Blood of Jesus Christ. The congregation asks for one more blessing of forgiveness prior to communion and as the priest consumes the Eucharist, he prays that the Body and Blood of Jesus Christ will protect him for eternal life.

 **CATHOLIC QUOTE**

Holy Communion is the shortest and surest path to heaven.

—Pope St. Pius X

There is a lot of confusion as to why Catholics change their position so much during Mass, but in actuality, each posture is used for a specific reason.

- Catholics stand during processions and prayers, during the entrance and closing processions, and any time the community prays together.

- Like the common practice of standing to honor the presence of an important person, Catholics stand during the proclamation of the Gospel, which contains the words of Jesus Christ.

- They sit during times of listening and quiet reflection such as the readings and during the homily.

- They kneel during the Eucharistic Prayer when Jesus becomes present through transubstantiation, and before and after the time of receiving communion, as a sign of adoration.

The Concluding Rites

After communion, any parish announcements are made and then the priest offers a prayer prescribed by the Church calendar as well as the solemn blessing. Once again, he tells the congregation that the Lord is with them and they respond, "And with your spirit." He or the deacon gives one of four dismissal commands to which the faithful respond, "Thanks be to God." The closing song is sung and the priest, deacon, servers, and ministers process out the same way they came in.

Interestingly, the name Mass comes from the Latin dismissal at the end of the celebration: *Ite, missa est.* "Go, you are sent." Catholics believe that the Mass is not just a good thing to participate in, but that it should send us out into the world nourished and strengthened by the Word of God and the Body and Blood of Christ to serve our brothers and sisters.

The Least You Need to Know

- The Mass has been celebrated in the same basic fashion for more than 1,800 years.
- The Mass is the single most important thing for a Catholic to participate in.
- The Mass is the same in every Catholic church all over the world.
- The Mass is comprised of the Liturgy of the Word and the Liturgy of the Eucharist.
- Every action, posture, song, and prayer has significant meaning within the Mass.
- The Mass nourishes the soul and sends Catholics out into the world fortified for the work ahead.

Living the Good Life

In order to live a good and virtuous life, a Catholic must do more than have faith in God, attend Mass, and participate in the sacraments on a regular basis. They must walk the walk at the same time they are talking the talk. In other words, they must cultivate and practice righteous habits in their everyday lives. This isn't always easy. Even though we know we are supposed to love the Lord God with all of our whole beings and love our neighbor as ourselves, we are still human and prone to making mistakes.

In this part, we will investigate moral decision-making: the virtuous qualities that raise us up, and the vices that set us back. We will explore the social teaching of the Church and what it means to live the Beatitudes. Finally we will uncover the consequences of our choices with a sneak peek into the hereafter: Heaven, Hell, and everything in between.

Morality

Living a moral life is about more than knowing the difference between good and bad or right and wrong. It is about living life with integrity, making ethical and responsible choices in an effort to follow God's plan in our life rather than our own agenda.

It's not always easy, and God knows that. No human gets it right 100 percent of the time; however, with their faith in God, participation in the sacraments, and reliance on their gifts of reason and intelligence, Catholics strive to model Christ's example in everything they say and do.

In this chapter, you will find out what it takes to live a good and decent life. You will discover why humans must wield their freedom responsibly, how they understand the consequences of their actions, and above all, how they seek forgiveness from God and one another when they fall into an occasion of sin.

In This Chapter

- Understanding free will and Original Sin
- How do we develop our conscience?
- The importance of using our own judgment
- Making decisions based on the Ten Commandments

A Stake in Salvation

Catholics believe that when God made man in His own image, He created a rational being and afforded him the dignity to keep his own council in the decision-making process. He was not looking to create a race of individuals who operated on a predetermined, uncontrollable life path, but rather hoped that this *free will* would enable them to seek out a relationship with Him and have a stake in their own salvation.

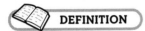 **DEFINITION**

Free will is the God-given ability to act on one's own behalf without being influenced by someone else.

Free will offers us the ability to grow in perfection or to fall deeper into sin, depending on the choices we make. Obviously the more good one does, the freer they become, while sinful choices lead one into futility. The concept of free will also forces us to take responsibility for our actions and to understand which decisions were made consciously and voluntarily, even if they were decisions made against God's will.

Original Sin

Ever since Adam and Eve disobeyed God in the Garden of Eden by eating from the Tree of Life, humanity has suffered the impact of Original Sin. As we have learned in previous chapters, Original Sin is a part of each of us that causes our will to weaken, and our mind to turn toward the dark side from time to time.

Like factory seconds, we arrive on this planet slightly imperfect, and although we are delivered from Original Sin through the Sacrament of Baptism, the effects linger on. We still have the inclination to do the wrong thing, and while Christ's death on the cross delivers us from evil and heals the lasting damage individual sins cause within us, it is not a free pass to do whatever we want. We must use our free will judiciously and consciously strive to be the person God created us to be.

 **CATHOLIC QUOTE**

Being free means self-possession.

–Dominique Lacordaire

It's not always easy, though. We are human and our human desires and stubbornness get in the way sometimes, and any time we go against the grain of what God has in mind for us, we commit a *sin*. While some religious traditions believe that all sins are equal and that the tiniest lie is comparable to murder, Catholicism classifies *sin* into two categories: mortal and venial.

Mortal sins are ones in which people knowingly and willfully commit an act that will drive a wedge between them and God. This kind of sin must be rectified prior to death if there is to be any hope of salvation in the afterlife. A venial sin is a little less serious and is the type of sin that merely puts a strain on one's relationship with God, but does not break it. Venial sins are usually our everyday failings that run counter to values such as honor and truth, and are typically committed when one is not fully aware of how serious the consequences are or without full consent of one's will. We'll go into more detail about mortal and venial sins in Chapter 11.

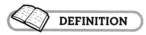 **DEFINITION**

> **Sin** is any thought, word, or deed that causes man to disrupt the natural order of things as God has arranged them.

To Whom Much Is Given

Jesus knew that with great power comes great responsibility. In order to find eternal happiness with God in this life and in the hereafter, one must wield the freedom he or she was endowed with responsibly. In Luke 12:48, Jesus says to Peter, "From everyone to whom much has been given, much will be required; and from the one to whom much has been entrusted, even more will be demanded." It is vital that we consistently opt for choices that are harmonious with God's laws and not choices that merely seem like "a good idea at the time."

In order to make good choices in our lives, three things must be considered. They're called the Sources of Morality:

1. Object: What are we doing?

2. Intention: Why are we doing it?

3. Circumstances: What are the circumstances surrounding it?

In order for a specific act to be considered morally good, the act itself must have a positive objective. A good intention alone is not a sufficient enough reason, especially if it goes against a fundamental human right. For example, when Robin Hood stole from the rich in order to give to the poor, he was still committing a crime, even though he had a good intention for doing so.

Secondly, the person's intent must be pure. Sometimes people do the right thing, but for the wrong reason or with an ulterior motive in mind. For example, putting a donation in a collection basket because you felt you had to rather than because you wanted to is an example of acting from impure intent. Walking someone home in order to find out where they live and later robbing them would be another example.

Finally, the circumstances surrounding the act have an impact on whether or not it is considered to be moral. The end does not justify the means. We cannot do something we know to be evil in an effort to bring about good. Sometimes it is better to simply tolerate the lesser of two evils rather than to cause a bigger evil to occur.

This can be a problem when passions and emotions get in the way. While passions and emotions can help identify those things that might be good and evil and enable us to discern between them in order to make good choices, they can overpower a person and cause them to lose control in the decision-making process.

KEEP IT SIMPLE

Passions are great, but it's all too easy to get carried away for the "cause." Someone who is passionate about caring for strays may have the best of intentions, but when they become an animal hoarder, they are actually doing more harm than good for the critters in their care. They are so determined to do the "right thing" that they fail to see the detriment to their actions and often lose control of being able to rectify the situation without help.

Making a "Conscience" Choice

In order to help us riddle out whether we are using our power of free will for good or evil, humans have been given a *conscience*. This is that inner voice inside that knows beyond a shadow of a doubt this is the right path to take and the voice that nags a little every time you know you've made the wrong choice.

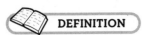

DEFINITION

Conscience is awareness of and attentiveness to the voice of God guiding our actions toward the good, the true, and the beautiful.

Like reason and intelligence, our conscience is something that must be developed over time. Think about it: when a two-year-old takes something from a store shelf and unwittingly leaves with the contraband in their stroller, no one threatens to call the police or send the child to jail. Mom and Dad take the item back into the store, apologize for the mistake, and issue a theatrical reprimand that has no impact on the child's logic. In time, however, the child becomes old enough to understand more. They realize that it's wrong to take what doesn't belong to them. Still later, they learn that it's more than wrong; it's illegal as well. Finally, they come to understand the big picture: stealing is against the law and can result in an arrest and charges being filed against them.

By the same token, the conscience also helps us discern the right choices in our lives. A child who is handed spare change to put in a collection basket at Mass may not understand why he or she is handing over cash, but they do understand the smiles of approval from those sitting around them. Giving must be good! Only later do they put together the whole idea that when they do something for the betterment of others, they make an impact in the world and feel good for having done so.

The conscience is not unlike our brains, our muscles, and our bones. It needs exercise. If we don't use it, we will lose it!

 **KEEP IT SIMPLE**

We are not permitted to do something bad in hopes that good will come out of it. There is never an excuse for murder, or other acts that threaten the dignity of human life. We also cannot be compelled to act against our conscience (aka "the devil made me do it").

Moral Decision-Making

When it comes to making moral decisions in our everyday lives, God was kind enough to provide the Ten Commandments to help us. The Ten Commandments are not a random list of rules and regulations that are out of date in the twenty-first century, but are a cohesive set of directives that include humanity's obligation to God and to each other.

The Ten Commandments

1. I am the Lord your God: you shall not have other gods before me.

2. You shall not take the name of the Lord your God in vain.

3. Remember to keep holy the Sabbath day.

4. Honor your father and mother.

5. You shall not kill.

6. You shall not commit adultery.

7. You shall not steal.

8. You shall not bear false witness against your neighbor.

9. You shall not covet your neighbor's wife.

10. You shall not covet your neighbor's goods.

(Adapted from Exodus 20:2-17 and Deuteronomy 5:6-21)

 CATHOLIC QUOTE

Anything that is done against conscience is a sin.

—St. Thomas Aquinas

Love God with All Your Heart

The first three commandments refer to man's relationship to God. In the first commandment, we are expected to love God with our whole hearts and souls and to place our relationship with Him above everything else in our lives. He is our top priority and it is in Him that we should place our full faith, hope, and trust. It is only in God that we as humans will find eternal happiness. God is not something that can be substituted or replaced by another deity, person, or material item. We are not permitted to allow our lives to be ruled by superstition. We are not to provoke God, to commit a sacrilege, or to attain spiritual power through exploitation.

In the second commandment, we are expected to honor God's name and keep it holy. It's a sign of trust. Think about it: have you ever been introduced to someone with an impressive title only to have that person say, "Call me Bill"? That invitation should not be taken lightly. By allowing you some familiarity, they trust you. God gave the people of Israel His name and He doesn't want it to be invoked for reasons that are not righteous. The name of any person is sacred and something that should be respected and treated with dignity.

Technically, when it was written, God's third commandment to keep holy the Sabbath day did not require one to attend a religious service, but it did require humanity to stop and smell the roses. We all need to take time out of our busy lives to recharge, re-energize, and to reflect on the wonder of God. No one should be so consumed with their work and their other commitments that they cannot rest and relax. Today, of course, Catholics honor the Sabbath by attending Mass on Sunday or a vigil on Saturday evening, and they make a point to suspend all work that would take them away from the focus of celebrating the wondrousness of God.

CATHOLIC QUOTE

Without Sunday we cannot live.

—The Christian Martyrs of Abitena

Love Your Neighbor as Yourself

The last seven commandments deal with how we treat each other. In the fourth commandment, we are directed to honor our fathers and mothers. We made it into this world because of these two people who created us out of the feelings they had in their hearts. For some this is easy, especially if they grew up in stable households. For others, this commandment can be difficult, but rest assured it can be applied to anyone in the proverbial village who helped raise the child. The spirit of this commandment goes beyond our DNA makeup and can include anyone who helped you along the way. This commandment also calls us to have respect for any person in a position of lawful or moral authority over us.

The fifth commandment is a big one, and there is no wiggle room on what it means. Murder is a sin against God, plain and simple. God created all human life and all human life is sacred, including our own. We are not permitted to destroy what God has made. It is up to God as to when we are born and it is up to God to decide when we die. Committing the sin of murder not only includes the act itself, but also serving as an accomplice.

KEEP IT SIMPLE

The Catholic Church believes that life begins at the moment of conception and does not end until the moment of natural death. Anything done to end a life otherwise is considered murder. There are a number of people who try to find exceptions to the fifth commandment by justifying their acts as "humane," but the Church does not recognize it. Abortion in the case of rape is still considered murder. Euthanasia, even in imminent death, is murder.

The sixth commandment deals with marital infidelity, adultery. From the Church's standpoint, God only sanctifies the sexual union when it occurs within a marital union between one man and one woman. The purpose of this union is twofold: to unite the spouses and to create new life. Adultery at its most basic is, of course, when at least one married person consents to have sexual relations with someone who is not their spouse. When one chases their desires only for the purpose of their own satisfaction, it damages what is special and beautiful between a husband and wife. Adultery betrays the love connection between two people and damages one's relationship with God as well. This commandment also guides Catholic beliefs on sexual morality beyond adultery.

Theft is the subject of the seventh commandment. It compels us to not take things that do not belong to us. This doesn't include only "things" we haven't paid for. This commandment also compels us to be good stewards of the earth's natural resources and to share the wealth with those less fortunate. Just as we are not entitled to claim something that we have not been given access to legally, through a gift or by inheritance, it is equally wrong to "rob" the planet of its riches so that they cannot be enjoyed by future generations.

 CATHOLIC QUOTE

To have and not give is in some cases worse than stealing.

—Marie Von Ebner-Eschenbach

In the eighth commandment, we are told not to lie. Lying is any word or act that goes against the grain of truth. When someone lies, they delude themselves into believing a falsehood and they mislead others who are entitled to hear the whole truth. By and large, lying is a pretty black-and-white concept. You either tell the truth, the whole truth, and nothing but the truth, or you don't. If you don't, that's a lie. Even if you tell the truth but eliminate a few facts to save face. That is a lie of omission. However, telling the truth does require one to use discretion. We are not allowed to be "brutally honest" in such a way that it would hurt others. If the comment we are about to make is neither true, kind, or helpful, then it is better left unsaid. By the same token, the willful spreading of confidential information breeches trust and falls into the category of dishonesty as well.

The last two commandments concern the same kind of thing, the disordered desire to possess something that does not belong to us. Unhealthy sexual desires plague the mind and have a tendency to destroy the soul. At the same time, when we are envious of what others have or strive to "keep up with the Joneses" at all costs, we fail to see the blessings in our own lives. These two commandments, though they deal with separate issues, essentially compel us to rely on God for our happiness and to rejoice in what we have rather than to despair over the things we do not.

You've Got to Stand for Something

For most of us, following at least some of the Ten Commandments is a no brainer. After all, we know the legal ramifications of murder, theft, libel and slander and the potential problems associated with adultery. But living a moral, commandment-based life requires us to do more than follow the rules associated with civil consequences. They ask us to stand for something so that we don't fall for everything. Throughout history, there have been men and women who put the commandments and their personal convictions above everything else, even if it cost them their lives.

St. Thomas More

Perhaps best known to people today because of the play and movie *A Man for All Seasons,* St. Thomas More lost his life because he refused to violate his conscience. Born on February 7, 1478, Thomas More was a young man with a bright future ahead of him. He was educated at St. Anthony's, one of London's finest schools, and as a child became a page for John Morton, who was not only the Archbishop of Canterbury, but also the Chancellor of England. He went on to Oxford University, where he mastered formal logic and studied Greek and Latin literature before returning to London at his father's behest to study law.

After passing the bar in 1501, More vacillated between his legal profession and the possibility of becoming a monk. Although he lived in a monastery for one year, he ultimately decided that his true calling was to serve his country. He left the cloistered life and concentrated full-time on law, becoming a member of parliament in 1504. He also married around this time. He and his wife had four children, and after his wife died at a young age, More married a widow, who became stepmother to his children.

A personal friend of King Henry VIII, More became Lord Chancellor of England and a royal advisor on matters both legal and spiritual. When reformer Martin Luther published his three-volume doctrine of salvation, which rebuffed certain Catholic practices and condemned others, the king responded with *Defence of the Seven Sacraments,* written with More's help, which extolled the Catholic theology of the sacraments.

As time went on, the relationship between More and the monarch soured. When his marriage to Catherine of Aragon failed to produce an heir to the throne, Henry was determined to secure an annulment and tried to use the Bible to prove his case. More refuted his logic and ultimately retired from his position, refusing to serve under someone who had such little regard for Church law that he would break from union with the pope in order to secure a divorce. Not only did More refuse to attend the coronation of Anne Boleyn in 1533, More also refused to pledge his allegiance to Henry's Act of Succession and Oath of Supremacy (which named the monarch the head of the Church of England).

For More, it was a matter of following his conscience. Because of his religious beliefs, he could not support Henry's claim to be the Supreme Head of the Church in England; it would violate his conscience to recite the Oath of Supremacy. For his treason, More was arrested and sent to the Tower of London, and was beheaded on July 6, 1535. His last words were "I die the king's good servant, but God's first." Not only did the Catholic Church canonize him in 1935 but More was also named a "Reformation martyr" by the Church of England as well.

St. Gianna Beretta Molla

Gianna Molla was born on October 4, 1922, in Magenta, Italy. She was the tenth of 13 children and grew up in the Lombardy region of Italy. She was plagued with chronic health problems from a very young age, which affected her studies. But she was eventually able to complete her education in 1942 and went on to study medicine in Milan. In September of 1949, she met the man she would eventually marry, Pietro Molla, at her brother's medical clinic and later that year she received her degree in medicine and surgery.

For a while, Gianna considered joining her brother as a missionary in Brazil, but she ultimately opted to open her own medical clinic in Mesero, Italy. She specialized in pediatrics and after her career was established, she married Pietro on September 24, 1955. They had three children in four years, and during her fourth pregnancy, doctors discovered that she had developed a tumor in her uterus, which caused her tremendous pain. Though benign, the doctors offered three solutions to the situation: to terminate the pregnancy, to have a complete hysterectomy, or to undergo a procedure to remove the tumor.

Guided by the fifth commandment and the Church's stance on abortion, even when the life of the mother was threatened, Molla opted to have the tumor removed in order to save the life of her child. Anything else would be a sin in God's eyes, and she did not want to have that decision on her conscience. The operation was successful, but complications in the pregnancy continued. Molla knew that she was headed for a difficult delivery and made it clear to everyone that if came down to her life or the child's, the child should be saved.

 CATHOLIC QUOTE

If one were to consider how much Jesus suffered, one would not commit the smallest sin.

—St. Gianna Molla

On April 21, 1962, which happened to be Good Friday that year, Molla gave birth to her third daughter and namesake via Caesarean section. However, septic infection set in, causing extreme pain and leading to Molla's death a week later.

Moral decision-making is never easy. Guided by Scripture and the tradition of the Church, St. Gianna Molla made the best possible choice in the midst of challenging and life-threatening situations. Ultimately, her choice was one of giving, to bestow the gift of life on her child through an act of selfless love, even knowing that she herself might not survive. That gift of life was the most precious gift she had to offer.

St. Pope John Paul II canonized Molla on May 16, 2004, with her husband and daughter present at the ceremony. (It was the first time a husband was able to witness his wife's canonization.) Pietro Molla died in 2010 at the age of 97 and today, Gianna Emanuela Molla, the child whom Molla died to protect, is a geriatrician in Milan who often gives speeches about her mother's life and legacy.

The Least You Need to Know

- Every human being has been born with Original Sin and given the free will to make their own decisions.
- God gives us a conscience and encourages us to develop it so that we can use our judgment in moral decision-making.
- The Ten Commandments are the rules for right and wrong concerning our relationship to God as well as our fellow man.
- Moral decision-making is never easy, but when coupled with Scripture and the tradition of the Church, it can lead us on the path of righteousness.

Virtues and Vices

Catholics not only have to listen to their conscience in order to live a moral life. They believe they must develop virtuous character traits needed to do the right thing and avoid the pitfalls and vices that threaten to undermine those good intentions.

A virtue is a quality that enables us to move in the direction of reason and faith, while a vice holds us back. A virtue encourages us to be like God, while vices encourage sinful behavior and hover over our all-too-human hearts like a rain cloud.

In this chapter, we will examine the virtues necessary to live the life God has planned for each and every one of us, as well as the vices that lurk in the shadows of our souls. You will learn how to avoid the occasion of sin and develop the dispositions that will lead to an eternity with God in Heaven.

In This Chapter

- Understanding cardinal and theological virtues
- Distinguishing mortal from venial sins
- Avoiding the vices that lead us into sin
- Following the "Be Like Jesus Attitudes"

The Cardinal Virtues

Just as every human being has been imprinted with the effects of Original Sin that cause us to constantly exercise our free will against God's divine plan, we have also been given the attitudes and dispositions that lead us to moral excellence. These *virtues* are not something we are born with, but are positive traits and habits we develop in our characters over time. They help guide our decisions, control our passions, and avoid the snares that lead us to sin.

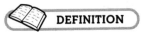 **DEFINITION**

A **virtue** is a positive character disposition that leads people to make good choices.

The most important virtues are the cardinal (or human) virtues, which include prudence, justice, fortitude, and temperance. The term comes from the Latin word *cardo* meaning "hinge" and is the category of virtues upon which all other virtues pivot. Humans acquire these habits by learning the behaviors associated with them, practicing the habits, seeing the cardinal virtues modeled in others, and being educated on the importance of virtuous behavior. We also grow in these virtues through prayer, participation in the sacraments, and God's grace, and through the seven gifts of the Holy Spirit:

1. Wisdom: The highest gift of the Holy Spirit, which calls us to perfect the virtue of faith.

2. Understanding: This offers Catholics the chance to grasp some of the essential truths about the faith.

3. Counsel: This gift calls us to perfect the virtue of prudence and helps us learn how to judge a situation and act according to our individual intuition.

4. Fortitude: This gift goes hand in hand with counsel because it encourages us to act on what our intuition tells us is the right move to make.

5. Knowledge: Unlike wisdom and understanding, knowledge calls us to perfect the virtue of faith and allows us to view situations in the way that our heavenly Father sees them.

6. Piety: This gift is about adhering to our religious practices and going beyond the ritualistic aspect of our Christian life to serve God in everything we do.

7. Fear of the Lord: Although the wording might seem odd, this gift enables us to place all of our hope in the Lord so that He will give us the graces we need to avoid offending Him.

Prudence

Prudence is considered the primary cardinal virtue because it enables us to determine what is truly essential and nonessential for happiness, to set proper goals, and to discern the best ways to achieve them. While prudence is often associated with timidity and cautiousness, it is more like far-sighted practicality.

Let's face it: few people would jump on a plane without knowing where it was going or without having plans in place upon arrival. We scour the internet looking for the best deals, talk to travel agents, book our itinerary as soon as possible, and try to foresee any potential problems long before reaching our destination. It's not that we aren't adventurous, but we are prudent when it comes to scheduling our experience with the most sensible choices.

Prudence is the virtue that guides the judgment of conscience and helps us know the right way to handle things. It is through this virtue that we apply moral principles to whatever situations we happen to be in and that we can remain confident in our choices despite all doubts and temptations that get in the way.

 CATHOLIC QUOTE

Prudence has two eyes, one that foresees what one has to do, the other that examines afterward what one has done.

—St. Ignatius Loyola

Justice

The virtue of justice is all about ensuring that every person on the planet is treated with the respect and dignity owed to them as a being made in the image of God. We are called to avoid partiality and to treat everyone fairly and honestly regardless of who they are, where they came from, or what they do. We are not permitted to be kind to the poor and suffering while taking advantage of the rich. By the same token we are not allowed to be in cahoots with the rich if the unfortunate are treated badly.

Justice is the virtue that promotes fairness and equity to the individual as well as the common good. Justice compels us to love our neighbor according to the Ten Commandments, to respect the rights of everyone without prejudice, and to remember that one's natural rights supersede any legal ones they may have. (This is especially important where the right to life is concerned according to the Church.)

Fortitude

The virtue of fortitude calls us to stand firm in our convictions and to push ahead even when we are frightened. Fortitude is all about courage and the ability to pursue good, to resist temptations, and to overcome the obstacles that get in the way of living a moral life.

When Jesus was arrested, his followers were scared to follow in His footsteps. They were so fearful at the time that they scattered like ashes in the wind rather than stand strong in the face of death; but when they were filled with the Holy Spirit on Pentecost, they were given the fortitude they needed to conquer their fears, to preach the gospel, to have faith in their abilities, and to confidently stand in the presence of their tormentors and cling to the beliefs they held to be true even when it meant they would be martyred for their convictions.

While few of us will ever suffer the way the apostles did for the faith, there have been news stories that cast the Church in a bad light and cause some of the faithful to "apologize" for what has happened in the past. God knows it is not easy to rely on one's faith when it is embroiled in controversy, but He calls us to rise above with the virtue of fortitude and to demonstrate the best that His Church has to offer rather than demure at its worse.

 CATHOLIC QUOTE

To live well is nothing other than to love God with all of one's heart, with all one's soul, and with all one's efforts; from this it comes about that love is kept whole and uncorrupted (through temperance). No misfortune can disturb it (and this is fortitude). It obeys only God (and this is justice) and is careful in discerning things so as not to be surprised by deceit or trickery (and this is prudence).

—St. Augustine

Temperance

Temperance is the virtue that moderates our actions and ensures that we maintain balance in our lives. Balance is very important because as humans, we tend to become consumed with those things that give us pleasure, which causes everything else to go out of whack.

When we do not eat a balanced diet, our health suffers. When we do not balance our bank accounts, we face financial difficulties. When we do not balance our schedules, we become overwhelmed by work or activities that leave little time for anything else.

The virtue of temperance helps us master those impulses to go overboard on any one aspect of our lives. Temperance understands that too much of a good thing is never the way to go and that it is important for us to keep everything in moderation so we can maintain sober lives focused on God.

The Theological Virtues

The cardinal virtues are rooted in the theological virtues of faith, hope, and charity (love). These supernatural powers are graces given to man by God so that we can share in His divine nature and act more like Him. They set the stage for all Christian moral behavior, give it life, and infuse it with special character. They are imprinted on the soul so that as God's children, we can live in a way that will lead us to eternal life with the Father, Son, and Holy Spirit.

Faith

As we learned in Chapter 1, faith is the foundation for our relationship with God. It is the path that causes us to seek something larger than ourselves, to acknowledge God's presence in our lives, to believe in His truth, and to commit ourselves to His plan.

Once the gift of faith has been received, it remains with us provided we do not sin against it. However, man cannot live by faith alone. Faith must be coupled with the other theological virtues in order to unite one more fully to Christ. It must also be professed through the Creeds; demonstrated, witnessed, and spread through our words and actions; and defended against all of those who would persecute against it.

Hope

The virtue of hope is about longing for something we have not yet attained. We hope for a new job. We hope to retire comfortably. We hope to achieve eternal life with God in Heaven.

Through the virtue of hope, we place our trust in God's promises and rely on His strength rather than our own to get through whatever life hands us. Hope is what responds to that internal happiness that God placed within us. It is what sustains us when times are tough. It is what encourages us when we feel like all is lost. It is what enables us to open our hearts and contemplate all that comes after this life, and causes us to look beyond ourselves to find satisfaction through charitable acts toward our fellow man.

Christian hope is based on the Old Testament hope of Abraham, who was willing to trust in God at all costs, even if it meant sacrificing his own son. It evolves through the ministry of Jesus and his directives (beatitudes) that trace the pathway to Heaven. We learn the importance of hoping against hope as we watch Jesus' trials and suffering, solid in the knowledge that God will not disappoint, and we rejoice in the triumph of the resurrection knowing that when Jesus conquered death, he gave us more hope for our own eternal salvation.

Charity

When it comes to understanding the theological virtue of charity, all you need is love. This is the virtue in which we are asked to love God above everything and everyone and to love our neighbor as ourselves.

When the Pharisees were trying to trap Jesus into saying something blasphemous, they asked Him to name the most important commandment in the Law of Moses. Knowing that there was an ulterior motive for their query, Jesus wrapped all of the Ten Commandments into a single statement:

> "'You shall love the Lord your God with all your heart, and with all your soul, and with all your mind.' This is the greatest and first commandment. And a second is just like it: 'You shall love your neighbor as yourself.'" (Matthew 22:36-39)

Love was the central theme to Jesus' ministry. Not only was He sent by God to show His love for humanity by dying on the cross and conquering death through the resurrection, but He also reached out to people from all walks of life and embraced them. He included them in His work. He assured them that they, too, were worthy of salvation. He gave them faith, He gave them hope, and He showed them love.

On the night of His final Passover meal with His friends, Jesus emphasized the importance of love when He commanded his apostles to love one another. "Just as I have loved you, you should love one another. By this everyone will know that you are my disciples, if you have love for one another." (John 13:34-35)

KEEP IT SIMPLE

Along with the gifts and fruits of the Holy Spirit, which give us powers beyond our natural aptitudes, our love helps us keep God's commandments. It is a symbiotic relationship. After all, one cannot be charitable and still commit a sin against the Law. It is only natural that if we abide in Christ's commandment to love, then we will naturally keep the other commandments as well.

St. Paul Explains Love

Throughout his writings, St. Paul emphasized love as the most important virtue one can have. Without it, all of the other virtues are empty and meaningless. He said that love is more than an abstract idea, but something that is practical and real. He said that all of us have a debt of love to one another and it is important to repay that love as often as possible, because in the end, that's what our lives will be judged on.

Of course, St. Paul's most famous statement on love comes from his first letter to the Corinthians, in which he says that no matter what gifts and virtues one possesses, if they lack love, they really have nothing. What follows is a definition of love that has been read at countless weddings and sets a tone for what love is as well as what it is not.

> "Love is patient; love is kind; love is not envious or boastful or arrogant or rude. It does not insist on its own way; it is not irritable or resentful; it does not rejoice in wrongdoing, but rejoices in the truth. It bears all things, believes all things, endures all things." (1 Corinthians 13:4-7)

St. Paul goes on to say that love never ends. Every other gift in our life will pass away, but love does not. He said we abide in faith, hope, and love, but the greatest of the three is love.

 **CATHOLIC QUOTE**

Love is repaid by love alone.

—St. Thérèse of Lisieux

Mortal and Venial Sins

As we mentioned in the last chapter, a sin is any thought, word, or deed that goes against the natural order of creation as God designed it. In Catholicism, sin is classified into two categories based on severity: mortal and venial.

A mortal sin is a willful act, committed out of free will, that violates the Ten Commandments in a severe way and causes a spiritual death between our Heavenly Father and us. It is a break in the bond we have, and if we were to die without rectifying that bond, we would spend eternity separated from the sight of our Heavenly Father.

In order for a sin to be mortal, three things have to have occurred:

1. The object of the sin must be grave in severity.

2. We must know that the action is sinful.

3. We must commit the act with full freedom.

The sins that qualify as grave include sins against the commandments, including murder, adultery, theft, lying, and anything that could be construed as disrespectful or dishonest. The severity of the matter is another issue entirely. Obviously, taking someone's life is more severe than lying about their whereabouts, and when it comes to a mortal sin, one must weigh who is being wronged by the act. For example, it is worse to steal from one's parents or other family member than it is to steal from a complete stranger.

When we consent to commit a mortal sin with full knowledge of the outcome, we are acting on the free will God gave us to choose between personal desires and his plan at any time in our lives. Only unintentional ignorance or mental instability has the ability to diminish the severity of a mortal sin, but when we choose the path that takes us away from God, that is considered to be the gravest sin of all.

FAST FACT

God offers forgiveness for mortal sins through the Sacraments of Baptism, Reconciliation, and the Anointing of the Sick.

A venial sin is a lesser matter, but still chips away at the love inside a person's heart and is not to be taken lightly. Venial sins weaken our ability to practice the virtues we need to in order to be more like God. When Catholics commit these lesser sins, they still believe it is important to participate in the Sacrament of Reconciliation so that these "lesser crimes" can be absolved and to pray for the strength to avoid the vices that triggered the behavior in the first place.

KEEP IT SIMPLE

How can you tell a mortal sin from a venial one? It starts with severity. A child who eats a cookie and then lies about it is technically breaking a commandment. But this is a venial sin compared to an adult lying about their whereabouts in order to have an affair in which he or she is turning away from God as well as the sacramental bond they share with their spouse. That would fall into the mortal category, if the person knows that it is a sin and commits it with complete freedom.

The Seven Deadly Sins

Just as we are given the seven gifts from the Holy Spirit to help us lead moral lives, there are seven perverse inclinations ready to dull our senses, cloud our judgment, and lead us into temptations. Don't misunderstand: these vices are not from God. These are human qualities that impede our spiritual progress and are in direct contrast to the virtues we hold dear in our hearts.

St. John called these tendencies the lusts of the flesh, the lusts of the eyes, and the pride of life. Within these three categories are the seven tendencies we struggle to overcome that create a breeding ground for sinful behavior and cause us to turn our backs on God. They are the seven deadly sins.

The Lusts of the Flesh

The lusts of the flesh include lust, sloth, and gluttony. Lust is an offense against the virtue of chastity and self-control and constitutes an unnatural appetite for sexual pleasure. This includes but is not limited to adulterous acts, masturbation, fornication, pornography, prostitution, and rape. The Catholic Church is firm in its belief that any sexual act outside of Holy Matrimony that is used for personal pleasure rather than procreative and unitive purposes, between one man and one woman, falls into the category of lust and is a sin against the theological virtue of love.

Sloth is a spiritual apathy or laziness that runs counter to the virtue of zeal, or the energetic response to God's commands. A good example of this would be parents who send their child to a Catholic school and to Mass each week, but stay home and do not practice their faith themselves. When we do not make God the center of our lives but treat His goodness with indifference, then over time the fire that was once inside of us becomes little more than a smoldering ember in danger of losing its light and warmth forever.

Gluttony is the sin that laughs in the face of temperance and does not believe there can ever be too much of a good thing. Gluttony has never heard of moderation and is willing to indulge in everything to excess. While most of us think of gluttony as having to do with food, in actuality it is anything that tips one's sense of balance or creates an addictive or habit-forming pattern that is difficult to equalize. Those who struggle with gluttony know that one of their vices is always too many and a thousand is never enough.

The Lust of the Eyes

Were you every guilty of taking more than your fair share at a family barbecue only to discover midway through the meal that you could not eat the quantity of food you took? Chances are, someone such as a grandmother or great-uncle looked at you and told you that "your eyes were bigger than your stomach." Greed is what this category of vice is all about. No matter if it's the biggest piece of birthday cake, the latest and greatest techno-gadget on the market, or hogging all of the praise and adulation for yourself, greed leaves no room for the virtue of generosity and constantly wants more, more, more for itself.

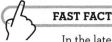

FAST FACT

In the late 1970s and throughout the 1980s, the TV show *Dallas* hit a chord with viewers because it featured an unapologetically greedy character who took pride in his ruthlessness and did it all with an evil grin. Actor Larry Hagman said he thought his character J.R. Ewing resonated with audiences because everyone in the world knows someone just like him.

The Pride of Life

The sins of pride, envy, and anger comprise this category, and like the other deadly sins, they focus on selfish behavior that does not lead to a virtuous model of living. Pride overshadows humility, which is the ability to see ourselves as we are without feeling compelled to compare what we see with someone else. Pride and vanity are all about keeping up appearances and cause us to be competitive about our looks and achievements in relationship to others.

Envy goes hand in hand with pride and, in fact, sometimes it is hard to tell the two apart. The sin of envy causes one to want what they don't have. This is usually because someone else has it and the individual believes they are entitled to it as well. This can lead to breaking commandments associated with theft, adultery, and coveting and creates an empty place in one's soul. Envious people resent the good things others receive, such as fortune, friends, happiness, and praise, and fail to see the blessings they have in their own life.

The last of the seven deadly sins is anger. Anger is the opposite of kindness, which calls us to reach out with compassion to others. Anger is often our first reaction to the problems brought to us by others. It's the feeling we have when we lash out rather than take a moment to process what is being said. Often anger presents itself as impatience, irritability, annoyance, or fury, but it is all the same premise of someone who refuses to take the tender approach and opts for more abrasive behavior instead.

This sinful anger, sometimes called wrath, is not to be confused with a nonsinful feeling that is sometimes called righteous anger. In the Gospels, Jesus himself got angry at the money changers in the Temple who were turning his Father's house into a marketplace. Yet this anger was not sinful; it was a righteous feeling that recognized that people were leading others into sin and away from God. The important thing to recognize is that not all anger is sinful.

Living the Beatitudes

In order to learn to live a good and virtuous life, Christians turn to the Beatitudes, the moral message at the heart of Jesus' teachings. Found in the Sermon on the Mount in the Gospel of Matthew, they are nine simple directives that compel us to live properly and walk in the ways of the Lord so that we can achieve happiness in this life and attain happiness in Heaven with God.

Often called the "be-like-Jesus-attitudes," the Beatitudes show us the charitable character of Christ and unlike the more general Ten Commandments, call us to recognize our individual places in society, confront ethical issues, and take a stand for what we believe in. They are the principles that, once absorbed, become a way of life and illustrate the promises that await those who choose to follow Christ's example in their human vocation.

"Blessed are the poor in spirit, for theirs is the kingdom of heaven.

Blessed are those who mourn, for they will be comforted.

Blessed are the meek, for they will inherit the earth.

Blessed are those who hunger and thirst for righteousness, for they will be filled.

Blessed are the merciful, for they will receive mercy.

Blessed are the pure in heart, for they will see God.

Blessed are the peacemakers, for they will be called children of God.

Blessed are those who are persecuted for righteousness' sake, for theirs is the kingdom of heaven.

Blessed are you when people revile you and persecute you and utter all kinds of evil against you falsely on my account. Rejoice and be glad, for your reward is great in heaven." (Matthew 5:3-12)

FAST FACT

The Gospels of Matthew and Luke both contain narratives that include the Beatitudes, but the location, content, and number of principles vary depending on which version is read. Matthew's Gospel, which contains nine Beatitudes, takes place during the Sermon on the Mount while Luke's version contains only four and takes place on a plain.

The Beatitudes serve as the backbone for Catholic social teaching, which, as you will learn in the next chapter, serves as a central and important component of the Catholic faith designed to help the faithful live holy lives as individuals as well as functional members of society.

The Least You Need to Know

- There are four cardinal virtues and three theological virtues.
- Sins are classified into two categories based on severity: mortal and venial.
- The vices that create a breeding ground for sinful behavior are known as the seven deadly sins.
- Christians rely on the moral message of the Beatitudes to help them live good and virtuous lives.

CHAPTER 12

Catholic Social Teaching

Every person who longs to achieve happiness and personal fulfillment on Earth and in the Kingdom of God needs directives upon which to model their lives. Like other Christian traditions, Catholics follow the "letter of the law" through the Ten Commandments and organize their priorities around the Beatitudes, but they also have the Church's teachings on social issues to help guide their lives.

Catholic social teaching focuses on four basic principles designed to help the faithful live a Christ-centered life in an increasingly secular world: Respect for Human Life and Dignity, the Common Good, Subsidiarity, and Solidarity. They are based on papal, episcopal, and council documents and are the core of the Catholic moral tradition.

In this chapter, we will explore the themes at the heart of the Church's social teaching. We will investigate the issues designed to create unity among the faithful as well as the hot-button topics that create the most controversy.

In This Chapter

- Respecting the dignity of all individuals
- Promoting the common good of society
- Giving help to those who are most in need
- Living life according to God's plan
- Taking a stand for freedom and fairness for all

Universal Guidelines

The Catholic Church is the only major Christian faith tradition with a unified body of social teaching. Most other denominations do not have a central teaching authority that proclaims their positions on social issues, and because of that, they have also not developed a body of social teaching. This is not to say that the global community does not adhere to many of the principles contained in Catholic social teaching, only that in many other religious traditions the guidelines have not been compiled in a formal manner.

Catholic social teaching is a way of ordering the elements of society in order to achieve individual and social justice for all humanity. It is not a set of rules made up according to the Church's institutional agenda, but the way in which the faithful learn how to apply the Ten Commandments, the Beatitudes, and the ancient doctrines of the Church to twenty-first-century issues.

Catholic positions on moral and social issues are interconnected and all based on the same basic, fundamental principles, which are drawn from Scripture and the tradition of the Church. Through the Church's social tradition, Catholics learn how they can effect social change, take responsibility for their fellow man, and contribute to the *common good*.

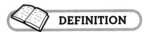

DEFINITION

The **common good** is that which benefits the interests of everyone involved.

Respect for Human Life and Dignity

The Catholic Church believes that every human being has been created equal in the image of God and is born with certain inalienable rights. This dignity is not dependent on what we do with our lives, but is guaranteed by the very fact that we exist.

The Church is very vocal in its assertion that all human life is sacred and that the basic rights and dignity of the individual must be respected and protected from the moment of conception to the moment of natural death. Although most people associate this "right to life" idea with the issues of abortion and euthanasia, it actually encompasses a wide range of topics including, but not limited to, cloning, embryonic stem cell research, care of the poor and suffering, the death penalty, and the quest for world peace.

The Fruit of Thy Womb

The Catholic Church believes that life is a precious gift from God and that children should be the result of a sexual union between a man and a woman whose relationship has been sanctified through the bond of matrimony. While the Church expects a couple to be responsible in the number of children they bring into the world, it does not authorize the use of external methods designed to prevent conception from occurring, terminate unwanted pregnancies, or manipulate life outside of the womb to either create families or eliminate undesired genetic traits or generate "spare parts." Catholic moral teaching prohibits …

- Artificial birth control medications, devices, and methods designed to prevent conception from occurring.

- Sterilization for contraceptive purposes.

- Cloning, which tampers with the natural method of reproduction designed by God.

- Surrogacy, any act in which a third party's body is employed to help a couple create a child and/or carry a pregnancy to term.

- In vitro fertilization, because it takes reproduction into the lab and often results in the creation of several embryos, most of which are either destroyed or frozen in the process.

- Genetic engineering to ensure that a child will be born a certain gender or to eliminate what is perceived to be an undesirable trait.

- The use of embryonic stem cells for purposes of research because it results in the destruction of human embryos, which Catholics view as full human beings with the right to a life of their own.

- The abortion of a pregnancy through medical procedure, regardless of the circumstances. The Church believes abortion is in violation of the fifth commandment forbidding murder.

 FAST FACT

In recent decades, the Catholic Church has been embroiled in the debate regarding stem cell research. Adult stem cell research is perfectly acceptable to the Church, and encouraged; however, embryonic stem cell research is condemned. Experience has shown that adult stem cells have been used to treat hundreds of thousands of people suffering from dozens of different diseases, whereas all the privately funded research on embryonic stem cells has not proven to benefit a single person.

Catholics are encouraged to regulate the number of children they bring into the world through natural family planning (NFP), which takes into account the nature of the female anatomy so that a man and a woman can mindfully choose the moments in which to celebrate their love.

Natural family planning is not the "rhythm method" of years gone by. For one, NFP actually works and is very reliable. It is a medically derived way of teaching a woman to know when she is naturally fertile and when she is naturally infertile, for the purpose of using that knowledge to aid in either achieving pregnancy or avoiding it at that particular time. When properly used, it is over 99 percent effective—better than any method of artificial contraception—and is completely natural and morally acceptable.

When a couple struggles with infertility, Church teaching does authorize them to seek alternative methods by which to have a family. In addition to adoption (whether infertility is an issue or not), the Church accepts some medical solutions that can promote their chances of conception. Some of these include hormone treatments or injections that help the fertilization process to happen naturally.

FAST FACT

The epidemic of HIV/AIDS in Africa has presented a unique challenge for Church leaders, who are torn between the Catholic position regarding condom use for contraception and advocating that same methodology as a means to preserve life. Though the Vatican has not wavered from its beliefs, in communities where as many as 50 percent of the people are HIV+, the local Church authorities may have grounds to allow the use of condoms for the purpose of protecting life by limiting the spread of HIV. Intention and circumstance are important components to determining morality, and they can lessen a person's guilt for committing what is normally considered a sinful act.

At the Hour of Death

The Church is very concerned with human dignity at the end of life as well. The Catholic faith is opposed to the use of the death penalty, euthanasia, and the intentional targeting of civilians during an act of war. The Church feels that all of these issues violate the fifth commandment prohibiting murder, that God alone has the right to end a life—not the state, nor the individual—even when quality of life has diminished, and that conflicting nations must constantly work together to find peaceful solutions to their differences.

So what about suicide? Strictly speaking, the taking of one's own life is murder and many people consider it the "unforgiveable mortal sin" because there is typically no chance to ask for absolution for the act. This thought is discomforting to those who have lost loved ones to this type of tragedy, so it is important to understand that Church doctrine does assure us that God has ways of providing for these souls. Many of those who commit suicide are plagued by psychological and emotional illness, which leads them to the ultimate despair culminating in this final act. The Church refrains from making judgment calls in these cases and believes that when suicide occurs, God alone knows the person's heart well enough to extend His mercy even in death.

The Common Good

Although God created us to be individuals, we are not allowed to be radical individualists. Christians are by nature social beings who are designed to interact with one another for mutual benefit—which is called the common good.

The common good occurs when ...

- Society recognizes every human person is sacred and has been made equal in the image of God.

- Every person is allowed to realize his or her intellectual and religious potential in a community rather than in isolation.

- A foundation of basic rights and minimum standards for life in society has been established.

The common good is both personal and communal. In order to achieve the common good, every society depends on an ethical, legitimate authority dedicated to the orderly promotion of societal development without oppression, and for every member of that society to assume responsibility for one another—especially those who are most vulnerable. This "preferential option for the poor" is critical to understanding Catholic social teaching. As Christians, we are called to assist those most in need first and provide for a distribution of goods and services that doesn't only benefit the rich, but provides for the poor as well.

Not only does this mean we are to help provide for the poor's basic needs, but also to give voice to the voiceless, defend the defenseless, and safeguard those who are in danger. In the Gospel of Matthew, Jesus tells his followers that society will be judged by their treatment of those who are hungry, thirsty, isolated, naked, and imprisoned. "Truly I tell you, just as you did it to one of the least of these who are members of my family, you did it to me." (Matthew 25:40)

Though the poor are always with us, working for the common good compels us to demand social justice for all of our brothers and sisters in Christ: to challenge regimes that squash individual rights, to work to alleviate poverty, and to rely on one another's gifts to charitably make up for what someone else lacks.

Subsidiarity

We all know people who are "trapped in the system." They have been marginalized for so long they cannot transcend their circumstances. While they would like to work and contribute to society in such a way that they can improve their quality of life, they can't afford to. For them, poverty has become a lifestyle.

The principle of *subsidiarity* warns against charity that becomes oppressive in nature or causes the governing authority to control rather than liberate the individual. It is an organizing principle of decentralization that calls for matters to be handled (whenever possible) at the lowest possible level of authority rather than the highest. Similar to an inverted pyramid or a chain of command, this idea suggests that the government should get involved only in those issues that go beyond the capacity of the local community to handle. This not only respects the dignity of the individual but also ensures that government concentrates on serving the community rather than micromanaging it.

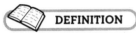 **DEFINITION**

> **Subsidiarity** is the principle that all matters should be handled at the lowest level of authority possible for a good solution rather than the highest, and that the governing body should not get involved in issues that can be handled on the local level.

If that seems a bit overwhelming, consider this: when you were a child and had a disagreement with a sibling that required intervention, did you pick up the phone and call local law enforcement to handle the matter? Of course not! Chances are you went to Mom and Dad in search of a fair and equitable solution. This idea of taking problems to one's immediate supervisor rather than the governing authority is the thought process behind the principle of subsidiarity.

Throughout life, there are a number of local organizations designed to handle issues at the local level (such as school boards, labor unions, charitable organizations, church elders). These entities have adopted bylaws and tenets to help them mediate solutions that respect the dignity of all parties involved, empower individual action, and link them to the larger society.

 KEEP IT SIMPLE

> Subsidiarity does not mean government doesn't have its place. On the contrary, it is imperative for communities to be built on a structure of principles that are executed through justice and charity and administered by an authentic and ethical authority for the benefit and interests of everyone involved.

The Church believes everyone has a responsibility to the common good. Just as we are dependent on others from time to time, we are called to serve our fellow man. We have the responsibility to be mindful of everyone's basic rights and to do what we can to ensure those rights are being met. This means we must ...

- Promote the dignity of the individual as well as the family unit.

- Reach out to the poor and suffering.

- Elect leaders who will impose just laws and regulations.

- Fight for workers' rights, fair wages, and appropriate working conditions.

- Work tirelessly for peace, stability, and justice for all people.

Solidarity

It is impossible for a Christian to be concerned only about his own needs. By their nature, Christians are compassionate and empathetic people who believe in the idea of justice for all. When tragedy strikes, they are quick to respond by organizing relief efforts. However, it's one thing to reach out and help those who are suffering in the moment and quite another to stand with those who suffer long-term through the principle of solidarity.

Solidarity is the principle of Catholic social teaching that calls the faithful to action in an effort to strengthen community and to create a civilization of love. Solidarity compels us to stand together for what is right, to make a difference in the world, and to respect every person as the unique individual God created them to be.

 KEEP IT SIMPLE

The principle of solidarity calls society to respond to people in the same manner as the Good Samaritan did when he reached out to care for the man who was attacked by robbers on the road to Jericho. By feeling compassion for the man's suffering and seeing to the man's needs as he would his own, the Samaritan showcases the idea behind this important aspect of Catholic social teaching.

The Catholic Church condemns the discrimination of anyone based on their race, creed, culture, sexual preference, gender, or the conditions under which they were born. Catholics believe that every individual has been called by God to serve in His divine plan, and regardless of the Church's doctrinal position regarding specific lifestyle choices, they feel that the global community should accept every individual and extend them nothing but love.

Solidarity occurs on a number of levels. It can be the child who reaches out to befriend the new kid in school. It can be the person who refrains from indulging in office gossip about a co-worker. It can mean dedicating one's volunteer efforts to an issue they feel particularly close to, such caring for the earth. But at the end of the day, solidarity is about redefining how we see our neighbors and how we respond to Jesus' command to love one another as He loves us.

The Values of Truth, Freedom, Justice, and Love

Although the principles of Catholic social teaching are put into place in order to help create a society based on the teachings of Christ, there must also be fundamental values that correspond to them.

Everyone has the duty to seek the truth and to bear witness to it in his or her daily life. When truth prevails, so, too, does the dignity of the individual. And when people use the truth to guide their decision-making process, it helps them avoid potential abuses and act according to the existing moral parameter.

KEEP IT SIMPLE

The Catholic Church often takes a lot of heat for some of the decisions it makes regarding societal issues. Some people say it is an entity that fails to move with the times or is unwilling to modernize, but in reality, the Church's job is not an easy one. Though there may be times the hierarchy would like to announce a more "popular" decision, its job doesn't work that way. It must weigh all of the facts in relation to Scripture and the accepted tradition, and make a decision according to the truth God has revealed.

The fact that we have been given the freedom to choose is the highest sign that humanity was made in the image of God. This freedom enables us not only to follow the vocation God has called us to fulfill, but also to profess our religious, cultural, and political ideas and opinions. Naturally, we are expected to exercise this freedom responsibly within the limits of the common good and for the betterment of mankind.

Through the value of individual and societal justice, Catholics strive to connect with the world at large through the principles of subsidiarity, solidarity and fairness for all.

When justice prevails, so, too, do truth, freedom, and unity. The value of justice compels us to view everyone as an individual with rights while still treating them from a neutral position as a way to achieve peace.

Justice alone can ultimately lead to destruction, so it is important to couple the value of justice with the value of love. Love does nothing more than restore man to himself. Love goes beyond how we feel about each other and asks us to embrace the larger idea. Love must operate for the greater good, and it must accept everyone as they are, not as we would like them to be. Though there are countless members of the Church who have exhibited these values throughout their lives, two standouts include Blessed (Mother) Teresa of Calcutta and activist Dorothy Day.

Blessed Teresa of Calcutta

Although she was small in stature, Blessed Mother Teresa of Calcutta was a tower of faith. Born Agnes Gonxha Bojaxhiu circa August 26, 1910, in Skopje, Albania (today the capital of Macedonia), she lost her father very early in life and was raised by a mother who instilled piety, compassion, and a commitment to charity in the young girl.

Teresa knew she had a call to the religious life at the age of 12, and in 1928, when she was 18, she joined the Loreto Sisters of Dublin. After taking her first vows, she was sent to Calcutta, India, where she taught high school classes in the Bengali language to some of the poorest families. She mastered both Bengali and Hindi as she taught, and hoped that she could help alleviate her students' poverty through education.

 CATHOLIC QUOTE

If we have no peace, it is because we have forgotten that we belong to each other.

—Bl. Teresa of Calcutta

In 1937, Teresa took her perpetual vows and was accorded the title "Mother" as per the custom of her order. She became the principal of her school in 1944, but two years later she had an experience that would change her life forever. While on board a train one day, Mother Teresa heard the voice of Christ calling her to leave the classroom and go to work in the slums. Though she wanted to do as Jesus asked, she also had taken a vow of obedience preventing her from leaving the convent without permission.

It took nearly 18 months for her to receive permission from her superiors, but in 1948, she was allowed to leave the Loreto Sisters of Dublin in order to work in the streets. She donned her trademark blue and white sari and set out to minister to all who were unloved, uncared for, and unwanted.

Before long, this simple call to action encouraged Mother Teresa to found an open-air school and a home for the dying, and even to secure donations from the city government. In 1950, she was authorized to begin a new congregation of women religious, which she named the Missionaries of Charity. Her efforts swelled throughout the latter part of the twentieth century, including the addition of a leper colony, nursing home, family clinic, orphanage, and several mobile health clinics. By 1970, her mission was an international one. She even opened a soup kitchen in New York City and expanded her efforts to care for those suffering the effects of HIV/AIDS. The Church, in addition to countless governments and other entities, honored her for her work, and in 1979 Mother Teresa was awarded the Nobel Peace Prize for her humanitarian efforts.

CATHOLIC QUOTE

Each one of them is Jesus in disguise.

—Bl. Teresa of Calcutta

By the time of Mother Teresa's death on September 5, 1997, the Missionaries of Charity numbered over 4,000, with thousands of lay volunteers, and included 610 foundations in 123 countries. St. Pope John Paul II waived three of the five years needed prior to opening a cause for canonization for his beloved friend, and in 2002 the Vatican recognized Mother Teresa's intercession in the healing of an abdominal tumor from an Indian woman and beatified the humanitarian on October 19, 2003.

Dorothy Day

Dorothy Day was a Catholic activist who never shied away from promoting the social causes she believed in or protesting those she opposed. Born on November 8, 1897, in New York City, Day's family relocated to California when she was only 6 years old. She grew up in a nominally Christian household, but very early on developed an aptitude for religious studies, read the Bible frequently, and eventually joined the Episcopalian Church.

A stellar student, Day was awarded a scholarship to the University of Illinois in 1914, but two years later she abandoned her studies to return to New York in order to become involved with the city's liberal crowd. She was a contributor to a number of socialist magazines and quickly became involved in political and social causes such as women's suffrage, which led to several arrests.

CATHOLIC QUOTE

We have all known the long loneliness, and we have found that the answer is community.

—Dorothy Day

Dorothy became involved in a love affair, which resulted in a pregnancy. Her lover insisted that she terminate the pregnancy, and not long after her abortion, the relationship ended. After a while, she entered another long-term relationship, which resulted in another pregnancy; but this time Day carried the child to term and gave birth to a daughter, whom she had baptized in the Catholic Church. This decision led to Day's own conversion in 1927. The relationship with the child's father also ultimately ended.

Enamored with her new faith, Dorothy was a rabid fanatic over Catholic social causes. In 1932, she met former Christian Brother Peter Maurin and together the two founded *The Catholic Worker*, a newspaper dedicated to Catholic teachings and the societal issues of the day. It was a classic example of advocacy journalism. The success of the publication led to the Catholic Worker Movement, which worked to bring awareness to issues and how these topics fit into the Church's social teaching. Another component of this movement was the establishment of special homes to help the poor and homeless.

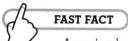

FAST FACT

A year's subscription to *The Catholic Worker* today is only 25 cents.

Day was an unapologetic pacifist who used the Sermon on the Mount as her manifesto. Throughout the 1940s and 1950s, she was a conscientious objector to all armed warfare and a fearless champion of workers' rights, yet her participation in the 1960s counterculture was mixed. Despite her poor health, Day continued her work throughout the 1970s and traveled the world as an advocate of peace. She was given the Pacem in Terris Award from the Interracial Council of the Catholic Diocese of Davenport, Iowa, as well as the Laetare Medal from the University of Notre Dame.

Dorothy Day died of a heart attack on November 29, 1980, at one of the homes she established. Her papers are on file at Marquette University. *The Catholic Worker* continues to be published and as of 2013 had a circulation of just under 30,000. The cover price remains the same as when Day started it: one penny. The Church has opened a cause for Day's canonization and she currently holds the title Servant of God.

The Least You Need to Know

- Catholicism is the only Christian faith that has a unified body of social teaching.
- Catholic social teaching focuses on four principles: Respect for Human Life, the Common Good, Subsidiarity, and Solidarity.
- The values of freedom, truth, justice, and love permeate Catholic social teaching.
- Two dedicated champions of Catholic social teaching were Blessed Teresa of Calcutta and Dorothy Day.

CHAPTER 13

Heaven and Hell

We know just enough about the one to know it's a really nice place to visit and enough about the other to know we never want to go there. They summon visions of a pearly-gated paradise and a fiery realm of eternal damnation, and are the two places where the promises or punishments of the afterlife await depending on how we spend our earthly lives. They are Heaven and Hell.

Home to the Holy Trinity and all the angels and saints, Heaven is naturally the preferable choice given the two. Scripture assures us that the faithful will find ultimate fulfillment in the hereafter, while those who shun salvation will be isolated for all time.

In this chapter, we will uncover the worlds that lie above us and below us, and why Catholics believe there is something in between. We will explore the domains of the dearly departed as we try to determine where we go from here.

The Day of Judgment

Although Catholics generally do not occupy themselves with doomsday prophecies and apocalyptic language, they do believe everyone will arrive at that moment when they will have to stand before God and account for their lives. No matter who they are, where they lived, how much money they made, or what level of fame they achieved, God will render His verdict based on what they have done and what they have failed to do. His decision will determine whether or not they climb the stairway to Heaven or find themselves on the highway to Hell.

For many of us, this particular judgment will occur at the moment of our death. It is our day in court, so to speak, and it is important for us to be the person He expected us to be when He created us. Assuming that we are fortunate enough to stand before Him, Catholics believe that one of three things will happen: either God will embrace us immediately as one of His own, or He will determine that we are in need of additional purification. Or if we are so full of evil and hatred and reject everything He has to offer us, we will opt for an existence of solitude devoid of His presence.

 CATHOLIC QUOTE

I am not dying; I am entering life.

—Thérèse of Lisieux

There is also the more "general" or "final" judgment associated with the "Last Days." This is the moment in which Christ will return to Earth in glory and according to the Nicene Creed, "will judge the living and the dead." This is the moment in which the sheep will be separated from the goats, the Book of Life will be consulted, the evildoers of the world will be thrown into the lake of fire, and the righteous will be led into eternal life with God. It's more than the Second Coming; it's the end of the world as we know it.

In the Book of Revelation, John offers a graphic (and often frightening) glimpse of the events leading to the Last Judgment and its aftermath. For thousands of years, the imagery in this text has been analyzed for clues that can help us riddle out its hidden meaning, but Catholics tend not to focus on the literary symbolism. After all, it was a popular style of writing geared toward a first-century audience. Catholics do, however, emphasize the apostle's overall message that Christ will come again, God will create a new Heaven and a new Earth, and His people will share in this kingdom with Him.

> "I heard a loud voice from the throne saying, 'See, the home of God is among mortals. He will dwell with them; they will be his peoples, and God himself will be with them; he will wipe every tear from their eyes. Death will be no more; mourning and crying and pain will be no more, for the first things have passed away.'" (Revelation 21:3-4)

Those who have already died and have been judged will not be judged again. They will remain where they are but they will no longer exist as a disembodied spirit. They will be reunited with their bodies (similar to the one Jesus had after His resurrection and not our current one) while those on earth learn their fate. Those who find favor with God will be taken to His realm where evil, suffering, and hatred no longer exists, their deepest longings will be fulfilled, and every day they will rejoice in the presence of God. It is nothing short of paradise.

Heaven Is Not Too Far Away

The world we live in is hardly the only construction project in God's portfolio. In addition to giving His humans the planet we call Earth, He also filled the universe with galaxies of stars and planetary systems that are awesome to contemplate. However, He also created a dominion of His own where he lives in an atmosphere of love alongside the angels and the saints. We know it as Heaven.

Though it is often depicted as a gleaming, golden city in the clouds, Heaven isn't a "place" in the classic sense. It's not located somewhere above our heads. There are no coordinates and we can't get directions to it from a GPS. It is where one is in the presence of God, face-to-face, and experiences nothing but pure love from Him. Heaven is an advanced state of being that defies description. It is a consciousness beyond this plane of knowledge where the lives of the faithful take on a deeper intensity and meaning and transcend what they can comprehend during their mortal existence.

Scripture tells us a little about what Heaven is like. John 14:2 says that "in my father's house, there are many dwelling places" and it is to this house that Jesus went to prepare a place for His people. In Revelation, John gives us a description of the New Jerusalem that includes many of the accoutrements we associate with the eternal kingdom (the streets of gold, pearly gates, throne of God, river and tree of life, and so on). However, no matter how we imagine it, the reality is better than anything we can come up with. As Paul wrote in 1 Corinthians 2:9, "What no eye has seen, nor ear heard, nor the human heart conceived, what God has prepared for those who love him."

CATHOLIC QUOTE

We long for the joy of Heaven, where God is. It is within our power to be with Him in Heaven even now, to be happy with Him in this very moment. But to be happy with Him now means to help as He helps, to give as He gives, to serve as He serves ... to love as He loves.

—Bl. Teresa of Calcutta

God always intended for His humans to live this kind of bucolic existence with Him. In the beginning He created the Garden of Eden and gave it to Adam and Eve in order for them to live in harmony with God and His creation. They did not have to work for it. There was no admission fee and no test to pass. It was all free and clear, but then sin entered the picture and all of it was taken away. From that moment on we would be expected to toil for our rewards, suffer for our choice, and face mortality before ever seeing paradise again.

So how do we get there? As we learned in Chapter 6, the Sacraments of Initiation are a great place to start; but merely participating in them all does not guarantee your soul a space in Heaven. "For just as the body without a spirit is dead, so faith without works is also dead." (James 2:26) Catholics believe that their faith leads them to perform good works out of obedience to God, that they must keep His commandments and live by His beatitudes so that by His grace they will be prepared for admittance into His kingdom at the end of their lives.

 CATHOLIC QUOTE

We have lost paradise but have received heaven, and therefore the gain is greater than the loss.

—St. John Chrysostom

Angels

Although we may not have a lot of details regarding what Heaven looks like, we do know a little about the beings that live there. In Chapter 17, we will discuss at length the concept of the saints and how we know they reside alongside God. For now we will concentrate on looking into the original heavenly inhabitants, the angels.

Out of all the creatures created by God, the angels are truly unique. Angels are immortal beings that are neither gods nor humans. They are noncorporeal, pure spirits who have intelligence and free will and who spend their existence serving as special emissaries of God.

They have been around since the beginning of creation, and throughout history have played significant roles in God's divine plan:

- They were placed at the entrance to Eden in order to guard it after the fall of Man.
- They protected Lot from the destruction of Sodom and Gomorrah.
- They saved Hagar and Ishmael (Abraham's firstborn child).
- They stopped Abraham from slaying Isaac.
- They protected Daniel while he was imprisoned in the lions' den.
- They assisted the prophets and led the people of God on countless occasions.
- They announced the births of John the Baptist and Jesus.

From the moment of the incarnation through the ascension, the heavenly hosts surrounded Christ's earthly life. They came to the shepherds in the fields to tell them the Messiah had been born in Bethlehem. They protected the child Jesus when Herod threatened His life. They ministered to Him in the desert, and in Luke's Gospel they proclaimed the good news of the resurrection to the women at the tomb. The Bible also tells us they will be the ones to herald the second coming, will be present when Christ returns, and will serve him during the Final Judgment.

CATHOLIC QUOTE

Make friends with the angels, who though invisible are always with you. Often invoke them, constantly praise them, and make good use of their help and assistance in all your temporal and spiritual affairs.

—St. Francis de Sales

The Catholic Church believes there is a distinction between humans and angels and that one cannot become the other. Humans were given a body and soul while angels are pure spirit. Although angels have appeared in human form, they are not humans. And when humans die, although we are temporarily separated from our bodies, we do not become angels because at the end of the world our bodies and souls will be reunited.

The Church also believes the human race is constantly under the watchful eye of the angels and that God provides everyone with a guardian angel who can be called upon in times of need. (They have also been known to act without being asked.) They are there to protect, guide, and sometimes intercede with God on behalf of their humans whenever necessary. In short, they are a constant spirit presence with powers greater than our own.

The God Squad

There are 227 references to angels in the Bible, and for the most part they are nameless agents sent by God. In the Catholic Scriptures there are three angels mentioned by name who have served very special purposes throughout history: Michael, Gabriel, and Raphael.

Michael ("he who is like God") is called an archangel in the Epistle of Jude and is mentioned in both the Hebrew and Christian Scriptures. Though he says nothing in the Bible, he is known as a chief prince, a fierce protector, and the leader of the army of God who will rise up at the end of time and defeat Satan once and for all. He is often depicted wearing armor and carrying a sword.

Like Michael, Gabriel ("God is my strength") is found in both the Old and New Testaments, and just like Michael, one of those times is in the Book of Daniel in which Gabriel (the "man in linen") interprets Daniel's dreams. In the Book of Ezekiel, it is implied that Gabriel is the angel sent to destroy Jerusalem.

In the New Testament, Gabriel is the angel who comes to Zechariah in the temple to tell him that God has heard his prayers. He assures the older man that he and his wife Anna will have a child and that he is to name him John. Zechariah challenges this announcement and for his lack of faith, the messenger issues a swift rebuke:

> "I am Gabriel. I stand in the presence of God, and I have been sent to speak to you and to bring you this good news. But now, because you did not believe my words, which will be fulfilled in their time, you will become mute, unable to speak, until the day these things occur." (Luke 1:19-20)

As we learned in Chapter 2, Gabriel then travels to Nazareth to tell Mary that she will be the mother of God. Many believe that Gabriel is also the "angel of the Lord" who tells Joseph that it is proper for him to take Mary as his wife and possibly that he was the chief being who came to the shepherds in the field, but the Bible is not clear on these last two points.

FAST FACT

Gabriel is often pictured with a horn befitting his tendency to make significant announcements. The origin of this instrumental connection is unknown, but in the English-speaking culture it was first referenced in 1667 in John Milton's *Paradise Lost*.

While he is not as well-known as Michael and Gabriel, the archangel Raphael ("God heals") is a powerful healer who appears in the deuterocanonical Book of Tobit. He appears as a human named Azarias who encounters the blind Tobit and is hired to be a traveling companion for his son Tobias. During the journey, Raphael binds the hands and feet of a demon, heals Tobit's blindness, and at the wedding feast of Tobias, offers his blessings on the couple and reveals his identity saying, "I am Raphael, one of the seven angels who stand ready and enter before the glory of the Lord." (Tobit 12:15) He assures the couple that he was not acting on his own accord but on the will of God, and asks them to praise Him for their blessings every day. (Raphael is also associated with the angel in the Gospel of John stirring the water at the healing pool of Bethesda, but it is not clear if it really is the same being.)

Lucifer and His Demons

Like all of the angels, Lucifer was created by God to be a force for good, but ultimately he became the agent of evil known as Satan. Although no one knows exactly what happened that led to the fall of Lucifer and his followers, the Church teaches that they ultimately rejected God and everything that he stood for. Their irrevocable choice means there is no chance for repentance. They committed the unforgivable sin.

From the Garden of Eden to the temptation in the desert and beyond, the Catholic Church teaches that Satan is the father of lies. He is the one who tells us it's no big deal when we want to do something we shouldn't. He makes promises that are always too good to be true, and when we choose his way over God's, we suffer from the consequences. (Yes, there are times we suffer for God as well, but only because He will make something better out of it.)

Although he is a powerful, pure spirit who cannot die, Satan is still a creature and not an infinite being. He can never stop God's reign. Even though he is 100 percent evil, he cannot triumph over something that is 100 percent good. At times it may seem like Satan is winning, and we've all pondered the great mystery of why God allows him to exist at all, but as Paul says in Romans 8:28, "We know that all things work together for good for those who love God."

There are 33 names for and references to Satan or the Devil in the Bible. Though these are his two most common monikers (aside from his angelic name Lucifer), some of his pseudonyms include:

- Abaddon

- Adversary

- Angel of the bottomless pit

- Antichrist

- Beelzebub

- The great red dragon

Purgatory

It is the teaching of the Church that most non-Catholics (and a few Catholics) have the hardest time with: the concept of Purgatory. Often thought of as a stop on the way to Heaven, Purgatory is the place where people who died in God's grace and friendship undergo a final purification in order to achieve the state of holiness required for entry into Heaven.

If the Church is right, then chances are most of us will end up there for a period of time before moving on to eternal glory with God. In Heaven, we are completely focused on God, nothing else is important to us, and we are able to completely receive God's love and love Him in return. However, even if we have lived fairly good lives, when most of us die, there are still things on Earth we are attached to: human relationships, material goods, successes, and dreams that prevent us from being completely focused on God. Purgatory is that process by which we are detached from the things of earth in order to be attached exclusively to God in Heaven. It is painful, because we have come to like our attachments.

KEEP IT SIMPLE

Another way to think about Purgatory is this: if Heaven is like a wedding banquet, Purgatory is like the process of getting ready for it—scrubbing off dirt and grime, getting clean, putting on our best clothes, and so on.

Purgatory is not a Catholic invention. While the doctrine for the belief in Purgatory was hammered out at the Councils of Florence and Trent, it is based on the scriptural account of Judas Maccabeus' practice of atonement for the dead. This event is recounted in the deuterocanonical book of 2 Maccabees when, after a battle, Judas discovers that his deceased warriors were all wearing sacred tokens of idols that were forbidden by Jewish law. He took up a collection in their honor and also felt compelled to pray for these otherwise righteous men who had died "so that they might be delivered from their sin." (2 Maccabees 12:45)

CATHOLIC QUOTE

Let us not hesitate to help those who have died and offer our prayers for them.

—St. John Chrysostom

The Loss of Limbo

Although the Catholic Church is an organization that firmly believes in baptism as the first step to salvation, in the fifth century, there arose a problem of how to explain what happened to those who died prior to the sacrament's institution as well as those who were too young to receive the sacrament prior to their death. Would God really exclude Abraham, Moses, and even Jesus' earthly father Joseph from his kingdom? And what about the infants who died free of mortal sin but still possessed Original Sin? Would their souls be banished to Hell? The Church's answer for hundreds of years was a place called Limbo.

St. Augustine was the first theologian to ascribe to the concept of Limbo. He was such a staunch supporter of the sacrament of baptism that he could not agree with heretical ideologies that said the innocent would be spared, but at the same time, he couldn't relegate their poor souls to eternal damnation. He conceived of the idea of Limbo, and it became a popular belief for hundreds of years.

Though it was never official doctrine of the Church (and has been omitted from the Catechism since 1992) there are actually two distinct Limbos that have been supposed to exist: the Limbo of the Innocents and the Limbo of the Fathers. The Limbo of the Innocents as outlined above offers an image of a celestial daycare where souls who were too young to know any better are relegated rather than shown mercy.

In 2007, Pope Benedict XVI closed the book on this idea with the publication of *The Hope of Salvation for Infants Who Die Without Being Baptized* and concluded that God has the ability to immediately transfer sanctifying grace to these children, perhaps even at the moment of their death. This explanation does not negate the importance of baptism, but rather it is a statement on God's mercy and love that He would not exclude an innocent child from Heaven due to circumstances beyond their control.

CATHOLIC QUOTE

> Limbo was never a defined truth of faith. Personally—and here I am speaking more as a theologian and not as prefect of the congregation—I would abandon it, since it was only a theological hypothesis.
>
> —Joseph Ratzinger (In *The Ratzinger Report*)

The Limbo of the Fathers is another matter entirely. The concept of this holding station is a step above Hell where it is believed that everyone who died after Adam and Eve but before Jesus were kept because Heaven had not yet been opened (it wasn't opened until the death and resurrection of Jesus). It is where the patriarchs of the Old Testament were kept until Jesus could die and "spring" them. It is supposedly a happy place, distinct from Purgatory, in which folks waited contentedly until Jesus could fulfill his mission.

The Apostle's Creed states that He descended into Hell not only to affirm that Jesus died a human death, but also to offer salvation to those people who had been in the waiting room, so to speak, for thousands of years. The Church still believes that Jesus descended to this realm as a savior delivering the good news and freeing the souls He found there, but the term Limbo is not really used.

Paradise Lost: The Reality of Hell

The opposite of Heaven is Hell, and just as Heaven isn't a country club in the clouds, Hell is not a fiery pit located below the earth where the devil and demons torture humans for their past crimes. In actuality, it probably isn't even hot. But make no mistake, it does exist and it is a possibility for those who see everything God has to offer and say, "No thanks."

Jesus offered up a compelling visual for believing it was just such a place. In the Gospels, he says that wicked people will be thrown body and soul into Gehenna (Hell) and made to suffer in an eternal fire for their sins, but archaeologists have learned that Gehenna may have been a real place.

Though the location is heavily debated, Gehenna was once a landfill somewhere near Jerusalem known as the valley of Hinnom where waste, corpses, and other trash were dumped and fires burned continually. It is referenced in the Old Testament as a place where children were involved in some kind of fire ritual, but it is not clear if the terms used reference a ceremonial event or possibly a child sacrifice. The prophet Isaiah refers to it as the "burning place" (Isaiah 30:33) the Lord has prepared as punishment for those who disobey him.

 CATHOLIC QUOTE

He fashioned hell for the inquisitive.

—St. Augustine

Whether Jesus was speaking about a literal realm beyond Earth or making an allegorical comparison to get His point across is unclear. Needless to say, no one enjoys the thought of being thrown into God's garbage bin—especially one that looks and smells like Gehenna.

Regardless of what Hell actually looks like, the real punishment of being sent there is the fact that it is the final isolation from God. It is a place where people live devoid of anything that could bring them comfort or joy. The Church teaches that God doesn't want anyone to go to Hell and that His love is so vast and infinite He will pursue a soul until the very end. But if anyone standing before His throne still refuses to atone for their sins and accept His love, He has no option but to allow them to make that choice. However, it is a fate far worse than death.

The Least You Need to Know

- Every individual faces a particular judgment at the end of their earthly life.
- The Final Judgment refers to the Second Coming of Christ and the Last Days.
- Heaven is the residence of God and is more beautiful than anything we can imagine.
- Angels are immortal spirits and emissaries from God that protect and guide the human race.
- Lucifer was once an angel but rebelled against God and became known as Satan.
- Purgatory isn't something the Church invented, but is based on 2 Maccabees.
- Hell is the final, eternal separation from God.

Prayer and Holiness

Open 24 hours a day, 7 days a week and with no busy signals, prayer is truly Heaven's hotline and a direct path to God. Although at times it may seem like a memorized conversation with no one, prayer is actually a dialogue between child and parent, servant and master, student and teacher, deity and devotee. By talking to God and listening patiently for his response in our hearts, we can better trust in His plan for our lives and strive ever harder to achieve holiness.

In this part, we will look at the many ways in which we can talk with God and take time out of our busy lives to reflect on His place in our world. We will explore the mysteries of the Rosary and why Mary holds such a prominent place in the Church. And we'll examine why saints are not gods to pray to, but rather God's role models to pray through in hopes that they can intercede with God on our behalf.

Prayer: A Two-Way Conversation

In order to have a relationship with God, one must first begin a conversation. This conversation is the doorway leading to faith and the manner in which we turn our hearts to God. We know it as prayer.

Prayer is the proverbial bridge over troubled water that comforts us when no one is available to talk and assures us that no matter where we are, God is always listening. Prayer is communal as well as personal. It strengthens us when we are weak, increases our stamina, removes fear, and enables us to turn our cares and concerns over to the only one who can take on our problems as His own.

In this chapter, we will fall to our knees in order to understand the power of prayer. You will discover why it matters and learn which prayers all Christians have in common and which are unique to the Catholic faith.

In This Chapter

- God is always listening to His people
- The way Jesus taught His disciples to pray
- The six categories of Catholic prayer
- Common prayers every Catholic should know

Dialing Up a Deity

We all have those moments when it feels like no matter how hard we spin our wheels, we just don't get anywhere. We run the numbers three times and still can't make ends meet. We read the directions time and time again, and still have problems with the end result. We start a project with the best of intentions, yet are still plagued by problems that undermine the objective. It's in those moments that we throw our hands up to the sky in defeat and yell, "I give up!"

It may be a rhetorical statement, or a way of releasing steam, but deep down inside there is a part of us that hopes someone will recognize the frustration we are having and magically solve all of our problems for us. The good news is that in those moments when we are most afraid, lost, or frustrated, God is listening to us. From the moment He created us, He put upon our hearts a longing that can only be filled by His presence. When we call out into the void, God is ready to answer. It may not always be the answer we would like to receive, but when we offer our concerns in prayer, we can trust that God will respond according to His will.

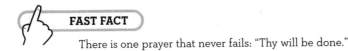

FAST FACT

There is one prayer that never fails: "Thy will be done."

Prayer is the primary way humanity communicates with God. It can be private or public, formal or informal, and can occur anywhere and everywhere at any time of the day.

Beginning with Abraham in the Old Testament, we hear about the patriarch setting up altars to praise God and offer sacrifices to Him. We also know that Abraham and God enjoyed a very interactive relationship and that he was an obedient servant who did whatever God commanded. However, there was one situation in which Abraham felt compelled to express his reservations about God's plan. When God told Abraham he was going to destroy the cities of Sodom and Gomorrah for their depravity, Abraham pleaded with the Lord to spare the righteous people he found inside:

> "Suppose there are fifty righteous within the city; will you then sweep away the place and not forgive it for the fifty righteous who are in it? Far be it from you to do such a thing, to slay the righteous with the wicked, so that the righteous fare as the wicked! Far be that from you! Shall the Judge of all the earth do what is just?" (Genesis 18:24-25)

God assures Abraham that he would spare the entire city for the fifty righteous He found there, which prompts Abraham to ask if He would do the same for forty, thirty, and so on …. God proceeds to promise that if He finds so much as ten righteous people, He will not destroy the cities. This exchange is considered to be the first great intercessory prayer in history.

Moses shows us that prayer is actually a two-way conversation with God in which we are allowed to raise questions, express uncertainties, and demure in the face of God's call. This doesn't make us cowardly, just prudent. God wants us to feel confident in following Him and He doesn't mind when we take the time to talk things over with Him, raise any objections, and contemplate our options in order to make the best decisions.

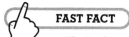

FAST FACT

The Psalms are a treasury of songlike prayers that remain a timeless part of the Catholic tradition.

Praying with Jesus

Because He was raised in a traditional Jewish household, Jesus was educated in the Jewish tradition. He learned to read the Torah and to pray not only in the synagogue but also at home with His parents and other family members. However, Jesus' prayer went beyond the usual boundaries between God and His people. When Jesus prayed, His words suggest a union with God that could only be possible because He was the Father's Son.

Jesus' whole life was a constant prayer, but at key moments in His life His prayer becomes especially intense. During the temptation in the desert after His baptism, Jesus contemplates the ministry that He is about to embark on and must decide how He will use His extraordinary position. He prays for the strength to serve humanity rather than to dominate it. In the Garden of Gethsemane, He begs to be spared from the horrific death that awaits him. Even on the cross he reaches out to God and asks forgiveness of those who have tortured Him and audibly gives up His spirit to the Father. The prayers of Jesus help us to ...

- Praise God as our Father.

- Trust that His will be done.

- Ask for the things we need to live the life He has planned for us.

- Ask God to forgive our own sins, and for the ability to forgive those who have wronged us.

- Ask for the strength to avoid sin and temptation in our lives.

- Commit our souls to Him in hopes that he will lead us to salvation in Heaven with Him.

Sound familiar? In the Lord's Prayer (or as Catholics typically refer to it, the "Our Father"), Jesus offers his disciples the words they need to engage in an effective conversation with God. When we pray the words Jesus gave us and with the spirit in which He prayed, we walk in His footsteps and trust that we can attain favor in the heart of God.

 CATHOLIC QUOTE

Prayer in my opinion is nothing else than a close sharing between friends; it means taking time frequently to be alone with him who we know loves us.

—St. Teresa of Avila

The Lord's Prayer

The "Our Father" is the only prayer that Jesus himself composed and gave to His disciples in response to their request to learn to pray as He did. It consists of seven petitions including three that relate to God's role in our lives and four that concern our basic needs. It is often the first prayer every Catholic learns, and if there is one prayer everyone should say each day, it's this one. It is the prayer that encompasses the entire message of the gospel in just a few words. And at the end of life, these are often the last words that a Christian remembers and says, even when all other words are lost.

The Crux of Christ's Words

According to St. Thomas Aquinas, the Lord's Prayer is the most perfect prayer ever written and serves as a direct pathway to Heaven. In order to understand what he means by this, it is necessary to break down the Lord's Prayer line by line:

- Our Father: Jesus encourages us to reach out to God as a father figure who wants to engage with us and provide for our needs.

- Who art in Heaven: This statement acknowledges where God is and the fact that He transcends the normal bounds of time and space.

- Hallowed be Thy name: As the Source of everything we have, God's name should be revered as the creator of the universe.

- Thy kingdom come: We ask God to make good on His promise to return one day in glory when He will reign forever and to bring about His kingdom on earth today.

- Thy will be done on Earth as it is in Heaven: This line prays for God's will to be accomplished in an imperfect world as it is easily accomplished in the far more perfect Paradise.

- Give us this day our daily bread: While man cannot live by bread alone, we implore God to give us what is vital for our spiritual and material survival.

- Forgive us our trespasses as we forgive those who trespass against us: This line asks God to treat us exactly as we treat others. (Note the irony and be careful what you wish for!)

- Lead us not into temptation: Asks God to help us avoid sin in our lives.

- Deliver us from evil: In the ongoing battle for the soul, we beg God to free us from all the evils of the world and take us into His arms in Heaven.

FAST FACT

The word *Amen* is an affirmation meaning "So be it!" This conclusion is added to the end of all prayers as a way of affirming the words that are spoken.

How to Pray

There are six main kinds of prayer in Catholicism: prayers of blessing, prayers of adoration, prayers of petition, prayers of intercession, prayers of thanksgiving, and prayers of praise.

A prayer of blessing is one that calls down God's consecration on an individual or individuals. Catholics bless themselves when making the Sign of the Cross or when they trace a small cross on their foreheads, lips, and hearts prior to the Gospel reading at Mass. Sometimes they offer each other a personal blessing in the same manner. Only priests, due to the nature of their office, can bless people and objects in a more forthright manner in the name of Christ and on behalf of the Church as well.

KEEP IT SIMPLE

To make the Sign of the Cross, use the first two fingers of your right hand to touch your forehead, heart, left shoulder, and right shoulder while saying "In the name of the Father (head) and of the Son (heart) and of the Holy (left shoulder) Spirit (right shoulder). Amen."

In a prayer of adoration, we humbly acknowledge God as the almighty creator and take the time to freely and devoutly marvel in His greatness. In prayers of petition, we humbly ask God for favors we desire. This may seem strange considering God knows every problem we have ever faced or will face. Nonetheless, He still wants us to call out to Him in our time of need to ask for the things we want, to cry out in our desperation, to raise whatever concerns we have, and even to question His will in our lives (especially when we don't agree with it).

Sometimes Catholics pray for their petitions through *litanies*, a series of call and response invocations used in liturgical celebrations as well as private prayer. There are six litanies approved for recitation in the Catholic Church:

- The Litany of the Holy Name of Jesus

- The Litany of the Sacred Heart of Jesus

- The Litany of the Most Precious Blood of Jesus

- The Litany of the Blessed Virgin Mary (also known as the Litany of Loreto)

- The Litany of St. Joseph

- The Litany of the Saints

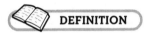 **DEFINITION**

A **litany** is a repetitive series of petitions used in formal services or private prayer.

In a prayer of intercession, we pray for the intentions of others. It doesn't matter who that person is. It may be a dear friend, a complete stranger, or even an enemy. When we call upon God to answer the prayers of others, we understand that we may be many parts but we are all one Body of Christ and that the power of prayer is strengthened through a spiritual family.

A prayer of thanksgiving is exactly what it sounds like. It is thanking God for the blessings He bestows on us. For the faithful, this type of prayer is as natural as breathing. They know God is behind everything that has been given to them and how important it is to acknowledge His generosity and goodness. In the Catholic Church, the greatest prayer of thanksgiving is the Eucharist because it offers thanks to God for all of creation, as well as for the gift of His Son who redeemed us all through His death and resurrection.

In a prayer of praise, we delight not only in the existence of God but also His goodness. It seems very similar to a prayer of adoration, but there is a difference. If a prayer of adoration is one of quiet awe, then a prayer of praise has a bit more exuberance to it. Think of it this way: a prayer of adoration is similar to walking through a fine china department where you are intensely mindful of the priceless items around you. A prayer of praise is more exuberant and joyful, where one is allowed to enthusiastically compliment God's work in our lives.

Catholic Prayer

Prayers come from a variety of places. The Bible provides some of the most beautiful prayers in all of Judeo–Christian history. Catholics also rely on the *common prayers* of the Church as well as the words we hold in the privacy of our heads and hearts. Jesus assures us that when we use the Holy Spirit to pray in His name, those prayers go directly to the heart of God where each is answered according to His will.

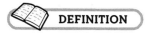

DEFINITION

> **Common prayers** are proscribed words that are adopted by a faith tradition and recited privately as well as in the structure of a religious celebration.

Prayer can literally happen anywhere and at any time of the day. However, Catholics often look to pray in those places where they believe God is present in a very special way. This includes Catholic churches where God dwells in the form of consecrated bread. When Catholics spend time in God's house, it enables them to reconnect on "His turf" and be renewed by His Spirit, which resides within.

From the early days of the Church, Christians made prayer part of their daily rituals. They prayed in the mornings to dedicate the day to God. They prayed before meals in thanksgiving and once again at the end of the day to "square accounts." That evening prayer was to ask forgiveness for any sins, to ask grace for themselves and others, and to pray for peace. Those early Christians knew that if they did not pray regularly, it would be a matter of time before they stopped praying altogether.

Catholics pray in three different ways. They pray vocally, they pray through meditation, and they pray in contemplation. Vocal prayers are those in which one "comes out with it," so to speak. In these types of prayers, we are polite but we dispense with the formality and say what is on our minds. It is in these words that we come to God with our needs, talk to Him about what is on our mind, and ask for guidance. While Catholics do not have to recite these prayers out loud in order for them to be heard, it is important that they connect the meaning of the words to the desire in their soul.

One of the best-known Catholic vocal prayers is a *novena*. This is a formalized prayer that is prayed over an extended period of time (the most common period is nine days, the origin of the word novena, which means "nine"). Novenas are usually connected to a specific intention or need, and though they have been connected to miraculous events, it is important to note that a novena is not a magic formula to make dreams come true. Rather, it is a way to channel our petitions into a cohesive prayer that can be recited over and over.

DEFINITION

> A **novena** is a vocal prayer (sometimes invoking a saint) that is prayed over an extended period of time and is usually connected to a specific intention.

Meditation is a type of prayer that compels us to think about a Scripture passage or image and absorb it. At first, the passage may not seem to have relevance for our lives, but when we take it in with an open heart, we can discern God's message and apply it to our lives. Contemplative prayer is one of silent, still, reflective love. It requires us to drop all pretenses in order to humble ourselves to listen for the voice of God calling out to us. Contemplative prayer is the one that seeks God within the heart of the person praying. There are no flowery speeches, no poetry, and no imagery, just the bare soul of someone who is willing to be still and know God on a deeply personal level.

The Purpose of Prayer

Catholics use prayer as a way to grow closer to God and as the first line of defense in the ongoing battle for the soul. However, it isn't always easy to remain prayerful when nothing is going right or when it feels as though God isn't listening. Rest assured, God got the memo; but it is important to remember that prayer is not a spiritual wishing well. We are not supposed to come to God with a laundry list of requests in hopes that He will grant some or all of them, but rather we come to God in prayer in order to enjoy a more intimate relationship with Him and to grow in devotion and faith.

God is not too picky about when we pray as long as we do so with a faithful heart. No one likes a fair-weather friend who only wants to hang out when it is convenient. God wants us to come to Him anywhere and everywhere, provided that we approach with an attitude of faith, hope, and charity and a readiness to resign ourselves to His will. One only has to look to the lives of some of the saints in order to find people who understand the restorative power of prayer.

St. Monica

St. Monica was born in AD 333 in Tagaste, North Africa. Though she was brought up a Christian, she was married off to a pagan man named Patricius and gave birth to two sons, Augustine and Navigius, as well as a daughter, Perpetua.

Monica's married life was far from a fairy tale. Patricius was an alcoholic who had an explosive temper, and she endured abuse from a critical mother-in-law as well as servants who had no respect for her position as the lady of the house. After much prayer for her husband's conversion to the faith, Patricius was baptized on his deathbed. (His mother converted to Christianity as well.) Two of Monica's children readily followed their mother into the Christian faith, but Augustine proved to be more of a challenge. Monica's wayward son wanted nothing to do with Christianity. One night, Augustine outlined his philosophies on Manichaeism, which rankled his mother and caused Monica to kick him out of the house. However, she later had a vision imploring her to reconcile with the young man.

Monica became the ultimate helicopter parent, following Augustine to Rome and later Milan praying for his change of heart along the way. She eventually befriended St. Ambrose, who ultimately became the catalyst for Augustine's conversion after 17 years of nonstop effort. St. Augustine would go on to become one of the most important theologians and writers in the history of the Catholic Church. Monica died in AD 387 in Ostia and was buried there.

Augustine paid tribute to his steadfast mother in his autobiography *The Confessions,* championing not only her strong faith, but also her perseverance in prayer. While she was not formally canonized a saint due to the fact that the process was not formalized until the twelfth century, she was proclaimed a saint by acclamation for her pious and holy life. She is the patron saint of mothers and alcoholics.

St. Teresa of Avila

Born on March 28, 1515, in Avila, Spain, Teresa grew up believing she was destined to screw up no matter how hard she tried. She was the daughter of an extremely pious man who worried she could not live up to his expectations. She loved beautiful clothes, romance stories, and flirting with boys, which convinced her that she was destined for an eternity in Hell. Her father agreed with this assessment and sent the out-of-control girl to a convent in order to straighten her out. Though she initially resisted convent life, she grew to love it. After all, it was a lot less strict than her father's household.

She struggled to decide between a religious vocation and a married one, choosing the former because she was convinced it was the best option for someone as prone to sin as she was. She was received in the Carmelite order and tried to enjoy her life of contemplative prayer, but didn't feel like she was getting anywhere.

It was especially difficult to live in an environment where not everyone had been called to the religious life, but some were "going through the motions" in order to help their parents save money back home. Teresa found that it was all too easy to slip back into her worldly ways and be flattered by those who were charmed by her countenance. She was more obsessed with flattery and ego than she was with improving her relationship with God.

After falling ill and being paralyzed, Teresa gave up on prayer altogether. It wasn't doing anything for her. Her heart wasn't in it, so why bother? A priest finally convinced her to give it another try, but she still found it difficult. However, she persevered and in time felt the Holy Spirit working within her. She gave up her friendships, eschewed public recognition, and in time was able to establish her own convent and reform her order to get it back to the basics—a contemplative place devoted to poverty and prayer.

More tears are shed over answered prayers than unanswered ones.

—St. Teresa of Avila

She also began to forgive herself for her all-too-human emotions. She realized that it was fruitless to beat oneself up over a mistake, and better to be proactive in changing it. Needless to say, all of this was easier said than done. She was denounced from the pulpit, threatened with legal action, and faced the Spanish Inquisition. (She was later cleared.)

No matter how she was scorned, she took all publicity as good. She shared her ideas about prayer and action widely and carried out her vocation faithfully before dying on October 4, 1582. She was canonized in 1622, and is a doctor of the Church. Her prayers are considered some of the most poetic writings of the Catholic faith.

Common Catholic Prayers

Are you ready to learn some of the most common prayers in the Catholic Church? In the next chapter, we'll look at some of the common Catholic prayers relating to Mary, the Mother of God. But for now, here are just a few important general prayers that will be helpful to know.

Our Father

Our Father, Who art in heaven, hallowed be Thy name; Thy kingdom come, Thy will be done on earth as it is in heaven. Give us this day our daily bread, and forgive us our trespasses, as we forgive those who trespass against us; and lead us not into temptation, but deliver us from evil. Amen.

Glory Be

Glory Be to the Father, and to the Son, and to the Holy Spirit. As it was in the beginning, is now, and ever shall be, world without end. Amen.

Blessing Before Meals

Bless us, O Lord, and these Thy gifts, which we are about to receive from Thy bounty through Christ our Lord. Amen.

Grace After Meals

We give You thanks, Almighty God, for these and all thy gifts, Who live and reign forever. Amen.

Guardian Angel Prayer

Angel of God, my guardian dear, to whom God's love commits me here, ever this day be at my side, to light and guard, to rule and guide. Amen.

Prayer to the Holy Spirit

Come, Holy Spirit, fill the hearts of your faithful and kindle in them the fire of your love.

Verse: Send forth your Spirit and they shall be created.

Response: And you shall renew the face of the earth.

O God, by the light of the Holy Spirit you have taught the hearts of your faithful. In the same Spirit help us to relish what is right and always rejoice in your consolation. We ask this through Christ our Lord. Amen.

Prayer to St. Michael

St. Michael the Archangel, defend us in battle. Be our safeguard against the wickedness and snares of the devil. May God rebuke him, we humbly pray, and do thou, O prince of the heavenly host, by the power of God cast into hell Satan and all the evil spirits who prowl through the world seeking the ruin of souls. Amen.

Prayer for the Deceased

Eternal rest grant unto him/her, O Lord, and let perpetual light shine upon him/her. May he/she rest in peace. Amen.

Prayer of St. Francis

Lord, make me an instrument of your peace. Where there is hatred, let me sow love; where there is injury, pardon; where there is doubt, faith; where there is despair, hope; where there is darkness, light; where there is sadness, joy. O Divine Master, grant that I may seek not so much to be consoled, as to console; to be understood, as to understand; to be loved, as to love. For it is in giving that we receive, in pardoning that we are pardoned, and in dying that we are born to eternal life.

The Divine Praises

Blessed be God.

Blessed be His Holy Name.

Blessed be Jesus Christ, true God and true man.

Blessed be the Name of Jesus.

Blessed be His Most Sacred Heart.

Blessed be His Most Precious Blood.

Blessed be Jesus in the Most Holy Sacrament of the Altar.

Blessed be the Holy Spirit, the Paraclete.

Blessed be the great Mother of God, Mary Most Holy.

Blessed be her Holy and Immaculate Conception.

Blessed be her Glorious Assumption.

Blessed be the name of Mary, Virgin and Mother.

Blessed be Saint Joseph, her most chaste spouse.

Blessed be God in His angels and in His saints.

The Least You Need to Know

- Prayer is the way Catholics converse with God and grow closer to Him.
- There are six types of prayers in the Catholic Church: prayers of blessing, adoration, petition, intercession, thanksgiving, and praise.
- The Lord's Prayer is the most perfect prayer and encompasses the gospel message.
- Catholics pray vocally, through meditation, and through contemplation.
- St. Monica and St. Teresa of Avila made prayer a central part of their lives.

CHAPTER 15

Mary and the Rosary

She was the teenage peasant girl whose affirmative response to God changed the course of human history. Born without the stain of Original Sin on her soul, she was the pristine vessel who would deliver the child who would in turn deliver the world. She was Mary of Nazareth.

Mary holds a special place in the hearts of Christians everywhere for her active participation in God's divine plan. However, in Catholicism, though the veneration of Mary does not go beyond the lines of the New Testament in which she appears, the devotion to her has developed through the centuries.

In this chapter, we will explore this extraordinary individual who said "yes" to God. We will discover the ways in which Catholics honor the Blessed Virgin and we will bust the myth of "Mary worship" once and for all. We will learn the prayers associated with the rosary and why Catholics believe that on occasion, the way to Jesus' heart is through His mother.

In This Chapter

- The handmaiden of the Lord
- Do Catholics really worship Mary?
- Common prayers associated with Mary
- How to say the prayers of the rosary

The Mother of God

She is called blessed among women, and yet we know very little about the adolescent Jewish girl who became the mother of Jesus. The Gospel of Luke tells us that Mary is a virgin living in the Galilean town of Nazareth and that she is engaged to a man named Joseph, who is a descendant of King David. The Bible says nothing about her early years or her family other than a cousin named Elizabeth, the aged wife of Zechariah and mother of John the Baptist.

However, it is generally accepted in the Church that Mary was the late-in-life, longed-for daughter of Anna and Joachim whose conception was extraordinary in and of itself. Unlike every other person born on Earth after Adam and Eve, Mary was given a unique grace by God and spared from the stain of Original Sin. This *Immaculate Conception* made her extra special right from the very start.

The scriptural origin for the Immaculate Conception comes from Luke 1:28, in which the angel Gabriel greets Mary as being full of grace. The term "full of grace" is the key to this fundamental belief, because while all human beings are given the gift of grace, it competes with our inherent concupiscence or inclination to sin. Mary is the only human being who is described in Scripture as being full of grace, completely gifted with God's grace. Being completely filled with grace and having Original Sin are incompatible. Catholics believe that Mary had to be born without Original Sin in order for Jesus to grow and develop in a spotless environment.

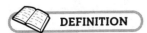 **DEFINITION**

> The **Immaculate Conception** refers to the conception of Mary, who was born without the stain of Original Sin on her soul.

Mary is about 14 years old when Gabriel comes to her and announces that she has found favor with God and will give birth to His son. When Mary questions the logic of this statement, the angel tells her:

> "The Holy Spirit will come upon you and the shadow of the Most High will overshadow you; therefore the child to be born will be holy; he will be called Son of God." (Luke 1:35)

Gabriel also tells her that her cousin Elizabeth, old and thought to be barren, is also pregnant, proving that nothing is impossible with God. It's a phenomenal encounter and a terrifying plan that is sure to result in great difficulties for the unwed teen, but in consenting to God's will, Mary exhibits a faith that surpasses even that of Abraham.

 **KEEP IT SIMPLE**

The issue of Mary's virginity has sparked considerable debate over the years. While Christians believe that Mary was pure at conception and remained so until after Jesus' birth in Bethlehem, there is a difference of opinion as to what happened after that.

Many denominations believe Mary and Joseph enjoyed a traditional marriage after the birth of Jesus and had many children together. However, Catholics believe that Mary remained a virgin, and those scriptural references to Jesus' siblings use a word that can also mean cousins or other family members.

Though she only has 14 lines of dialogue in the New Testament, Mary's words offer a hint of the kind of woman she was. She was first and foremost a woman of great faith. After learning of her impending condition, Mary makes plans to visit her cousin in order to confirm the angel's message that the older woman is in fact six months pregnant. Elizabeth, who has been told about Mary's pregnancy, is overjoyed that the mother of the Messiah would pay her a house call. She blesses Mary and the child within her, which prompts Mary to rejoice in her condition and offer God a song of praise known as the *Magnificat*:

> "My soul magnifies the Lord and my spirit rejoices in God, my Savior, for He has looked with favor on the lowliness of His servant. Surely from now on all generations will call me blessed; for the Mighty One has done great things for me and holy is His name. His mercy is for those who fear Him from generation to generation. He has shown strength with His arm; He has scattered the proud in the thoughts of their hearts. He has brought down the powerful from their thrones, and lifted up the lowly; He has filled the hungry with good things, and sent the rich away empty. He has helped His servant Israel, in remembrance of His mercy, according to the promise He made to His ancestors, and to Abraham and to his descendants forever." (Luke 1:46-55)

DEFINITION

The **Magnificat** is a song of praise found in the Gospel of Luke and is often called "Mary's Hymn."

Mary's faith is exhibited even further when she agrees to travel with Joseph to Bethlehem for the Roman census, despite the late stage of her pregnancy. Luke's Gospel tells us "While they were there, the time came for her to deliver her child. And she gave birth to her firstborn son and wrapped him in bands of cloth, and laid him in a manger, because there was no place for them in the inn." (Luke 2:7)

A Very Special Son

In Matthew's Gospel, we learn that a few days after Jesus' birth, Joseph learns that King Herod has issued a death warrant on any child under the age of 2 years. He's heard that the promised Messiah has been born and wants to end any threat to his throne. At the urging of an angel, the Holy Family puts all of their trust in God and flees into Egypt, remaining there until Herod's death.

Mary's words also tell us she was not merely a conduit to bring Jesus into the world, but she was also His mom—and a very typical mom at that. Though her presence in the Gospels is sporadic, we know that when Jesus was 12 years old, He traveled with His family to Jerusalem for the festival of Passover. When the festival was over and their caravan left for home, Mary and Joseph notice that Jesus wasn't with them. The couple races back to the city in search of the boy, but cannot find Him anywhere. After three days of looking, they go into the temple to pray and find their wayward Son sitting with the elders and having a deep theological conversation.

Relieved to have found Jesus, but furious at the worry and anguish He'd put them through, Mary quickly rounds on the preteen, "Child, why have you treated us like this? Look, your father and I have been searching for you in great anxiety."(Luke 2:48) Jesus offers a cheeky response in defense of His actions, saying that they should have known where to find Him, and while Luke does not elaborate on the confrontation, He does note that Jesus returned to Nazareth and was an obedient child after that, so perhaps there were a few consequences for His actions.

"Do Whatever He Tells You"

Several years later, Mary, Jesus, and His disciples are guests at a wedding in Cana when Mary learns that the host has run out of wine for the feast. Sensing the embarrassment that will follow, Mary tells Jesus about the dilemma and sets the stage for His first public miracle. Jesus doesn't want to do it and tells His mother that this is not the time for His public debut, but she insists (in a way only a mother can) and instructs the waiters to "Do whatever he tells you." (John 2:5)

In Matthew 12, Mary appears again; this time she is accompanied by other family members who are concerned that Jesus' controversial teachings and associations are becoming a problem. They arrive at one of His public appearances determined to talk some sense into Him, but when Jesus learns that His mother and kin are waiting for Him, He replies, "Who is my mother and who are my brothers?" (Matthew 12:48) It's an allegorical statement about how we are all family, but to those family members who heard it, it sounded like a public rebuke.

 CATHOLIC QUOTE

Never be afraid of loving the Blessed Virgin too much, You can never love her more than Jesus did.

—St. Maximilian Kolbe

Still, Mary took it all in stride. She knew her son had a mission to fulfill, and it was one in which she could not interfere. Despite the trials Jesus must have put her through as a very human son who was also divine, it's obvious how much Jesus loved her in return. As He hung on the cross at Golgotha, Jesus' last thoughts were of His mother as He charged His beloved disciple (John) with Mary's safety and security. Mary remained a source of strength and comfort to the apostles after Jesus' resurrection and ascension, and was even present at the feast of Pentecost when the Holy Spirit descended upon them.

It is unclear when or if Mary died. The Catholic Church believes that when she reached the end of her earthly life, Mary was assumed body and soul into Heaven where she rejoined her son and was crowned queen of all things. This was dogmatically defined in 1950, though the question of whether or not she died first was not. References to Christian belief in her assumption date back to the fourth century, but there is also a biblical reference alluding to it in the Book of Revelation when John describes "a woman clothed with the sun, the moon under her feet and on her head a crown of twelve stars" (Revelation 12:1) who gave birth to a son that would rule next to the throne of God.

Another "proof" of Mary's assumption is the fact that no place claims to have her body or tomb—you would think that the tomb of Mary would be a site of extraordinary veneration and pilgrimage, but no place claims to have her body. There are two competing traditions as to where Mary lived at the time of her assumption into heaven—Jerusalem and Ephesus—and both have places commemorating that event, but without a tomb.

The Myth of Mary Worship

Catholics feel a strong connection to Mary because, in a sense, she is a mother to us all. Though she is not the source of Christ's divinity, and is not worshiped as a goddess, she did give birth to Christianity and is someone we can turn to for comfort and support just as Jesus did when He was a child. The veneration of Mary is an important practice in Catholicism, but Catholics do not worship Mary as they do God. Catholics turn their intentions over to Mary and ask that she bring those concerns to God. They pray through Mary, not to Mary.

 CATHOLIC QUOTE

> In dangers, in doubts, in difficulties, think of Mary, call upon Mary .... With her for guide, you shall never go astray ....
>
> —St. Bernard of Clairvaux

Over the years there have been numerous claims by people who have actually seen and spoken with Mary. These supernatural appearances by the Blessed Mother are called Marian apparitions and they have made headlines, and been written about, profiled on television, and dramatized on film. Out of the numerous claims, the Holy See has studied 295 causes. After intense scrutiny, they have deemed 12 "worthy of belief." This does not mean that the others are somehow false, but most agree that the apparitions are largely a question of faith. Though impossible to prove or disprove, there is no question that the phenomena has had a tremendous impact on the Church. They have been responsible not only for the construction of some of the largest Marian churches in the world, and the spread of Marian devotion, but also for millions of conversions to the Catholic faith. Following are some samples of the most well-known stories.

Our Lady of Guadalupe

In 1531, Mary appeared to St. Juan Diego, an indigenous farmer and widower, on the Hill of Tepeyac in Mexico and asked that he build a church there in her honor. He took her request to the bishop, who was skeptical of the story and demanded a sign proving the claim. When Juan Diego tells the Blessed Mother what has transpired, she instructs him to go back to where they first met and gather the roses that he finds miraculously blooming there. He does as she asks and carries the flowers back to her in the fold of his tilma, or poncho. Mary arranges the flowers and tells him to return to the bishop. When he does, he opens his tilma and the flowers fall to the floor. To everyone's astonishment, a full-color portrait of Mary appears on Juan Diego's garment as well, just as he has described her.

Today, the tilma is on display at the Basilica of Our Lady of Guadalupe in Mexico City. It has never decomposed or faded. The imprinted pictograph was full of symbolism that was understood by everyone who saw it, and it is said that it is responsible for the conversion of eight million natives in an incredible seven years.

Our Lady of Lourdes

In 1858, Mary appeared to St. Bernadette Soubirous, a 14-year-old uneducated and sickly shepherdess in Pyrenees, France. She visited the girl 18 times over a six-month period, and during one visit Mary instructed the girl to dig a hole, which exposed a buried spring. She told Bernadette to bathe in and drink from the water, which had healing properties, and to build a chapel there in her honor. When Bernadette told the local pastor about the lady's request, he demanded that she find out who the lady was and request a sign from her. During their last visit, Mary revealed, in Latin, that she was the Immaculate Conception (a dogma that had only been defined four years earlier). Bernadette took the message back to the pastor, who knew there was no way an illiterate shepherd girl could know such a thing and that the message must have come from Mary herself.

Lourdes is a major Catholic pilgrimage site, and the water of Lourdes has been attributed to thousands of cures, of both a spiritual and physical nature. Today there is a clinic to support the millions of pilgrims who find their way to the site each year. Bernadette died in 1879 and was canonized a saint in 1933.

Our Lady of Fatima

In 1917, Mary appeared six times to Lucia dos Santos and her cousins, Jacinta and Francisco Marto, at the Cova de Iria near Fatima, Portugal. It was the height of World War I, and during the first visitation, the lady asked the children to say the rosary every day and to meet her on the thirteenth day of each month until October, when she would tell them who she was and what she wanted. The children agreed and returned each month, with increasing numbers of people in attendance. However, only the children could see or hear the lady to whom they were speaking.

 CATHOLIC QUOTE

There is no problem, I tell you, no matter how difficult it is, that we cannot resolve by the prayer of the Holy Rosary.

—Sister Lucia dos Santos

On October 13, Mary revealed herself and promised to give a sign that everyone would see and believe. On that day, the thousands in attendance reported that they saw something unique in the sky as if the sun wobbled and fell to earth before returning to its regular position. During her visits with the children Mary revealed a number of alarming prophecies, which proved to be accurate. Although the event was deemed worthy of belief in 1930, five popes expressed support of the Fatima messages, and over the years Mary's revelations, which were chronicled by Lucia, have been shared with the world. The two youngest children died shortly after their visits with Mary and have since been beatified by the Church. Lucia became a Carmelite nun and lived mostly in seclusion until her death in 2005.

Praying with Mary

There are a number of prayers and devotions dedicated to the Blessed Mother, but a few of the most common are the Hail Mary, the Memorare, and the Hail, Holy Queen. The Hail Mary (Ave Maria in Latin) comes from the greetings Mary received in Luke's Gospel and was added to by Pope Pius V, while the Memorare began as a portion of a much longer thirteenth-century prayer known as the "Ad sanctitatis tuae pedes, dulcissima Virgo Maria." The Hail, Holy Queen (Salve Regina in Latin) was written by Adhemar of Monteuil, the Bishop of Puy, France, and was originally used as a war chant in the Crusades. The triple invocation at the end was not originally included but was later added by St. Bernard of Clairvaux.

Hail Mary

Hail Mary, full of grace! The Lord is with thee; blessed art thou among women, and blessed is the fruit of your womb, Jesus. Holy Mary, Mother of God, pray for us sinners now and at the hour of our death. Amen.

The Memorare

Remember, O most gracious Virgin Mary, that never was it known that anyone who fled to your protection, implored your help, or sought your intercession was left unaided.

Inspired by this confidence, I fly unto thee, O Virgin of virgins, my mother; to thee do I come, before thee I stand, sinful and sorrowful. O Mother of the Word Incarnate, despise not my petitions, but in thy mercy hear and answer me. Amen.

Hail, Holy Queen

Hail, Holy Queen, Mother of mercy, our life, our sweetness, and our hope! To you do we cry, poor banished children of Eve! To you do we send up our sighs, mourning and weeping in this valley of tears!

Turn then, most gracious advocate, thine eyes of mercy towards us; and after this our exile, show unto us the blessed fruit of thy womb, Jesus!

O clement, O loving, O sweet Virgin Mary!

The Rosary

If you were to ask people what objects they associate with the Catholic Church, the *rosary* would probably be near the top of the list. The rosary is the most common Marian devotion, though the origin of the beads themselves is sketchy at best. The use of repeated prayer recitation and meditation comes from the earliest years of the Church and has ties to the pre-Christian era. However, we do know that beads were used in the Middle Ages to count prayers and that the basic structure of the rosary we know today developed between the twelfth and fifteenth centuries. St. Dominic, who died in 1221, is credited with spreading the practice of praying the rosary throughout the Church.

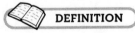 **DEFINITION**

The **rosary** comes from the Latin word *rosarium,* meaning "garland of roses." It is used to describe both the sequence of prayers related to it and the beaded chain used to mark them.

The rosary is a Scripture-based set of prayers that commemorate four sets of five specific events, or mysteries in the life of Jesus and His mother. A traditional set of rosary beads contains five decades (sets of ten) of beads in a circular fashion on which to say the Hail Mary and intermediate beads on which to say the Our Father. The five decades are connected to a medallion, which has a shorter strand of five beads and a small crucifix hanging at its base.

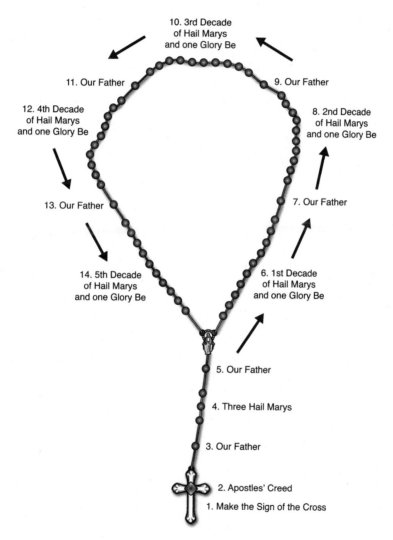

10. 3rd Decade of Hail Marys and one Glory Be

11. Our Father

9. Our Father

12. 4th Decade of Hail Marys and one Glory Be

8. 2nd Decade of Hail Marys and one Glory Be

13. Our Father

7. Our Father

14. 5th Decade of Hail Marys and one Glory Be

6. 1st Decade of Hail Marys and one Glory Be

5. Our Father

4. Three Hail Marys

3. Our Father

2. Apostles' Creed

1. Make the Sign of the Cross

How to Pray the Rosary

1. Make the Sign of the Cross with the crucifix.

2. Recite the Apostles' Creed.

3. Say an Our Father while holding the first bead of the short strand.

4. On the next three beads, recite a Hail Mary on each bead for the virtues of faith, hope, and love followed by a Glory Be.

5. Introduce the first mystery and reflect on its significance. Then say an Our Father. (This should be the final bead of the shorter strand.)

6. For the decades, say a Hail Mary for each of the beads. When all 10 are completed, follow it with a Glory Be, typically while touching the chain or rope between the last Hail Mary bead and the next Our Father bead.

7. Introduce the next mystery and repeat steps 5 and 6 until you work your way around the circle of beads.

8. After all five decades have been completed, say a Hail, Holy Queen prayer followed by:

    V: Pray for us, O holy Mother of God.

    R: That we may be made worthy of the promises of Christ.

    Let us pray: O God, whose Only Begotten Son,

    by His life, death, and resurrection,

    has purchased for us the rewards of eternal life,

    grant, we beseech thee,

    that while meditating on these mysteries

    of the most holy Rosary of the Blessed Virgin Mary,

    we may imitate what they contain

    and obtain what they promise,

    through the same Christ our Lord. Amen.

9. A Memorare may also be added, if desired.

 FAST FACT

After reciting the Glory Be at the end of each decade, some people choose to add the prayer the Virgin Mary gave the children to whom she appeared at Fatima, Portugal, in 1917: "O my Jesus, forgive us our sins, save us from the fires of hell, lead all souls to Heaven, especially those who have most need of your mercy."

The Joyful Mysteries

The Joyful Mysteries are prayed on Mondays and Saturdays as well as on Sundays from Advent to Lent. They cover events found in the first two chapters of the Gospel of Luke.

1. The Annunciation: The angel Gabriel appears to Mary and announces that she will be the Mother of Christ. (Luke 1:26-38)

2. The Visitation: Mary visits her cousin Elizabeth, who is also miraculously expecting despite her age. (Luke 1:39-56)

3. The Nativity: Jesus Christ is born in Bethlehem. (Luke 2:1-20)

4. The Presentation in the Temple: The baby Jesus is presented in the temple where Simeon and Anna rejoice at the sight of the Messiah. (Luke 2:22-38)

5. The Finding in the Temple: Jesus is located in the temple after being lost for three days. (Luke 2:41-52)

The Luminous Mysteries

The Luminous Mysteries were added to the rosary in 2002 by then pope St. John Paul II. They are traditionally prayed on Thursdays (except during Lent) and concern the public ministry of Jesus.

1. The Baptism of Jesus: Jesus meets John in the Jordan River and is baptized by him. (Matthew 3:13-17)

2. The Miracle at the Wedding of Cana: When the host of the reception runs out of drink for his guests, Jesus takes ordinary water and turns it into wine. (John 2:1-11)

3. The Proclamation of the Kingdom: Jesus begins His Galilean ministry by telling His followers that the Scriptures have been fulfilled and the kingdom of God has arrived. (Mark 1:15)

4. The Transfiguration: Jesus is transfigured into a vision in white and joined by Moses and Elijah. The apostles with Him hear the voice of God proclaim Jesus His Son. (Matthew 17:1-13)

5. The Institution of the Eucharist: The night before His death, He institutes the sacrament at the core of the Catholic faith. (Matthew 26:26-30)

The Sorrowful Mysteries

The Sorrowful Mysteries are said on Tuesdays and Fridays through the year and every day from Ash Wednesday until Easter. They center on the Passion and Death of Christ.

1. The Agony in the Garden: After His Last Supper with His friends, Jesus prays in the Garden of Gethsemane where He asks God to let the cup of death pass over Him. (Mark 14:35)

2. The Scourging at the Pillar: Pontius Pilate orders the flogging of Jesus. (Mark 15:15)

3. Jesus Is Crowned with Thorns: As a way of mocking the King of the Jews, Roman soldiers fashion a crown of thorns and place it on Christ's head. (Mark 15:17)

4. Jesus Carries His Cross: After being sentenced to death, Jesus is forced to carry His cross to the place of execution. (John 19:17)

5. The Crucifixion: Jesus dies on His cross for the sins of humanity. (Luke 23:33-46)

The Glorious Mysteries

The Glorious Mysteries are prayed on Wednesdays (except during Lent) and on Sundays from Easter to Advent. They focus on the events after the Crucifixion and two central Catholic beliefs regarding the Blessed Virgin Mary.

1. The Resurrection: Jesus is resurrected from the grave three days after His crucifixion. (John 20:1-18)

2. The Ascension: Jesus ascends to the father 40 days after His resurrection. (Luke 24:50)

3. The Descent of the Holy Spirit: The apostles receive the Holy Spirit on the feast of Passover. (Acts 2:4)

4. The Assumption of the Blessed Virgin Mary: Jesus assumes Mary's body and soul into Heaven at the end of her earthly life.

5. The Crowning of the Blessed Virgin Mary: Jesus crowns Mary as the Queen of Heaven and Earth.

The Least You Need to Know

- Mary was born without Original Sin and was chosen to be the mother of Jesus.
- Catholics believe Mary was taken body and soul into Heaven where she was crowned the Queen of Heaven and Earth.
- Catholics feel a strong connection to Mary; however, they do not worship her.
- The rosary is the most common Marian devotion, and many Catholics pray it daily.
- Catholics believe that Mary has appeared to many people all over the world.

Spiritual Growth

Even with regular Mass attendance, participation in the sacraments, and a daily dose of prayer, a Catholic needs to fuel their spiritual fire from time to time. Experts say that conviction without journey can quickly stagnate and it's important to spend some one-on-one time with Christ in order to better understand what they already have through faith.

Catholics participate in a number of activities designed to renew the heart and reinvigorate the soul. They retreat from their busy lives to commune with the Holy Spirit, travel the world, read inspirational material, and attend conferences where they strengthen their bond with God and commit more deeply to their faith.

In this chapter, we will examine the benefits of taking part in these opportunities and how even if faith blooms where it is planted, it needs fertilizer, sunshine, and even the occasional storm to help it grow.

In This Chapter

- What is spiritual direction?
- Getting away from it all on retreat
- Mission trips: helping humanity
- Catholic tourism sites around the world

Spiritual Direction

Everyone has those moments when they need guidance to help them discern God's plan for their life. Perhaps they are being called to the religious life, or perhaps they are considering marriage, additional education, or a career change and want to make the best decision for themselves as well as their family members. Whatever the situation, as Christians we often need spiritual direction in order to gain insight, distinguish God's will from our personal preference, and find the right path to follow.

In addition to reading Scripture, Church documents, and the writings of the saints, Catholics also turn to spiritual directors for guidance in helping to discern how the Holy Spirit may be working in their lives. A spiritual director is a fancy term for someone who is willing to listen and mentor us on the path of self-discovery. Our earliest spiritual directors are our parents, who create a miniature church within our homes, and also our godparents, clergy members, teachers, and confirmation sponsors. As adults we may continue to turn to our priests, deacons, and consecrated religious for advice, as well as pastoral associates, counselors, and other professionals who can help guide our footsteps and encourage a life of vocal, meditative, and contemplative prayer.

KEEP IT SIMPLE

A spiritual director serves as a mentor and a cheerleader on one's life path. They are usually individuals whose faith we admire or who have particular expertise in the situation we are facing who can listen and pray with us and for us as we listen for God's voice.

Although it may feel therapeutic, spiritual direction is not designed to be a therapy session. It is assistance given by one member of the faithful to another in order to help that person learn to listen for God's guidance and to deepen their relationship with Christ. Through this relationship, one learns to pray as effectively as possible, to hear God's call, and to act with confidence to live out the consequences of decisions they make. While there may be someone listening and praying for and with the individual, above all, the true spiritual director is the Holy Spirit who wants us all to enjoy the deepest and most intimate relationship possible with Him.

Spiritual Reading

As you might expect, the book most Christians rely on for spiritual guidance is Sacred Scripture. Catholics not only read the texts as prescribed by the liturgical year, but many also take the time to read each book chapter by chapter, either on their own or as part of a Bible study group. There are a number of resources available to help one work out an effective reading strategy, as well as study guides to help them understand the more difficult passages of text.

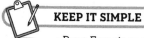

KEEP IT SIMPLE

Pope Francis suggests keeping a pocket Bible on hand to read during commutes, or anywhere people have a minute or two of free time. He says we all have the time to listen to the radio or television in sound bites, but we should take the time to listen to the Word of God as well.

Official Works and Papal Documents

The *Catechism of the Catholic Church* is another great resource for spiritual reading and a guide for living. It is written as a universal overview of Catholic beliefs for people of all ages and backgrounds. Many countries have adapted this universal Catechism for their own situation. The United States Catholic Catechism for Adults was published in 2006 as a U.S. adaptation of the universal Catechism. In 2011, the Church authorized the *YouCat*, which is a young person's guide to the Catechism containing much of the same material but in an easy-to-understand format.

Papal Encyclicals, council documents, and books written by the popes themselves are also great resources. A few titles to consider include:

- *Jesus of Nazareth* by Pope Benedict XVI (2007–2012): A rich and sophisticated three-volume series on the life of Christ written by the former Cardinal Joseph Ratzinger.

- *God Is Love* (*Deus Caritas Est*) by Pope Benedict XVI (2005): a Papal Encyclical or letter to all people of the world on the characteristics of God's love and how Christians are called to put love into action.

- *Crossing the Threshold of Hope* by St. Pope John Paul II (1995): An international bestseller that takes some of the most profound theological concepts and presents them in an easy-to-read text.

- *The Pastoral Constitution on the Church in the Modern World: Gaudium et Spes* (1965): This final major document of the Second Vatican Council sets out a framework for how the Church is called to interact with the modern world.

- *The Joy of the Gospel: Evangelii Gaudium* by Pope Francis (2013): A document called an Apostolic Exhortation written by the current pope that discusses ways to proclaim the gospel in today's world.

Saint Stories

Biographies of the saints as well as writings by the saints are also of particular interest to Catholics who rely on these ordinary mortals to act as role models in their lives. Many of these books are easy to understand and provide spiritual comfort, while others are more theological in nature. Some texts to consider include:

- *Our Lady of Fatima* by William Thomas Walsh (1954): Recreates the events that happened to three Portuguese shepherd children in 1917.

- *Story of a Soul: The Autobiography of St. Thérèse of Lisieux:* One of the most accessible, yet spiritually profound, writings of a canonized saint, advocating the "little way" of serving God.

- *St. Francis of Assisi* by Omer Englebert: One of the best-known and most beloved saints of all time is brought to life in this classic reissued for a modern audience.

- *The Curé d'Ars* by Francis Trochu (TAN 1992): Recommended by St. Pope John Paul II, this biography of St. Jean-Marie-Baptiste Vianney is a grace-filled story of the total love of God.

- *Confessions* by St. Augustine: The autobiography of this fifth-century bishop is remarkable for how well it relates to people's lives today.

Catholic Newspapers, Magazines, Journals, and Media

Catholics also turn to faith-based periodicals and news agencies to receive a "Church spin" on the stories of the day as well as inspiring features and information that may be appropriate to their spiritual growth. Here are a few excellent sources:

- *National Catholic Register:* America's most complete Catholic news source. Affiliated with ETWN, the global Catholic television network. www.ncregister.com

- *Envoy Magazine:* An award-winning online and print journal of Catholic thought that seeks to equip the modern-day faithful to respond to Christ's call. www.envoymagazine.com

- Our Sunday Visitor: Publisher of several Catholic publications including *Our Sunday Visitor Newsweekly, The Catholic Answer, The Priest, Take Out,* and the U.S. edition of the Vatican newspaper, *L'Osservatore Romano.* www.osv.com

- *Magnificat:* A monthly pocket-sized publication that contains all the prayers and readings for Sunday and daily Masses as well as Morning Prayer and Evening Prayer for each day and lives of the saints. www.magnificat.com

Faith Formation

No matter if you are a "cradle Catholic" or if you've recently converted to the faith, the Church believes everyone should constantly strive to grow in their understanding of the gospel throughout their lives. Adult faith formation ministries are designed to do just that. Though they vary from parish to parish, they strive to meet the specific needs of adults in the local community they serve. They offer a comprehensive exploration of the Catholic faith and its practices in an accessible way.

According to the United States Conference of Catholic Bishops (USCCB), there are three major objectives associated with adult faith formation ministries:

1. Invite and enable ongoing conversion to Jesus in holiness of life.

2. Promote and support active membership in the Christian community.

3. Call and prepare adults to act as disciples in mission to the world.

The first objective helps Catholics remain focused on their ever-evolving relationship with God, the promises that were made at their baptism and affirmed in the Sacrament of Confirmation. It encourages them to seek reconciliation while deepening their faith and following God's plan in their life.

The second objective urges Catholics to become involved in the faith community. This doesn't mean only at the parish level, but in service organizations that mean something to them and anywhere they can be a witness of Christ to their neighbor.

The third objective calls Catholics to serve God in the world at large. This may mean taking a mission trip or working to effect social change. This goal commands Catholics to share the gospel with others, to renew their own and each other's spirits, and to transform the public and secular order.

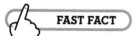 **FAST FACT**

Some Catholics enhance faith formation classes with an "apologetics class" designed to help them skillfully and confidently defend their beliefs. Through these courses, Catholics learn to articulately present the Church's worldview to others, without apology.

Retreats

Years ago there was a television commercial in which an overwhelmed woman bemoaned the cares of her daily life. Like many of us, she was a parent and a professional trying to strike a balance between home and the workplace. At the apex of the commercial, she utters the tagline that became a popular catchphrase for stressed-out people everywhere: "Take me away!"

Sometimes we need to get away from it all, but those quiet moments of rest and relaxation are all too elusive in an era when everyone is on the run 24 hours a day, 7 days a week. That's what makes a spiritual *retreat* an important component of Catholic spiritual growth. A retreat enables people to take a "time out" from their life and to work on their relationship with God. It is an event that refreshes, revitalizes, and allows for that one-on-one time with Christ minus life's daily distractions that all too often get in the way.

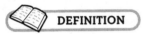

DEFINITION

A **retreat** is a withdrawal from daily life in order to renew and rejuvenate. From a religious perspective, it is an opportunity to help people improve their relationship with God.

Retreats can take a variety of forms and can be enjoyed by individuals as well as groups. They can be led by a spiritual director or undirected. They can be silent or more interactive. They can be single-day events or occur over an extended period of time. Some can last as long as a month, but these are usually sponsored by a religious congregation and designed to help someone discern how God is calling them to follow Him. Most Catholics, however, associate a retreat with an organized program of related activities scheduled over a specific period of time. All of the activities are geared toward guiding retreatants along the theme of the event and helping them deepen their relationship with God.

FAST FACT

A retreat is not the same thing as a conference or seminar, where there may be a lot of presentations to choose from or a wide variety of things to do (though these are great to attend as well). Rather, the primary objective of a retreat is interior spiritual growth through a prolonged period of introspection.

Mass is the perfect example of a "quick" retreat. When Catholics attend Mass, they leave the world outside in order to spend a contemplative hour listening to the Word of God and participating in the Sacrament of the Eucharist. Through the words of Sacred Scripture and being fortified by His body and blood, we are renewed and reinvigorated to serve the Lord for another day, weekend, or week. Catholics augment the Mass with other contemplative activities such as praying before the Blessed Sacrament in an adoration chapel, reading the Bible, or taking in the wonders of God's creation by getting out and enjoying nature.

Sometimes, though, Catholics need to change things up. They need to connect with God in a new location or hear His words in a new way that pertains specifically to them. Perhaps they want to strengthen their marriage or celebrate their gender roles with activities specifically geared toward those needs. Or perhaps they are preparing for a sacrament and need time to reflect on the momentous occasion ahead.

There are several basic elements of the Catholic retreat:

- A specific time frame: A day, a weekend, or one week tend to be the typical retreat lengths.

- Meals: Communal meals give a nod to the meals Jesus shared with his disciples. Sometimes these meals are taken in silence to encourage a continuing atmosphere of prayer.

- Plenty of time for reflection: Though there are often organized presentations, a retreat also offers ample time for personal prayer, group meditation, and Mass.

- A peaceful setting: Though they do not have to occur in nature, a retreat setting should invoke peaceful relaxation and serenity with a degree of isolation from the outside world.

- Personal space: Overnight retreats include lodgings, but even during day retreats there should be places where people can get away from the group activities as the need arises.

- Spiritual direction: The purpose of a retreat is to offer one a sense of renewal and spiritual direction, and there should be a trained professional onsite to listen and offer guidance.

 KEEP IT SIMPLE

Even Jesus understood the importance of retreats. Luke's Gospel tells us that shortly after His baptism, Jesus wandered in the wilderness for 40 days in order to contemplate His life and the ministry he was about to begin. After fasting for this period and enduring a rigorous temptation by the devil, "Jesus, filled with the Holy Spirit, returned to Galilee, and a report about him spread through all of the surrounding country. He began to teach in their synagogues and was praised by everyone." (Luke 4:14-15)

Mission Trips

Catholic social teaching commands us to attend to the common good with a preference to those in most need around us. This can happen in a number of ways, and while each act of charitable giving or service work has a way of enhancing one's spiritual development, a mission trip is one way Catholics go beyond their comfort zone in order to make a difference in someone's life.

A mission trip has a positive impact not only on the people who are served, but also the ones doing the serving. Missionaries often find that their lives are transformed by their mission work and that they receive much more than they actually give. Through their work, they see the face of Christ in those they assist and come to understand what Jesus means when He says that every time someone reaches out to those in need, they are serving Him as well:

> "For I was hungry and you gave me food, I was thirsty and you gave me something to drink, I was a stranger and you welcomed me, I was naked and you gave me clothing, I was sick and you took care of me, I was in prison and you visited me ...." (Matthew 25:35-36)

A mission trip is a rewarding experience that requires one to take a leap of faith, to go outside of one's regular environment, and to trust in God as they never have before. It's challenging to minister to the poorest of the poor and to experience suffering in such a radical way. However, the values of faith, hope, and love take over and they enthusiastically pitch in wherever they're needed.

Mission trips can take people to a variety of locations. Many parishes have a "sister church" relationship with a parish in another country, especially in Latin America. Parishioners will form teams to regularly travel to the same church in Haiti, Honduras, or elsewhere to provide medical care, assistance in building water purification systems, or job training. But you don't have to travel far away to go on a mission trip. Many parishes also sponsor trips to rural parts of the United States to help build homes or assist in recovery after a natural disaster. And don't forget your own town: home mission trips to the inner-city or a local neighborhood in need can make a great impact.

Ready to hit the road and help your fellow man? Here are a few tips to help ensure a successful trip:

- Remember that God is in charge of the mission.

- Don't forget that God has been in the community longer than you have.

- Keep in mind that God has a plan for the community as well as the people you will encounter.

- Know that God will be with you always.

- Meet every soul with an open heart.

- Be flexible, be focused, and be present!

- Build relationships on your journey.

- Practice humility as you serve.

- Try new things and do your best to fit in to the culture around you.

Places to Go, Things to Do, Relics to See

Making a pilgrimage is another great way to deepen one's personal faith, foster lifelong faith formation, and have a once-in-a-lifetime experience you will never forget! A pilgrimage is a faith journey that takes one to locations associated with Christianity and with Catholic tradition. These pilgrimage sites can be local, regional, national, or global and can include churches, graves, shrines, or cultural touchstones connected to Church history.

The Vatican

The Vatican is the epicenter of Catholicism and is possibly the closest thing to Heaven on Earth for Catholics. Tourists and pilgrims can visit St. Peter's Basilica for free and experience the majesty of Michelangelo's dome, the Pieta, and the tomb of St. Peter, the apostle and first pope.

The Vatican offers three different guided tours, including the gardens and the Necropolis archeological site, but the most popular tour is the art and faith tour of the Vatican Museums, which hold some of the most priceless art in Christendom. The tour takes visitors along hallways laden with the most renowned artwork of the Church, and includes the famous Sistine Chapel, whose ceiling was painted by Michelangelo in the early 1500s. The Chapel is also the place where the College of Cardinals convene to elect a new pope.

The Holy Land

It is the land of Jesus' birth and earthly journey, and the most sacred place on the planet. The Holy Land is an awesome experience for Christians who want to see the places connected with the Gospels and walk the same terrain Christ himself traveled during his public ministry. There is a lot to see and do in this region, but if you book a package or put together a good itinerary for a self-guided tour, you'll have no trouble seeing many of the most holy sites in the world. Some of the top pilgrimage spots include:

1. The Basilica of the Annunciation in Nazareth: Where the angel Gabriel told Mary that she would be the mother of Jesus.

2. Mary's Well in Nazareth: Located across the street from the Church of St. Gabriel, the water is said to have healing properties.

3. The Church of the Nativity in Bethlehem: The site of Jesus' birth.

4. The Church of John the Baptist in Ein Kerem: Built over the place where John the Baptist was born.

5. The River Jordan: The site of Jesus' baptism by his cousin John the Baptist.

6. The Sea of Galilee: The place where Jesus calmed the waters and called Peter, Andrew, James, and John to follow him.

7. The Mount of the Beatitudes: Where Jesus gave his famous Sermon on the Mount.

8. The Garden of Gethsemane: The site of Jesus' arrest.

9. The Church of the Holy Sepulcher: The site of the crucifixion, burial, and resurrection of Jesus.

10. The Upper Room or Cenacle: The site of the Last Supper, many of the resurrection appearances, and the first Pentecost.

 CATHOLIC QUOTE

Antiquity is never close to the parking lot.

—Erma Bombeck

Our Lady of Aparecida, Sao Paulo, Brazil

In preparation for a 1717 visit by the Count of Assumar to the state of Minas Gerais, a group of fisherman cast their nets in hopes of catching a feast, but after hours of attempts, the fish weren't biting and the only thing they had to show for their efforts was an odd-looking statue less than three feet tall. It was muddy and had clearly been submerged for a number of years, but when they cleaned it up they realized it was the figure of the Blessed Virgin Mary of the Immaculate Conception. All of the men were pious and took care to wrap the statue carefully before calling it a day. Someone suggested that they cast their nets out one more time in honor of the Virgin who had unexpectedly appeared (aparecida) and suddenly, after a day of nothing, their nets were full. It was a miracle.

After that day, Felipe Pedroso took the statue home and began to venerate it with his family and neighbors. In 1732, he moved to Proto Itagussu, where his son built the statue's first shrine. It wasn't long before word spread and people came from far and wide to see the statue, which was made around 1650. A church was built to house the statue and was opened to the public in 1745.

Today, an embroidered cloth allowing only Our Lady's hands and face to be seen covers the rich brown statue. In 1904, she was crowned with an imperial crown encrusted with precious jewels. In 1930, Pope Pius XII proclaimed her the Patroness of Brazil and today, more than five million pilgrims visit the statue annually. The current church, consecrated by Pope St. John Paul II in 1980, has a seating capacity of 45,000 people.

Santiago de Compostela Cathedral, Galicia, Spain

The Way of St. James is the name of the Christian pilgrimage leading to the remains of St. James the Great located at the cathedral of Santiago de Compostela. Tradition says the apostle's remains were taken to Northwestern Spain by boat from Jerusalem after he was beheaded in AD 44, and the site became an important pilgrimage destination during the Middle Ages.

Today, thousands of people begin their journey to Santiago de Compostela from a variety of points in Europe and travel to the site via bicycle, horseback, donkey, or on foot. They attend the pilgrims' Mass that is held each day at noon in honor of all the pilgrims who have journeyed to the shrine of the saint. Their groups are announced during the Mass as well.

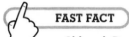

FAST FACT

Although Pope Leo XIII accepted that the remains of St. James the Great are interred at the shrine of Santiago de Compostela, the Vatican has never formally declared their authenticity and prefers to promote the overall benefits of making a pilgrimage to the site.

Basilica of the National Shrine of the Immaculate Conception, Washington, D.C.

Dedicated to the Blessed Virgin Mary, the Basilica of the National Shrine of the Immaculate Conception is the premier Marian shrine in the United States and one of the largest Catholic churches in the world. There are over 70 chapels and oratories, which highlight the diversity of the Catholic culture in the country, and the shrine is considered "America's Church."

The National Shrine is home to the world's largest collection of contemporary ecclesiastical art, contains statues of all of the canonized saints that came from or made their home in the United States, and is a church unlike any other with Romanesque–Byzantine architecture made entirely of stone, brick, tile, and mortar—without steel structural beams, framework, or columns. Masses from the National Shrine are often televised live and streamed on the internet for major celebrations throughout the year.

Mission San Xavier del Bac (Arizona)

Mission San Xavier del Bac is the oldest European structure in Arizona. Although the mission was founded in 1692 by Father Eusebio Kino, construction on the actual church was not begun until 1783 and completed in 1797. The building is full of original statuary and paintings that enable visitors to truly experience unique eighteenth-century Baroque architecture in the American southwest.

When the church was constructed, Southern Arizona was considered part of New Spain. It was financed by money loaned to Fr. Juan Bautista Velderrain from a Sonoran rancher. When Mexico won its independence in 1821, the mission became part of Mexico and with the Gadsden Purchase of 1854, the mission joined the United States. The Mission School has been educating students since 1872, the majority from the Tohono O'odham Native American Nation. The mission is still an active parish church, but also attracts more than 200,000 visitors from all over the world who tour the church and its museum and see what is considered the finest example of Spanish Colonial architecture in the United States.

Cathedral Basilica of Our Lady of Chartres, France

Built between 1194 and 1250, the basilica dedicated to Our Lady in Chartres has had a few traditions associated with it that make it a popular pilgrim destination for Christians from around the world. During the Merovingian and early Carolingian eras, pilgrims traveled to Chartres to visit what was believed to be the final resting place of early Christian martyrs. Around 876, the cathedral secured the Sancta Camisa, a tunic supposedly worn by the Blessed Virgin Mary at the time of Jesus' birth.

Though the authenticity of the holy maternity garb is almost impossible to verify, it is believed that the relic was a gift to the cathedral from Charles the Bald. By the twelfth century, pilgrims flocked to the cathedral for four great fairs, all coinciding with the feasts of the Blessed Virgin, in order to see the garment she wore. Today, Chartres Cathedral continues to draw pilgrims to one of the largest and most beautiful French Gothic churches and home to some of the most stunning stained glass windows anywhere.

Following are a few more popular sites where Catholic pilgrims travel to pay homage:

- The Shrine of Our Lady of Lourdes (France)
- The Shrine of Our Lady of Czestochowa (Poland)
- St. Patrick's Cathedral (New York City, USA)
- The Shrine to our Lady of Guadalupe (Mexico City, Mexico)
- The Basilicas of St. Francis and St. Clare (Assisi, Italy)
- The Shrine of Our Lady of Fatima (Portugal)

The Least You Need to Know

- Catholics need spiritual direction to follow God's plan for their lives.
- Catholics often read the Bible, the Catechism of the Catholic Church, and papal documents for spiritual enlightenment.
- Retreats offer a break from everyday life and the chance to spend some one-on-one time with God.
- Mission trips are a great way to grow spiritually while serving others and making new friends.
- Catholic pilgrimage sites enable the faithful to connect with the history of Catholicism in all parts of the world.

The Saints: God's Role Models

They are ordinary human beings venerated for their extraordinary sanctity and virtue by the Catholic Church. They include more than 10,000 men and women from throughout the world whose lives set the bar for Christian living and offer us a glimpse of what we are all called to be. They are the saints.

Saints represent the best of what humanity has to offer. Catholics are not only inspired by their lives, works, and words, but turn to them as patrons in hopes they can achieve a small portion of their infectious faith and love for God.

In this chapter, we will tour the halls of the holy in order to find out what a saint is and why some are given special recognition by the Church. We will explore the road to sainthood and explain why Catholics consider saints to be friends in high places.

In This Chapter

- Saints are admired, not worshipped
- Having a home in Heaven
- Saints do not make miracles happen
- Patron saints and affiliations
- Six key saints to know

What Is a Saint?

Has there ever been anyone in your life whom you really admire? Perhaps it was someone you've never met like a famous athlete, musician, or historical figure. Maybe it was someone a little closer to home, such as a favorite teacher or a beloved grandparent. Regardless of who it was, there was something about that individual that resonated with you in a deeply personal way. Not only were you inspired by their spirit or the way they lived their life, but on some level you probably longed to be like them. They served as your role model; and for Catholics, a *saint* is just such a person.

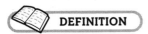

DEFINITION

A **saint** is any deceased individual who is believed to be residing in Heaven.

There is a lot of confusion about what a saint is, what purpose they serve, and why Catholics recognize them in the first place. While some Christian and non-Christian traditions view the veneration of saints as nothing short of idol worship, strictly speaking, a saint is any deceased individual who is believed to be in Heaven with God. This does not include only the men and women whose names and likenesses appear on religious articles throughout the world, but everyone who has passed from this life and is enjoying everlasting life in paradise.

That being said, there are those men and women whose lives have been carefully examined by the Church, have been deemed worthy of veneration, and have been distinguished by the Vatican through the process of canonization. As official "on the books" Catholic saints, these individuals may be called upon by the faithful to pray for them and to take their intentions directly to the throne of God.

Make no mistake, Catholics do not worship these individuals and do not pray to them. They may invoke the name of a saint in prayer to God, but it is for intercessory purposes only. The hope is that the saint will hear the special need, take the petition to God, and pray for the appropriate outcome. Saints do not have super powers, cannot guarantee a favorable answer to a request, and—contrary to popular myth—do not spend their time convincing God to grant our wishes. They are holy human beings, not religious genies.

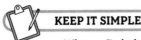

KEEP IT SIMPLE

When a Catholic calls upon a saint in Heaven for intercession, it is no different than asking a friend to pray for you on earth. Many religions acknowledge that there is strength in numbers and plenty of power in prayer, no matter where it comes from!

A Good and Holy Life

The process that leads to canonization is intense, very thorough, and can be quite lengthy—though technology has made communication a lot faster! It consists of a full investigation of an individual's life, along with evidence of two miracles that resulted from the person's direct mediation with God.

In the early days of the Church, the road to sainthood was not quite so complicated. Anyone who had a reputation for holiness, a spirit of charity, and reports of miracles happening when their name was invoked could be named a saint. However, in the Middle Ages it was decided that rumors of being an all-around good person were not enough reason to be enrolled into the canon of saints and, in 1234, Pope Gregory IX determined that a more formal process needed to be put into place. He developed many of the criteria that are used today to investigate a person's reported sanctity.

Before a person can be considered for canonization, he or she must be deceased at least five years. This is to ensure that the individual has an enduring reputation for holiness among the faithful and is not being venerated out of grief. During this time, the bishop in the diocese where the individual died conducts a preliminary investigation into the person's life and writings to identify evidence of heroic virtue, and when the five years (or more) have concluded the bishop can petition the Vatican to officially open a Cause for Beatification and Canonization.

FAST FACT

Obviously not every person who has lived a virtuous life can be considered for publicly recognized sainthood, so how does the Church know whom should be looked into? One way that has stood out for bishops is the incorruptibility of the individual's body. When someone's body does not decompose, as it should after death, it can indicate that the person is worth an investigation. While this is rare—even among the saints—it has happened in numerous cases, such as St. Bernadette of Lourdes, St. Padre Pio, St. John Vianney, and St. Catherine Laboure.

The pope can waive any or all of the five-year waiting period (beginning the "fast track" to sainthood), but this has only happened twice. Pope John Paul II waived three of the five years for Blessed Teresa of Calcutta in 1997, and in 2005, Pope Benedict XVI waived all five years for his predecessor and now St. Pope John Paul II.

When a Cause is opened, the core group promoting this person's journey to sainthood appoints a *postulator* (Latin for "one who asks") to the case. This person is trained in Church law and acts as a liaison between the group and the Holy See. During the first phase of investigation, a diocesan tribunal gathers testimony regarding the person's life and virtues. No stone is left unturned in this process, in which one's public and private documents are combed through and held up to rigorous scrutiny. This can take a number of years and concludes with a judgment from a local Church court and ultimately the bishop stating that this person's life does (or does not) exemplify the heroic virtues associated with canonized saints.

The results—complete with volumes of documentation, or Acta (Acts)—are filed with the Congregation for the Canonization of Saints at the Vatican. If the decision is favorable, they are entrusted to a member of the Congregation's College of Relators who sees the Cause through the rest of the way. This person works with a theological commission to ensure that the *Positio*, a document about the person's life, is properly written. When that is completed, the commission votes on the Cause and makes a recommendation to the members of the Congregation, who render their vote. If the vote is no, the Cause is defeated. If the vote results in a yes, the Cause is presented to the pope with a recommendation of a Decree of Heroic Virtue. The pope's decision on the matter is final.

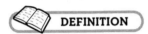

DEFINITION

> A **positio** is a documented account of the life, work, and writings of an individual being considered for eventual canonization.

When the Holy Father has given recognition to the person's heroic virtues, he or she is then referred to as a Venerable Servant of God. At this point, the wait for the first miracle begins.

Why Miracles Matter

Miracles are an incredibly important part of the canonization process, and they are difficult to prove. From a scientific standpoint, of course, they can't be proven. However, every other reasonable explanation is eliminated, leaving the possibility of a miraculous occurrence. Despite being an organization built on faith, the Catholic Church takes a skeptical approach to any potential miracle they investigate. People often refer to this as a "devil's advocate" position.

While any saint can intercede with God on one's behalf at any time, the types of events that are considered to be miraculous (and can be distinguished as such) are limited. Someone getting a new job, for example, is not a miracle because prayer is not the only mitigating factor. The miracles that are investigated for a canonization are almost exclusively medical in nature. They have the most documented history, there is a lot of research available in various conditions, and there are experts who can be brought in to weigh their professional expertise (versus an opinion) in the matter.

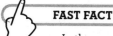

In the case of martyrdom, the miracle required for beatification can be waived as a miracle of grace. When the Congregation investigates and approves this type of case, they recommend a Decree of Martyrdom to the Holy Father.

When an alleged miracle has taken place and has been reported to the diocese in which it occurred, local scientific and theological tribunals are assembled to investigate it. In the case of a supposed healing, the person's medical history is examined, including the condition itself and treatments as well as the progression of recovery. The scientific tribunal must determine that there is no natural or scientific reason for the phenomena to have occurred, while the theological tribunal must attribute the event solely to the intercession of prayer through the venerated person in question.

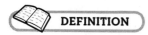

CATHOLIC QUOTE

The prayers of the Saints in heaven and of the just on earth are a perfume which never will be lost.

—St. Padre Pio

There are a number of things that can muddle this portion of the process. Praying for the intercession of more than one saint, unexpected scientific discovery, and so on can cloud the issue and cause the process to begin over again, but assuming that the two tribunals are satisfied with their findings, the Cause can move forward to the Congregation in Rome. When they receive the case, they, too, assemble a scientific and medical commission to review the conclusions and note any potential for error. If the findings are affirmed, the case is given to the General Meeting of the cardinal and episcopal members, who must also agree with the conclusions. They pass it on to the Holy Father, and if he finds everything in order, he approves it and *beatifies* the individual.

DEFINITION

Beatification is the term used to denote that a venerated servant of God has used his or her intercessory power to secure a miracle for someone on earth. The term is used for those who are one step away from becoming a saint and distinguishes them as "Blessed."

With beatification, the person is declared Blessed and is cleared to be venerated at the local or regional level in areas that have a particularly strong tie to the individual's life. The reason veneration is limited at this stage is because beatification is not considered an infallible papal act, and therefore it is not appropriate for the Church as a whole to sing the individual's praises, so to speak. This can only occur after a second miracle is investigated and approved and the person has been canonized.

The process for the second miracle follows the same format as the first. No corners are cut to allow one to "skate through." If anything, it is even more intense because its occurrence confirms that the person, who died in Christ, is now in Heaven with Him. A deceased person cannot ask God for a favor unless they are in Heaven, and as you may recall, this is the only real qualification to be a saint. Miracles are the only evidence we have to support this hypothesis.

If all parties approve the second miracle, the pope formally canonizes the individual in an elaborate liturgical celebration. This is considered an infallible act that is protected from error by the Holy Spirit, and it allows the individual to be venerated by the entire Church. Though this does not mean Catholics can worship the saints, they are allowed to look to them as positive role models, pray through them, and entrust that they can communicate people's needs to God.

KEEP IT SIMPLE

If the process of canonization seems overwhelming, think of it this way: when a notable athlete has demonstrated excellence in every aspect of his or her sport, a team often retires the athlete's "number." This is similar to a beatification. While most players are honored in this way only on the organizational level, Jackie Robinson's "42" was retired across all of Major League Baseball. This distinction is similar to a canonization because it showed that Robinson's achievements were venerated not only among the Dodgers, but throughout the entire baseball community.

Can St. Joseph Help You Sell Your House?

Once saints have been canonized, they often become the patron saint of something or affiliated with a particular area or need. The habit of adopting a patron saint goes back to the construction of the first public churches, which were built over the graves of martyrs and named after them. It was believed that the martyr would then act as a special intercessor for the congregants who worshipped there.

Eventually, churches were named for other holy men and women who were not martyred, and by the Middle Ages, the adoption of patron saints spread to occupations, locations, and other areas of life. For example, St. Veronica is known as the patron saint of photographers. St. Cecilia is the patron saint of musicians. St. Nicholas became the patron saint of sailors, children, and the country of Greece, and St. Roch is the patron saint of second-hand dealers and gravediggers. (Yes, really!)

Because they have their specific niches, patron saints can be called upon to help with certain problems. Misplaced your car keys? Call on St. Anthony. In addition to being the second-fastest saint ever canonized (after St. Peter of Verona), he is exceptionally good at finding lost articles and lost people. This stems from an event in which a book of Psalms belonging to Anthony was stolen by one of his students. Anthony prayed for its return and the thief was moved to give it back. It is believed that the stolen volume is kept in the Franciscan friary in Bologna, Italy.

FAST FACT

When someone chooses a confirmation name, they usually choose the name of a saint they admire. It is believed that this saint becomes their personal patron and someone they can turn to in good times and bad.

St. Jude is your man if you have a lost cause in need of resolution. Known also as Thaddeus, Jude was an apostle of Jesus whose letter in the New Testament encourages folks to persevere even when all hope seems lost. He truly believes that one can take a sad song and make it better.

Of course, there is also St. Joseph. As the earthly father of Jesus, he is the patron saint of carpenters, paternal figures, and real estate. One of the most peculiar practices regarding patron saints involves the burial of a St. Joseph statue on the property a homeowner wants to sell. Stores that sell religious articles actually carry the St. Joseph sell-your-house statue and kit complete with instructions on how he must be placed and in which direction he must face, and a prayer for a speedy escrow. While most Catholics firmly believe that saints have specific areas of expertise, they stop short of calling the traditions superstition. After all, it can't hurt to try, right? All houses sell sooner or later, and sometimes it's a question of waiting and having faith.

Key Saints to Know

There is no shortage of important men and women included in the canon of saints; however, there are a few key names to know. While some may be very familiar, others might be new to you. But all of the following are among the superstars of the Catholic Church.

St. Augustine

Born on November 13, 354, in Tagaste in northern Africa, the famous son of St. Monica spent a number of years living the life of a pagan. Despite his intellect and having been brought up a Christian, he simply could not let go of his wicked ways, and his pride kept him from seeing the truth about God.

Thanks to the prayers of his holy mother and the influence of his mentor St. Ambrose, Augustine finally became convinced that Christianity was the only path to eternal life. However, he was not ready to convert. He was too afraid that he would never have the strength to live a pure life. Eventually he realized how silly his line of logic sounded. No longer willing to continue wallowing in sin, he was baptized, became a priest, a bishop, one of the most famous Catholic writers, and one of the greatest saints to have ever lived.

Not only is his story of conversion remarkable, but throughout his ministry, Augustine overcame strong heretical opposition, lived a life of poverty, supported the poor he encountered, and preached with fervor until the very end of his life. He felt that he had waited too long to love God, but it was clear that his enthusiasm and zeal more than made up for his sins of the past. He died on August 28, 430, at the age of 76.

St. Francis of Assisi

St. Francis of Assisi was born around 1181 and was known as the spoiled son of a wealthy cloth merchant who liked to live the good life. He spent lavishly, had a rowdy rabble of friends, and never turned away from a good fight.

After being taken as a prisoner of war during a conflict with a neighboring town, suffering two major illnesses, and having his plans to join the military fall through, Francis turned to religion, and one night he heard the voice of God tell him to "rebuild the Church." Taking the order literally, he stole a bundle of his father's drapery material, mounted a horse, and sold the lot in order to restore the nearby St. Damian's. The priest refused the money because of the way it was procured, and when his father found out what his son had done, he dragged the boy home, beat him, and locked him in a dark room.

Francis's and his father's relationship never improved. When his father threatened to cut him off financially, Francis stripped off his clothes in the middle of the street and emancipated himself from the family. He devoted himself to his calling, emptying himself in pure obedience to God. He founded the order of the Franciscans, and later in life he had a vision that left him with the *stigmata* of Christ—the first recorded incident. He died at the age of 44.

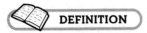 **DEFINITION**

The **stigmata** are to the sores, marks, or sensations of pain that occur on the human body in locations corresponding to the crucifixion wounds of Jesus.

Known for his passion for animals and ecology, Francis was canonized on July 6, 1228, and today his legacy resonates with millions of followers across the globe.

St. Catherine of Siena

Born Caterina Benincasa on March 25, 1347, Catherine of Siena began following a path of Christian devotion very early in life. She received her first vision at the age of 6, and took the oath of chastity a year later. When she was 15, Catherine entered the Dominican Tertiary Sisters and worked tirelessly to help the hospitalized at Santa Maria della Scala in Siena.

Catherine's reputation spread throughout the Christian world and while visiting Pisa, Italy, she became even more famous after receiving the stigmata from a cross hanging in the Church of Santa Christina. She traveled extensively and acted as a mediator for the papacy. One such trip was a journey to Avignon, where she convinced Pope Gregory to return the Papal Court to Rome after having been exiled in France for over 70 years.

After founding the monastery of Santa Maria degli Angeli Catherine found herself embroiled in what would later be referred to as the Great Western Schism. When Pope Urban VI succeeded Pope Gregory XI in 1378, there was strong opposition from some of the cardinals, who elected a second pontiff named Pope Clement II and created a great divide in the Church. Urban relied on Catherine to act as a mediator with prominent members of the faithful in order to legitimize his papacy.

In 1380, Catherine died at the age of 33. She is buried at the church of Santa Maria sopra Minerva in Rome, and in 1461 Pope Pius II proclaimed her a saint. Along with St. Francis of Assisi, Catherine is a patron saint of Italy and one of the co-patron saints of Europe. In 1970, she was named one of the Doctors of the universal Church. For a young woman in fourteenth-century Europe, she had an enormous influence on the Church and the world.

St. Theodora Guérin

Anne Therese Guérin was born on October 2, 1798, in Etables, France. Raised in the aftermath of the French Revolution, "Mother Theodore" knew by the age of 10 that she would dedicate her life to God. Her plans were derailed when bandits killed her father when she was only 15 and her mother fell into a deep depression, causing the young girl to assume responsibility for the household (which included a younger sister).

The call to the convent never subsided, however, and eventually Theodora's mother gave her permission to enter the Sisters of Providence at the age of 20. After serving as an educator at a number of Providence-led schools and earning a solid reputation throughout the community, Theodora answered the call to travel to America and establish an order near Terre Haute, Indiana.

CATHOLIC QUOTE

What must we do in order to become saints? Nothing extraordinary; nothing more than we do every day. Only do it for His love.

—St. Theodora Guérin

The journey was a difficult one, but it was only a precursor to the hardships that were in store for her. Despite poor health, primitive frontier conditions, and a contentious bishop, Theodora persevered, opening Saint Mary-of-the-Woods College (the oldest Catholic women's liberal arts college in the United States), as well as schools in three other communities, before her death on May 14, 1856. After miraculous healings involving two people within the Indiana community, Pope Benedict XVI canonized her on October 15, 2006.

St. Thérèse of Lisieux

Born on January 2, 1873, in Alençon, France, Thérèse Martin (the "Little Flower") knew from a young age that she was called to the religious life. Her mother died when she was only 4 and after two of her sisters entered the Carmelite convent, she wanted nothing more than to follow them.

At the age of 15, she made her intentions known, but the order told her to come back when she was a grownup. She took her petition to Rome, speaking directly to the pope, who granted permission for her to enter the community.

Though she achieved her dream, things were difficult behind the wall. Not everyone was thrilled that Thérèse had been admitted, and many of the sisters were less than charitable to the teen—who returned nothing but love to them. Her kindness not only warmed their hard hearts, but she realized that showing God's love in "little ways" was just as important as great works. She believed that with a heart full of love and the right attitude, there wasn't much one couldn't accomplish.

CATHOLIC QUOTE

Love is repaid by love alone.

—St. Thérèse of Lisieux

Thérèse tragically died after a bout with tuberculosis at the age of 24. She instinctively knew she would spend her time in Heaven doing good upon the earth and on May 17, 1925, she was canonized by Pope Pius XI. Her writings and autobiography (*Story of a Soul*) have been read all over the world, and in 1997 she was named one of four female Doctors of the universal Church.

St. John Paul II

Born Karol Józef Wojtyla in Wadowice, Poland, John Paul was an athletic young man with a keen interest in poetry, theater, and his faith. After the Nazis closed his university in 1939, he followed his call to the priesthood but was forced to study in secret. He was ordained in 1946 and after ascending through the church hierarchy as a bishop, archbishop, and cardinal, he made history in 1978 when he became the first non-Italian pontiff in over 400 years.

John Paul was an immediate hit with the faithful. He traveled extensively, visiting over 100 countries during his pontificate. He was a champion of human rights and an advocate for the youth of the Church, and used his influence to bring about political change throughout the world. (John Paul is credited with the fall of communism in his homeland of Poland.) He also survived an assassination attempt in 1981 and famously met with his attacker to offer forgiveness.

After an extended battle with Parkinson's disease, John Paul died on April 2, 2005, at the age of 84. An unprecedented three million people waited in line to pay their respects to their beloved leader, and at his funeral there was a cry for immediate canonization. Pope Benedict XVI ultimately waived the customary five-year waiting period so that a Cause for Canonization could open as quickly as possible. It seemed that it took no time at all for two healings (both involving Parkinson's patients) to emerge, paving the way for the former pope to achieve sainthood. St. John Paul II was canonized on April 27, 2014.

The Least You Need to Know

- Saints are people who are believed to be in Heaven with God.
- Canonized saints are upheld as religious role models for Catholics everywhere.
- Saints often become patrons of different locations, occupations, and other areas of life.
- Saints are considered the "best of the best" humanity has to offer and lived extraordinary lives of holiness.

Catholic Life and Culture

It's hard to imagine the Catholic Church as an organization that keeps its finger on the pulse of society. After all, it's an institution that tends to measure time by the century rather than the decade. However, the Church is keenly interested in current events, and its influence can be felt throughout the world at large—not only in formal church programs and ancient rituals, but also in science, technology, art, literature, and even trends in popular culture.

In this part, we will look at Catholic culture and what it means to be Catholic in the twenty-first century. We'll examine how the past affects the present, and how the Church makes an impact on the local, national, and global community in everyday life. It's not something that happens from the top down, but often blooms from the people in the pews. They are the ones who carry their faith into the streets and who share their wisdom and values in countless visible and invisible ways.

Balancing Faith and Fact

F. Scott Fitzgerald once said, "The test of a first-rate intelligence is the ability to hold two opposed ideas in the mind at the same time and still retain the ability to function." At no time is that ability more critical than when an individual is trying to balance matters of faith and fact.

Though it may come as a surprise to some, the Catholic Church does not see these two issues as an either/or proposition. Rather, the Church prefers to find common ground in opposing viewpoints rather than limit itself to one way of looking at things.

In this chapter, you will learn that despite a tumultuous history with science, the Church is actually quite progressive in its thinking. You will meet some Catholics who have been on the cusp of innovation and discovery, and learn how the Catholic Church reconciles seeming paradoxes in its beliefs.

In This Chapter

- Not the Church of either/or
- Holding two beliefs at the same time
- How the Church supports scientific research
- Scientists can be saints, too

The Church of Both/And

As we learned in Chapter 1, Catholics are like other monotheistic religions that believe in one all-powerful and infinite deity for whom nothing is impossible. As children, we hear the creation accounts in the Book of Genesis and are amazed by the Almighty's ability to do so much so quickly.

However, in time, the story we took on faith sounds more like science fiction than science fact. We note the differences between the creation stories in Genesis and wonder why there are two stories instead of one. Our belief in *creationism* is further challenged by theories that contradict this supernatural event, and we ask ourselves how we are supposed to resolve the idea that all creation came from God when scientific evidence suggests that *evolution* has something to do with it?

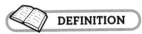 **DEFINITION**

Creationism is the theory that God created the universe and all life in existence in its present form in six 24-hour days. **Evolution** is the theory that all life was formed over millions of years and that each species is derived from one that existed before it.

Actually, we don't have to. We can believe in both/and. Like Fitzgerald's quote in the introduction to this chapter, Catholics open their minds to two thought processes at once and accept the possibility that both creationism and evolution are valid concepts that, when held together, neither eliminate God nor challenge His omnipresence. Each perspective answers different questions: science tells us the how, when, where, and what about how the universe was created, while only faith can answer the question of why the universe was created. Faith and science are asking and answering different questions, and thus complement each other.

So make no mistake about it: Catholics firmly believe that God created the world and everything in it, but they also believe that God could have developed the evolutionary process to allow His creation to grow and change over time. In other words, God is not absent from evolution. He engineers it. This idea is called *theistic evolution,* and while it is a theory that the Church leans toward, it is still possible as a Catholic to believe in creationism alone.

The belief in a Church of both/and eliminates the need to make everything an either/or proposition. It's not a game with words or an attempt to make the corners line up, but it is a way to acknowledge more than one school of thought without giving up another.

KEEP IT SIMPLE

In the movie *Oh, God! Book II,* a young girl asks God why He allows bad things to happen. He responds by telling her that no matter how infinite His power, He's never been able to create something with only one side to it. There cannot be a front without a back, a top without a bottom, or, sadly, good without evil. There must be both/and.

G.K. Chesterton discusses this paradox at length in his 1908 work *Orthodoxy,* a short volume on Christian apologetics. He argues that it is important for Christians to fill their lives with a "combination of something that is strange with something that is secure" and to "combine an idea of wonderful with an idea of welcome." Sometimes it is hard to wrap our brain around two conflicting theories, and we feel that we must define one as the be-all and end-all when the other feels correct as well. By allowing two different ideas to mutually inform each other, we are able to live with the tension that exists in nature and acknowledge that:

- God is both one divine being and three divine persons.

- We can know God through both faith and reason.

- The world's origin is a result of both divine creation and natural evolution.

- Jesus was both fully human and fully divine.

- The Bible is both read literally and interpreted spiritually.

- We must work both to build the Kingdom of God on Earth and to prepare ourselves for the Kingdom of God in Heaven.

- Humans are both individuals and social beings.

- The final judgment will be both particular and general.

The list goes on and on, but ultimately, the Church of both/and allows for two sides of the coin to coexist and gives Catholics a framework to understand the complicated world God has created. This way of looking at things doesn't apply across the board to every opposing idea, but it often provides a helpful Catholic way to look at seeming paradoxes. Throughout this book, we have tackled a variety of these both/and concepts in order to understand the Church's viewpoint. However, there are a few things we have not covered, and in this chapter we will attempt to do so.

CATHOLIC QUOTE

Let your religion be less of a theory and more of a love affair.

—G.K. Chesterton

Both Faith and Works

As we learned in Chapter 13, every human being will have the opportunity to stand before the throne of God and account for his or her life. We are told that it will not matter how we "won" at the game of life. God won't care how good we looked, how well we dressed, how big our house was, what kind of car we had, or whether we saved enough for our retirement. He will be more concerned with how we responded to His love and how we infused that love into the world.

Historically, the idea of faith and works has been a sticking point between Catholicism and other Christian traditions that believe an acceptance of Christ and the sacrament of baptism is the only cover charge to get into Heaven. They often confuse the Church's position on faith and works as a rejection that God's grace is all one really needs for salvation.

Actually, the Catholic Church very much believes that it is through God's grace and God's grace alone that one merits salvation. There is no ambiguity in that teaching. One cannot bribe/buy their way into Heaven based on attendance at Mass, participation in the sacraments, or even the amount of charitable works they complete in their lifetime. However, these works are a manifestation of our faith and a response to Christ's command to love one another.

The apostle James unravels the important both/and concept of faith and works when he famously tells the early Christian communities that faith without works is dead: "But someone will say, 'You have faith and I have works.' Show me your faith apart from your works, and I by my works will show you my faith. …" (James 2:18) He goes on to tell his readers that a person is shown to be a Christian disciple not only by his or her faith, but by works as well, and that "Just as the body without the spirit is dead, so faith without works is also dead." (James 2:26)

Both Catholic and SSA

If there are two words that, for many, seem as if they do not belong in the same sentence, it is Catholicism and homosexuality. For years the Catholic gay community has struggled to find a way to live their faith without hiding who they are. Truth be told, they don't have to and they never did. An individual can have both a same-sex attraction (SSA) and still be a practicing Catholic without feeling as if they have to live in a closet all their lives.

This is not a radical idea. It's the way it has always been, though in the attempt to clarify its position on the issue, the Church has added to the confusion with harsh-sounding language that is often misunderstood by the public. Paragraph 2357 of the *Catechism of the Catholic Church* makes it clear that homosexual acts are a messy business; however, they are no more disordered than any other sexual act prohibited by the Church (that is, anything outside of the bond of matrimony). In the next paragraph, the Church acknowledges the struggles the gay community faces and encourages the faithful to welcome these individuals with love and respect. So what's going on? Is the Church talking out of both sides of its mouth?

 CATHOLIC QUOTE

If a gay person is in eager search of God, who am I to judge them? The Catholic Church teaches that gay people should not be discriminated against; they should be made to feel welcome.

—Pope Francis

Not at all. It's more rational than that. The Church believes that God created the sexual act with two end goals in mind—the loving union of two persons and natural procreation. The proper use of our sexuality is one in which a couple must be open to both goals. The only way natural procreation can come about is by a union between a man and a woman, and the only way this act is sanctified is through the Sacrament of Holy Matrimony. Any union outside of this sacrament is considered sinful, and any sexual act that precludes the possibility of new life is considered a misuse of God's gift of sexuality.

The Church's position is not one of judgment on the individual. To the contrary, the Church does not believe that those with a same-sex attraction are better or worse than anyone else or that they are somehow more in need of saving than heterosexuals are. In fact, it holds those with a same-sex attraction to the same standards that every other single Catholic is expected to adhere to. They are to focus their lives on God, work hard to serve Him, participate fully in the sacraments, live chaste lives, and work to defeat the sins of the flesh that affect everyone regardless of sexual preference.

 KEEP IT SIMPLE

In 2014, Blackstone Films released *The Third Way*, a 38-minute film that explains the Church's position on homosexuality and how one can be gay and Catholic at the same time. The production team's mission is to honor and glorify God by active participation in the New Evangelization of the twenty-first century through the effective use of moving and uplifting films. For more information, visit www.blackstonefilms.org.

Both Scripture and Tradition

Imagine being handed a complicated set of instructions for how to complete a project without any explanation as to their logic or order, or why at times the words seem to contradict each other. Imagine if you read through them without a complete understanding of the overall objective. Imagine that these instructions were originally written for a primitive people in another land and had been given multiple translations that leave you guessing even if you do understand the words. You might need a little bit of help, right?

One of the biggest differences between Catholicism and other Christian faiths is the Church's reliance on both Scripture and tradition for its doctrinal teachings. Most Protestant Christians maintain that the Bible is the only divine source of information needed to achieve eternal life and that it is sufficiently written in a way that everyone can understand.

While Catholics do not discount the Word of God and absolutely see the Bible as a divinely inspired work, the Church does allow for ideas outside of the Bible to influence the faithful and its doctrinal teachings, provided that those teachings do not contradict Sacred Scripture. We call this Sacred Tradition. In fact, without Sacred Tradition, we wouldn't have a Bible at all—it was the leaders of the early Church who discerned which books were divinely inspired and would make up the Scriptures. That process in itself was a living act of Sacred Tradition.

 CATHOLIC QUOTE

> So then, brothers and sisters, stand firm and hold fast to the traditions that you were taught by us either by word of mouth or by our letter.
>
> —St. Paul (2 Thessalonians 2:15)

Sacred Tradition allows the Church to interpret the teachings of Jesus and to show Catholics how the Scriptures apply to their daily lives. Christ handed his ministry on to the apostles and their successors so that they could interpret his words and actions for the people of this new movement. This didn't end with the authors of the Biblical texts, but continues to this day. The Church has had any number of thinkers who have read and analyzed the Scriptures so they could continue to make the same passages relevant for generations to come.

In the Second Vatican Council's document on divine revelation, *Del Verbum* ("The Word of God"), the Church maintains that Sacred Tradition passes on the Word of God or the Sacred Scripture faithfully through the apostolic succession of bishops who not only preach it, but also explain it and help make it more widely accessible to a larger audience. Both Sacred Scripture and Sacred Tradition are a means to the same end.

Both Science and Religion

It's no secret that over the years the Catholic Church and science have enjoyed something of a love/hate relationship. Although the Church has been one of the longest patrons of science in history, the relationship has experienced a rather tumultuous past.

Who can forget the Church's reaction to a certain seventeenth-century astronomer who dared to teach the Copernican theory that the Earth rotated around the sun? Although Galileo was himself a Catholic, the papacy labeled him a heretic, which forced him to retract his statements and live out the rest of his days under house arrest. Though history would prove the general thrust of Galileo's scientific theories to be fact (although the actual scientific evidence he gave as proof of his theories was flawed), it would be 367 years before the Church offered a formal apology for their actions.

Although it may seem that the Catholic Church is not the most progressive organization where science is concerned, rest assured it has always kept its finger on the pulse of science, has learned from its mistakes with Galileo, and continues to be keenly interested in new developments in scientific innovation and discovery. Some of the most well-known Catholic scientists throughout history include:

- Nicolas Copernicus: Developed the theory that the sun was the center of the universe rather than the Earth

- Gregor Mendel: An Augustinian friar who is considered the father of genetics

- Roger Bacon: A Franciscan friar and father of the scientific method

- Georges Lemaitre: A Belgian priest who developed the Big Bang theory

 CATHOLIC QUOTE

I do not feel obliged to believe that the same God who has endowed us with sense, reason and intellect has intended us to forego their use.

—Galileo Galilei

The Pontifical Academy of Sciences

Located in the heart of the Vatican Gardens is the Pontifical Academy of Sciences. It is a scientific academy supported by the Holy See that was established by Pope Pius XI in 1936. It has roots in the Lincean Academy in Rome, founded by Federico Cesi in 1603. It was the world's first exclusively scientific academy but, sadly, it was an institution that did not survive the death of its founder. In 1847, Pope Pius IX wanted to resurrect the idea of a Vatican-supported scientific academy and established the Pontifical Academy of New Lincei, but that, too, didn't last.

Since its inception in the pre-World War II era, the Pontifical Academy of Sciences has grown into a diverse organization of men and women who come from a variety of nations, cultures, and religions who are all committed to research and discovery in six major areas of scientific study: fundamental science; science and technology of global problems; science for the problems of the developing world; scientific policy; bioethics; and epistemology. Its roster has included some of the most respected names in the scientific community and includes such Nobel laureates as: Max Planck, Otto Hahn, Niels Bohr, Ernest Rutherford, and Charles Hard Townes.

According to its website, www.casinapioiv.va, the goals of the academy are:

- Promoting the progress of the mathematical, physical, and natural sciences, and the study of related epistemological questions and issues

- Recognizing excellence in science

- Stimulating an interdisciplinary approach to scientific knowledge

- Encouraging international interaction

- Furthering participation in the benefits of science and technology by the greatest number of people and peoples

- Promoting education and the public's understanding of science

- Ensuring that science works to advance the human and moral dimension of man

- Achieving a role for science which involves the promotion of justice, development, solidarity, peace, and the resolution of conflict

- Fostering interaction between faith and reason and encouraging dialogue between science and spiritual, cultural, philosophical, and religious values

- Providing authoritative advice on scientific and technological matters

- Cooperating with the members of other Academies in a friendly spirit to promote such objectives.

 FAST FACT

Galileo Galilei was the president of the original Lincean Academy.

The Vatican Observatory

Established by Pope Leo XIII in 1891 and headquartered at the Papal Palace in Castel Gandolfo, Italy, the Vatican Observatory is one of the oldest research facilities in the world.

Like the Pontifical Academy of Sciences, it was not the first such establishment. Over the years, there had been three observatories founded by the papacy, including the Observatory of the Roman College (1774–1878), the Observatory of the Capitol (1827–1870), and the Specula Vaticana (1789–1821) in the Tower of the Winds within the Vatican.

With this rich tradition of Church-sponsored scientific research, Pope Leo XIII re-established the Vatican Observatory in 1891 as an answer to long-standing accusations that the Catholic Church was fundamentally opposed to science. He felt it was important for the world to see that the Church wanted to "embrace it, encourage it, and promote it with the fullest possible devotion." (www.VaticanObservatory.org)

 CATHOLIC QUOTE

The Bible shows the way to go to heaven, not the way the heavens go.

—Galileo Galilei

The observatory was originally located on a hillside behind St. Peter's Basilica, but by the 1930s, the light pollution from the surrounding city prompted the need to relocate the facility to its present home 25 kilometers southeast of Rome.

This proved to be a temporary solution. According to its website, after re-founding the observatory at Castel Gandolfo, the Jesuits (who were entrusted with the facility) oversaw the construction of "two new telescopes, the installation of an astrophysical laboratory for spectrochemical analysis, and the expansion of several important research programs on variable stars." (www.vaticanobservatory.org/about-us/history)

A Schmidt wide-angle telescope was added in 1957 and research spread into other areas of study, such as new methodologies for classifying stars according to color. This is a program that continues to this day.

In 1981, light pollution became a problem once again and rather than move, the observatory opted to found a second research center, the Vatican Observatory Research Group (VORG), in Tucson, Arizona, in the United States.

The VORG is one of the world's largest and most modern centers for observational astronomy. Observatory staff maintain offices at Steward Observatory at the University of Arizona and together the two entities completed construction of the Vatican Advanced Technology Telescope (VATT) at Mt. Graham, Arizona.

FAST FACT

The library at the Vatican's Castel Gandolfo site contains more than 22,000 works, including a valuable collection of antique volumes on the efforts of Copernicus, Galileo, Newton, Kepler, Brahe, Clavius, and Secchi. It also boasts a unique meteorite collection from which knowledge concerning the early history of the solar system is being examined.

Saintly Scientists

Now that we know the Church is not against empirical research and scientific innovation, it's time to meet a few saints who are "living proof" that faith and science are not mutually exclusive:

St. Albert the Great (c. 1200–1280)

Considered one of the Church's great intellects, St. Albert the Great was born into a wealthy family circa 1200. He was educated at the University of Padua, where he studied the liberal arts prior to joining the Dominican order in 1223 against his family's wishes.

He continued his education through his religious vocation and taught theology at a number of schools throughout Germany. He eventually moved to France, where he became a guest lecturer at the University of Paris and eventually earned his doctorate in 1245.

In Paris, he became enamored with the work of the ancient philosophers as well as the natural world. Albert wrote commentaries on the complete works of Aristotle and became an authority in a broad range of fields, including physics, geography, astronomy, mineralogy, zoology, chemistry, and biology. His work also included logic, metaphysics, mathematics, and theology. He spearheaded the Scholastic method, a system designed to use reason to explore the great philosophical and theological questions. (This was later perfected by Albert's protégée and friend St. Thomas Aquinas.)

His long journeys throughout Europe as the Bishop of Ratisbon earned him the nickname "the bishop with the boots" and over time, it was his friends who nicknamed Albert "The Great" due to the "wonder and miracle" of his "godlike knowledge."

CATHOLIC QUOTE

The aim of natural science is not simply to accept the statements of others, but to investigate the causes that are at work in nature.

—St. Albert the Great (*De Mineralibus*)

Albert was still in the classroom when his memory failed in 1278. Though it was not yet called dementia or Alzheimer's disease, Albert's mental faculties continued to decline, and two years later he died. It is believed that he was in his 80s at the time. Tradition says that when he was a young boy, Albert had a vision of the Blessed Virgin who told him that God would give him extraordinary intellectual talent, but that this talent would be reclaimed in his old age. This story and the resulting mental deterioration have been used to emphasize Albert's sanctity and to prove that the scientist knew that God was in charge of his brilliance and without Him, Albert was nothing.

Albert was canonized in 1931 by Pope Pius XII and named one of the Doctors of the Church. He is the patron saint of scientists and a number of Catholic schools are dedicated to him.

St. Joseph Moscati (1880–1927)

He was the "holy physician of Naples" and known for his holistic approach to health care. Joseph (Giuseppe) Moscati believed that a doctor must not only treat the body but also the soul "with counsel that appeals to their minds and hearts rather than with cold prescriptions to be sent in to the pharmacist."

Born on July 25, 1880, Moscati was the seventh of nine children born into an aristocratic Italian family. His father was a judge and Moscati, who inherited his father's intellectual gifts, had every intention of following in the judge's footsteps. However, he opted to study medicine after his brother sustained an incurable head injury in 1893.

He attended the University of Naples, a school well known for its openly agnostic and anti-clerical atmosphere, but Moscati was able to put those influences aside in order to concentrate on his studies and practice his Catholic faith. He graduated with honors in 1903. After receiving his degree, he practiced medicine at the Hospital for the Incurables and taught classes on the side. It wasn't long before he became the hospital's administrator and well known for his ability to diagnose his patient's conditions.

Moscati was renowned for the way he cared for the afflicted with warmth and charity. He saw his medical practice as a ministry and often treated patients for free, and he was not shy about handing over cash along with a prescription in hopes of making a small difference in their lives. He truly believed that it was a doctor's duty to prioritize the needs of the patient in his career rather than to get caught up in the nepotism and bribery that often accompanied the medical profession at the time.

A lifelong bachelor, Moscati understood what it meant to be a lay Catholic with a mission to evangelize the world, in his case through medical care. In 1927, prior to his 47th birthday, Moscati passed away peacefully after attending Mass and making his rounds at the local hospital. He was canonized on October 25, 1987, by then Pope John Paul II after his intercession was credited with the cure of a young man who was dying of leukemia.

Though Catholic physicians are not uncommon, it is unique when someone with a medical degree from a modern university is canonized as a saint. It is even rarer when they have "office hours" when they listen to the needs of patients and refer their cases to the one who can heal the body, mind, and spirit—the true heavenly miracle worker, God.

The Least You Need to Know

- The Church of both/and suggests that two bodies of thought do not discount one another.
- The Church believes that science and theology, faith and works, Scripture and tradition help to compose a well-rounded Christian.
- A person with same-sex attraction (SSA) can be a practicing Catholic.
- Over the centuries, the Church has been and continues to be one of the strongest supporters of scientific research.

People and Places of the Church

The Catholic Church is composed of a diverse group of individuals and entities all committed to promoting the gospel message and the overall mission of the Body of Christ. There are subsections of the faith that comprise and intersect the hierarchal structure and include everything from the smallest family unit to the highest offices of the Vatican.

Each part of the Church is designed to serve as a microcosm of the universal faith within its parameters and uphold the beliefs and philosophies that have been the cornerstone of the religious institution Jesus founded over 2,000 years ago.

In this chapter, we will explore the various groups within the Church. From parishes to papal offices and everything in between, we will uncover the entities that serve as the foundations of faith for people throughout the global community.

In This Chapter

- Practicing the Catholic faith at home
- What is a Catholic parish?
- Catholic charitable organizations of the diocese
- The Vatican: the global headquarters of the faith

We Are Many Parts; We Are All One Body

As we learned in Chapter 4, every person has been created by God not only to serve an individual purpose, but also to contribute to the larger society. He calls all of us to a specific vocation and gives us the tools and talents we need to fulfill His purpose for our lives. No matter who we are, where we go, or what we do, we are compelled to live and spread the gospel message in everything we say and do.

The Catholic Church is truly a universal entity and one whose members can be found in all socioeconomic classes and in virtually every country throughout the world. No matter if they are laying the groundwork of faith in the domestic church; serving their local parishes, schools, and service organizations; working at the diocesan level; or serving as part of the global community of God, each member of the Church is just as important as the next. All have a role to play in the hierarchal structure. Each unit serves the overall mission and reflects the face of Christ to all who come into contact with it.

As an extension of Jesus Himself, the people and places of the Catholic Church prove that although we are many parts, we are all one Body of Christ.

The Domestic Church

Catholicism begins at home. Family plays an important role in God's overall plan of creation. It is an institution that should be promoted, strengthened, and supported. When God created man and woman, He did so knowing that they would not only draw each other closer to Him, but also that the result of their conjugal union would be the procreation of children raised to love and serve Him.

From the moment we are born, we are welcomed into a family unit where we join our mother, father, any siblings, and extended family members who have pledged to raise us in a secure, loving environment centered on Christ. It is in this environment, known as the *domestic church,* that the faith is shared and where we learn the values and principles we are expected to live by.

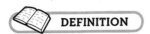 **DEFINITION**

The **domestic church** refers to the faith environment within the home.

When God sent His Son to live among us, He didn't arrive on a cloud as a fully grown deity ready to take over the world. He was delivered into a family where He was expected to grow, develop, and experience life as any other human child. Mary and Joseph not only modeled their

Jewish faith, they took Jesus to the synagogue and educated Him in the customs and traditions that were important to their culture. He was taught to obey the fourth commandment, to honor one's father and mother, and His parents committed to remain steadfast in their faith in order to model the lifestyle He was expected to adhere to as an adult.

In gratitude for their unconditional and unwavering love, Jesus not only respected their rules as a child but also ensured His widowed mother's security and well-being even as He was hanging on the cross:

> "When Jesus saw his mother and the disciple whom he loved standing beside her, he said to his mother, 'Woman, here is your son.' Then he said to the disciple, 'Here is your mother.' And from that hour, the disciple took her into his own home." (John 19:26-27)

By honoring His mother even at such a crucial hour, this act signifies the importance of the domestic church.

What Does a Catholic Home Look Like?

In terms of architectural structure, a Catholic home looks like any other residence, but it's built on a spiritual foundation that places God above everything and everybody. In a Catholic home, parents strive to love their children as God loves them. They all take the time to listen to the others' stories, champion each other's successes, and comfort one another during times of sorrow. It is a place where children are taught to respect their parents and to be grateful for the family God has given them. They are expected to follow the fourth commandment just as Jesus did not only through obedience and saying "please" and "thank you" when they are little, but also through understanding that honoring one another is a two-way street that doesn't end in adulthood.

The Christian home should resemble a miniature church and should be a place where family members strengthen each other's faith. Tradition says the father serves as the head of household with his wife as his beloved (and equal) spouse. Together, they strive to love one another and to educate their children in the faith so they can develop their own relationship with Christ.

CATHOLIC QUOTE

Children ought to receive two things from their parents: roots and wings.

—Johann Wolfgang von Goethe

Creating the Domestic Church

The Catholic home is a place where God comes first and family comes second. It is characterized by the customs and traditions that a family celebrates (especially the Mass and the sacraments), the service work in which the family participates, and the sacramental décor dotting the house.

Some of the most popular Catholic symbols found in the home include a Bible, a crucifix, dried palms from Palm Sunday, statues, blessed candles, a small advent wreath, a photo of the Holy Father, a rosary, and prayers printed and magnetized to the refrigerator.

Some of the ways a family can build up the domestic church include the following:

- Pray as a family and read Sacred Scripture on a daily basis.

- Pray a family rosary and include each other's intentions.

- Hang a crucifix in a prominent place to remind the family of Christ's sacrifice and to ward off evil. (Some families place one in every bedroom.)

- Attend Mass regularly and participate in the sacraments as a family (especially the Eucharist).

- Create family traditions based on liturgical seasons. (See Chapter 22 for more information on the liturgical year.)

- Plan vacations around shrines, churches, and other holy places. (Chapter 16 includes some suggestions.)

- Get involved in service work in order to teach children the value of stewardship and charity.

- Demonstrate your love for your spouse, as well as your children, and love them in the same way God loves them.

- Celebrate sacramental anniversaries, such as the anniversary of each family member's baptism.

- Welcome clergy members, consecrated religious, and members of the laity into the home in order to create vocational awareness in your children's hearts.

- Participate in the parish community by serving on committees, organizing events, fundraising, and welcoming new members to the Church.

The Local Church

When one thinks of the local Catholic community, chances are the *parish* church usually comes to mind. A parish is both a place and a group of people. It is the name for the local campus where Catholics attend Mass and participate in the sacraments, as well as the collection of people who worship at that place. It is the lowest subdivision of the Church governing structure and is the primary unit of a diocese that may be grouped with other parishes to form deaneries.

A parish is overseen by a bishop; administered by a priest (known as a pastor); and may include additional support personnel, such as other priests, deacons, a parish secretary, pastoral associates, and pastoral or parish councils. The grounds of the parish do not just contain the church building itself, but may also include administrative offices and auxiliary organizations, such as a school, rectory, convent, and parish center.

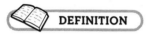 **DEFINITION**

> A **parish** is the name for the local Church structure where Catholics attend Mass and participate in the sacraments, as well as the group of people who gather there.

A Place to Fit In

Today's Catholics find their parish community in a variety of ways. Once upon a time, parish affiliation was largely determined by geography or nationality. Families moved into a neighborhood and registered at the nearest parish where they remained members until they moved or died. Or, if they were of a particular nationality, some parishes were erected to cater to specific ethnic groups, such as a Polish parish or an Irish parish.

Parish "boundaries" are put in place in order to gather a cross-section of a community's demographic and to ensure that no parish is overwhelmed (or underwhelmed) by its membership. However, today's Catholics tend to shop around and try out several parishes in order to find a place they can call home.

It's a little like buying a house. Some like the familiarity of the parish in which they grew up, while others look for a community that is the right size for their family and has the demographics and ministries that they may be looking for (for example, lots of young people or a parish school). The point being that even though parish boundaries still exist, Catholics don't always attend the nearest one. If a pastor allows one to register at a parish, he assumes the spiritual responsibility of that individual or family.

Ideally, a parish should have a good mix of individuals from a variety of backgrounds and talents. Like the family, the parish should serve as a microcosm of the church and offer its members the opportunity to participate in the life, mission, and work of the faith community. Some of the typical parish ministries and activities include the following:

- **Ladies and men's clubs:** These clubs help raise funds and sponsor parish-wide social events.

- **Youth and young adult ministries:** These ministries enable young Catholics to network and fellowship with other Catholics in their age group.

- **Prayer and rosary guilds:** These guilds convene to pray for specific intentions, as well as the parish and global Catholic community.

- **Catholic Youth Organization (CYO) groups and sports organizations:** These groups and organizations are designed to offer athletic and other opportunities for young people to participate in.

- **Religious education opportunities:** These include education for those in the RCIA program, faith formation for adults, and catechism classes for those who do not attend a parochial school.

- **Soup kitchens or food pantries:** Some parishes house ministries that serve the specific material needs of the poor in the community.

- **Parish festivals:** Festivals are usually one of the biggest fundraisers of the year. These include carnival games and, in some cases, midway-level rides.

- **Lenten fish fries:** These fundraisers combine food and fellowship during the Lenten season. (Cheese pizza is usually on the menu as well for those who do not like fish.)

- **Bingo/Monte Carlo nights:** These standard Catholic pastimes benefit the parish, as well as the individual winners.

- **Pancake breakfasts:** Another type of food fundraiser sponsored by any number of parish organizations, these can occur numerous times throughout the year.

The Four R's: Reading, 'Riting, 'Rithmetic, and Religion

When parents choose a Catholic education for their child, they do so knowing they are making an extraordinary sacrifice for their offspring. Unlike public education opportunities provided and funded by the government, parochial schools are primarily tuition-based institutions focused on educating the body, mind, and spirit of each child in their care.

Catholic schools enable children to explore their faith through daily religion classes, frequent opportunities to attend Mass, regular prayer services, and service projects in the local community. They are staffed by consecrated religious and lay teachers who share their faith, talents, and time with the community and are committed to seeing each student reach their full potential according to the social teaching of the Church.

FAST FACT

Not all students or teachers in a parochial school are Catholic; however, they are all people of faith who are willing to share their Christian values in order to build the future community of God.

Catholic schools recognize the parents and family members as the primary educators of an individual. Therefore, the faculty and staff of the school are committed to the following:

- Helping students understand they are a unique and special creation of God

- Teaching students how to play an important role in the family, Church, and society at large

- Encouraging parental involvement in the ongoing education of their children

- Creating a special bond between the students, domestic church, school, and parish in order to foster a strong sense of community

The Diocese

The *diocese* (or archdiocese) is the regional structure of the Catholic Church that encompasses several local parishes and Catholic organizations within a certain geographical area. Its size varies depending on the population, and it is led by a bishop, archbishop, or cardinal charged with teaching, governing, and blessing the faithful entrusted to his care.

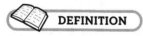

DEFINITION

A **diocese** is the regional Catholic structure led by a bishop, archbishop, or cardinal that oversees a number of parishes within a specific geographical region.

The central offices of the diocese include the administrative departments necessary to help the bishop execute his position faithfully and ensure the fair and equitable sharing of resources throughout the Catholic community, as well as cohesion among the various parish entities. Some of these offices include the following:

- **Education offices:** These departments may include Catholic schools, evangelization, religious education, and faith formation opportunities for all ages.

- **Catholic charities:** These charities coordinate the social service ministries of the local Church and various ways of outreach to the local community.

- **Office of Worship and Spiritual Life:** This office promotes the celebration of the liturgy and sacraments, as well as spiritual renewal programs, such as retreats and pilgrimages.

- **Vocations office:** This office promotes vocations to the priesthood and religious life and coordinates the education and formation of seminarians preparing for the priesthood.

- **Communications department:** This is comprised of diocesan media relations, including print, online, and broadcast communications and services.

- **Finance and administrative services:** These are charged with the responsible accounting of diocesan funds to promote generous sharing and responsible use of all human and material resources.

- **Multicultural ministry offices:** These offices honor and respect the cultural heritage of Catholics in the diocese, with many dioceses placing a particular emphasis on Hispanic ministry.

- **Tribunal:** This group is charged with helping the bishop execute his judicial responsibilities in accordance with the Code of Canon Law.

- **Pro-life and family life offices:** These offices promote Church teachings on the dignity of human life and support and strengthen families through marriage preparation, enrichment, and family-based ministries.

Other Local Entities

If you think the local Catholic community begins and ends at the parish or diocesan offices, you would be mistaken. There are a host of other entities affiliated with the Church that work tirelessly to promote the overall Catholic mission and serve the community at large. These include Catholic colleges and universities, hospital and health care facilities, and service organizations, among others.

Catholic colleges and universities are some of the oldest academic institutions in the world. Many of these are sponsored by a religious congregation or a diocese and are committed to the advancement of scholars from all walks of life. Throughout history, these institutions have worked tirelessly to inspire their students and serve the larger community. They continue to be leaders in the field of education and never shy away from moving with the times, employing new technology in the classroom, and adjusting to meet the needs of the students through traditional classroom settings, as well as alternative formats.

Catholic hospital and health care facilities are so ingrained into the local community that few people ever think about the fact that they are Catholic institutions. The Catholic health care industry includes everything from full hospital campuses to surgery centers, clinics (in the field, as well as traditional brick and mortar facilities), nursing homes, senior living communities, home health care services, hospice units, and more.

These institutions are unique in the fact that they have a responsibility to not only the Church but also the wider community they serve. Employees are expected to maintain ethical professional standards while caring for the sick in accordance with the gospel, as well as the moral teachings of the Church. They are to adhere to and uphold the religious mission of the institution and promote the entity's commitment to the dignity of the individual and to the common good.

There are a number of Catholic charities and service organizations that serve the needs of the less fortunate on the national and international level. One of the biggest in the United States is Catholic Charities USA, which has offices at the diocesan and national level and partners with local service agencies to meet the needs of the poor and underserved. These needs may include housing, food, basic necessities, employment, and disaster relief.

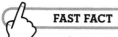

FAST FACT

The Knights of Columbus is an international Catholic men's organization founded by Father Michael McGivney in 1882. They operate through local councils throughout the world and focus on four core principles: charity, unity, fraternity, and patriotism. The Knights give extraordinary amounts of time and money to charitable organizations and work to support vocations, the pro-life movement, and the ministries of local parishes. Most Knights of Columbus councils have their own council hall that is used for meetings, events, and meals and is available for rent for large gatherings.

Catholic Relief Services (CRS) works with the United States Conference of Catholic Bishops (USCCB) to assist the poor and vulnerable in other parts of the world. One of the ministries they are most well known for is Operation Rice Bowl during Lent, which encourages the donation of spare change to help relieve hunger all over the world.

The Society of St. Vincent de Paul offers tangible assistance to those in need on a person-to-person basis. Through local councils based in parishes, the society operates a myriad of programs and services, including food programs, emergency financial services, transportation, disaster relief, low-cost housing and homeless shelters, thrift stores, counseling services, social justice programs, and more.

The Gabriel Project is an organization in which parish women provide crisis pregnancy support for expectant mothers. They help these women not only with their gift of friendship, but by helping to coordinate their transportation to medical appointments, making sure they eat properly, meeting their material needs, and helping them to prepare for a new life. The local parish also provides pastoral care if it is asked for as well.

The Global Catholic Community

As you may have guessed, the global headquarters of the Catholic Church are located in Vatican City, the small, independent sovereignty situated in the heart of Rome, Italy. It is home to the Holy See, the religious organization that governs the city-state through the papal offices and the *Roman Curia*.

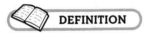 **DEFINITION**

The **Roman Curia** is the administrative body of the Holy See and through which the pope governs the Catholic Church.

Vatican City is more than a popular tourist destination known for its religious significance, rich history, and collections of priceless artwork and writings. It is a fully functioning country of 900 whose infrastructure includes a police force, a newspaper, a bank, a post office, retail stores, a telephone system, a radio station, a soup kitchen for the poor, and a heliport. It employs 2,000 people, and its citizenry is made up almost exclusively of clergy and Swiss Guard, the official bodyguards of the pontiff.

The Vatican is unlike any other place on Earth. It is a country where there is no separation of Church and state. The Holy See not only has the responsibility of overseeing the spiritual lives of more than 1 billion people, but it also must maintain diplomatic relations with countries all over the world and participate in a number of geopolitical organizations both as a permanent observer (the only other nation with this status being Palestine) and as a full member.

The Roman Curia

The Roman Curia oversees the day-to-day operations of the Church and is charged with helping the pope execute his office faithfully and assisting in his worldwide spiritual mission to promote human rights, interreligious understanding, peace and conflict prevention, development, and environmental protection. It is the people who work in these buildings and departments that give the universal Church its soul.

While we discussed the pope's duties in Chapter 4, the Secretariat of the State is one of the Vatican's most senior positions after the pontiff. He is responsible for all diplomatic and political functions of the Holy See. Until recently, this office was the only secretariat in the curia, but in 2014, Pope Francis established a new office called the Secretariat for the Economy that is designed to exercise authority over all economic concerns within the Vatican City State.

The Congregations

Nine congregations serve as the central administrative organization for the Catholic Church. A prefect, who is also a cardinal, leads each congregation, which includes the following:

- **The Congregation for the Doctrine of the Faith:** Ensures the unity of the Church's teachings on faith and morals.

- **The Congregation for the Oriental Churches:** Oversees the life and ministry of the various Eastern Catholic Churches.

- **The Congregation for Divine Worship and the Discipline of the Sacraments:** Promotes the correct celebration of the liturgy and sacraments, including ensuring accurate translations of various liturgical texts into different languages.

- **The Congregation for the Causes of Saints:** Coordinates the process leading to possible canonization of saints.

- **The Congregation for the Evangelization of Peoples:** Oversees the work of spreading the gospel throughout the world, especially in missionary areas.

- **The Congregation for the Clergy:** Ensures adequate training and formation for clergy and regulates policies for the life and ministry of priests and deacons.

- **The Congregation for Institutes of Consecrated Life and Societies of Apostolic Life:** Promotes and supervises the various religious orders in the Church.

- **The Congregation for Catholic Education:** Has oversight over Catholic schools and universities throughout the world.

- **The Congregation for Bishops:** Serves as a resource for bishops in their administration of dioceses and makes recommendations to the Holy Father for the appointment of bishops.

The Tribunals

The tribunals are the judiciary arm of the Holy See whose job it is to oversee the proper execution of the Code of Canon Law. The tribunals are comprised of:

- **The Apostolic Penitentiary:** This is responsible for the forgiveness of sins reserved to the Holy See.

- **The Supreme Tribunal of the Apostolic Signatura:** This is the highest judicial authority in the Church after the pope.

- **The Tribunal of the Roman Rota:** This is the appellate "court" of the Roman Curia and fosters unity of jurisprudence within its own area, as well as assisting other tribunals.

 CATHOLIC QUOTE

It often happens that I wake up at night and begin to think about a serious problem and decide I must tell the Pope about it. Then I wake up completely and remember that I am the Pope.

—St. Pope John XXIII

The Synod of Bishops

Formed during the Second Vatican Council, the Synod of Bishops is the pope's advisory council. It is made up of a cross-section of bishops from around the world and assists the pontiff by expressing its opinions on matters when he asks. The Synod does not make any formal decrees or resolution, and its agenda, members, and existence is at the sole discretion of the pope.

Meetings of the Synod of Bishops are held on a regular basis and are always on a particular theme of importance to the mission of the Church. Recent Synods have been on the family, the Church in the Middle East, the Eucharist, the Word of God, and the formation of priests. Following the meetings of the Synod, the Holy Father typically writes a summary document based on the discussions, called an *Apostolic Exhortation,* that is sent to Catholics throughout the world.

The Offices of the Roman Curia

The offices of the Holy See help coordinate the various ministries of the worldwide Church, as well as advise the Holy Father on particular areas of study:

- **Pontifical councils:** These advise the pope on such issues as culture, interreligious dialogue, social communications, and the family.

- **Pontifical commissions:** These assist in the governance of Vatican City State and oversee the preservation of the cultural and archeological heritage of the Church.

- **Pontifical academies:** These are more research-based organizations that bring Catholic teaching to such areas as science, fine arts, and the social sciences.

- **Prefecture for the economic affairs of the Holy See:** This oversees all of the offices of the Vatican that deal with financial issues. It balances the accounts and establishes a budget for the other departments and publishes an annual report.

Though it sounds like a lot of bureaucracy, the offices of the Holy See are at the service of the bishops and dioceses of the world and help to coordinate the complexities of a worldwide organization. They have undergone significant change as the church and the world have changed in order to best serve current needs, and the pope and bishops regularly assess the organizational structure of the Roman Curia to be sure it is effective and a good use of resources.

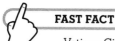

FAST FACT

Vatican City is the only place in the world that has an ATM machine with instructions in Latin.

The Swiss Guard

If you have ever visited the Vatican for a papal audience or Mass, chances are you've seen the Swiss Guard. They are kind of hard to miss. They are the pope's bodyguards bedecked in colorful uniforms designed by Michelangelo who have sworn to protect the pontiff even if it costs them their life.

In order to qualify for this Secret Service—level department, which is the smallest military force in the world, one must be a citizen of Switzerland, Catholic, and at least 5'8" in height. Although their Renaissance-style uniforms do not seem particularly menacing, make no mistake—these men have endured rigorous training and are proficient in all manner of combat. Along with the Vatican police department, they make up the nation's security detail.

The Least You Need to Know

- The home should serve as a miniature church, with celebrations reflecting the liturgical year.
- The parish is not only the local Catholic Church building but the people who worship there as well.

- The diocese is the regional epicenter of the Catholic community, with offices that oversee activities at the parish level.
- Vatican City is home to the Holy See and the Roman Curia, which governs the sovereignty and oversees the activities of the global Catholic community.

The Role of Beauty
in Catholicism

They are the works in which the terrestrial meet the transcendent—the paintings and sculptures synonymous with the Catholic faith, the notes that sing a new song unto the Lord, and the words that inspire the icons that draw thousands of people to the Church every year. They are the sacred arts.

The sacred arts go hand-in-hand with Catholicism. They are inspired works that showcase not only the beauty found in this world thanks to God's creation, but also give hope for all that God promises in the next.

In this chapter, we will explore the role of beauty in the Catholic Church and how these sacred arts reinforce the traditions of the faithful. We will highlight some of the most well-known pieces of art, music, and literature in the world and talk a little about the people who created them.

In This Chapter

- The masters of the visual arts
- The most famous works of Christian art
- When you sing, you pray twice
- Catholic authors who inspire the secular world

What Makes Art Sacred?

The sacred arts consist of any medium in which an artist uses his or her God-given talent to create works inspired by faith and designed to uplift those who experience them. They can take the form of iconography, two-dimensional and three-dimensional artwork, architecture, musical compositions, literary compositions, and more.

Sacred art is not something that is uniquely Christian. In fact, sacred art predates Christianity by quite a bit. The first mention of art in the Bible can be found in Exodus 31, when God instructs Moses to build a tent for the Ark of the Covenant and even commissions specific artisans to complete the project:

> "See, I have called by name Bezalel son of Uri son of Hur, of the tribe of Judah: and I have filled him with divine spirit, with ability, intelligence, and knowledge in every kind of craft, to devise artistic designs, to work in gold, silver and bronze in crafting stones for setting, and in carving wood in every kind of craft. Moreover, I have appointed with him Oholiah, son of Abisamach, of the tribe of Dan; and I have given skill to all the skillful, so that they may make all that I command you …."
> (Exodus 31:1-6)

Later, in 1 Kings, Solomon builds his great temple to the Lord, which measured 60 cubits long, 20 cubits wide, and 30 cubits high. So sacred was this piece of architecture that all of the materials used in its construction were "finished at the quarry so that neither hammer, nor ax, nor any tool of iron was heard in the temple while it was being built." (1 Kings 6:7) The designs included in Solomon's temple, including its famous columns, were so special that they continued to inspire artisans throughout the centuries and are still found in modern architecture.

The Book of Psalms, written by a number of authors, including King David, are a collection of 150 songs that evoke lament, thanksgiving, praise, adoration, blessing, anger, repentance, and more. Their lyrics have been used in countless compositions and are incorporated into several Catholic rites and liturgies. The most famous is Psalm 23, David's ode to the Divine Shepherd.

Throughout the Old Testament, we hear about those who have been called to serve as weavers, engravers, stonecutters, carpenters, and sculptors. We hear about musicians like King David who are called to glorify the Lord. In the New Testament, Jesus is born into a craftsman's household, and no doubt, Joseph took pride in his work, offering it up to the Lord. No matter what talent an artist has received, they know that it comes from God and must be returned to him in some way. After all, "we are the clay, and you are our potter, we are all the work of your hand." (Isaiah 64:8)

Visual Arts

Christian art is more than a pious picture used to accent the home or a church. It is a particular form of visual art containing images created by a person of prayer and designed to connect the viewer to the sacred in a deep and meaningful way.

Church tradition tells us that St. Luke was in fact the founder of Christian art when he painted a portrait of the Virgin Mary on a panel after spending time with the Blessed Mother during his travels. He is said to have painted images of both St. Peter and St. Paul as well. Other early Christian art was found on the walls of the catacombs, the burial grounds of the early Christians. In these images, Christ is depicted symbolically as the Ichthys (fish), peacock, lamb, or anchor.

By the third century, there is a definite image of Christ healing the paralytic found in the Syrian city Dura Europos, though it looks nothing like the traditional long-haired, bearded image we normally associate with Him. Around the same time, an image of Jesus as the Good Shepherd appears in a catacomb rendering, gathering His lambs to Him, though He is still clean shaven and sporting a short 'do.

KEEP IT SIMPLE

The definitive "look" of Jesus is partially inspired by the Shroud of Turin, a piece of linen fabric that many believe to be His burial cloth. The origins of the shroud remain a mystery, but experts agree that the image contained within the cloth show a long-haired, bearded man who has injuries consistent with crucifixion. We know that Joseph of Arimathea wrapped Jesus' body in linen and that Peter found multiple pieces of the cloth lying in the tomb after the resurrection.

Types of Images

In the early days, Christian art was used to convey deep theological concepts in an easy-to-understand way. Often, converts to the Christian faith could not read but could understand the imagery contained in a visual form in art.

Images of Mary with and without the Christ Child became popular in the Christian East, along with the image of Christ the Pantocrator (almighty). In the West, standard images of the saints emerged that gave each individual a common appearance (to represent what they may look like in heaven) along with the specific symbols that defined their earthly life.

It is not surprising that Christian art has not always been looked upon favorably. In the seventh and eighth centuries, the iconoclasts (image smashers) viewed the images as heretical and were determined to destroy them, since they dared to venerate humans or depict God Himself. Art supporters defended the place of sacred art in the Church and ultimately it was upheld.

Sacred Symbolism

As Christian art grew in popularity and acceptance, so, too, did the number of objects, animals, colors, and symbols used within the iconic images. We know that a halo denotes someone who is holy—usually a canonized saint—while wings on a human form indicate an angelic presence. We know that the Alpha and Omega symbols of the Greek alphabet represent God, the beginning, and the end; the cross, lamb, and fish continue to represent Jesus Christ; and the dove is almost exclusively used to evoke the Holy Spirit. Martyrs are often depicted with the instrument of their death, such as St. Paul being shown with the sword with which he was beheaded. The color blue is often affiliated with the Blessed Virgin Mary, and the presence of keys on a statue or painting distinguishes St. Peter from the other 11 apostles.

What were originally designed to be simple pieces of artwork developed into a sophisticated system that included several layers of meaning. Artists often hid their personal convictions or ironic statements in seemingly innocuous paintings that were only discovered later. Robert Campin's Mérode Altarpiece of 1425–1428, for example, has a highly complex iconography that is still debated. Although on its surface it is a simple depiction of the Annunciation while Joseph labors in his workshop, art experts wonder if Joseph's construction of a mousetrap is a symbolic reference to a remark of St. Augustine that Christ's incarnation was a trap to catch men's souls.

 CATHOLIC QUOTE

Where the spirit does not work with the hand, there is no art.

—Leonardo da Vinci

Another image whose meaning has been debated in recent years thanks to novelist Dan Brown is Leonardo da Vinci's *Last Supper* (1498). Da Vinci's fresco is dense with symbolic references, with a number of attributes that identify each apostle. Judas Iscariot not only reaches for the plate at the same time as Jesus, but he is also clutching the pouch containing his reward for the betrayal. St. Peter is holding a knife, foreshadowing his act of violence against a soldier that will occur later in the evening. The apostles are arranged in four groups of three, the three windows denote the Holy Trinity, and even the majestic landscape behind Christ suggests that the only way to get to this paradise is through Him.

This kind of sacred art is still an important element in the Church today. These images can be found on a number of religious articles that enable Catholics to proclaim their faith and give them a visual upon which to meditate. Modern artists continue to use a variety of media to create works that connect the image and the viewer on an ethereal level and to couple various elements to create a piece that serves both as a devotional image, as well as a work of art.

Catholic Artists

The Catholic Church is home to a wide variety of paintings, sculptures, mosaics, metalworks, textiles, and even architecture created by artists who are as diverse as the media in which they worked. Throughout history, it seems that every prominent name in the art world has been affiliated with the Catholic Church. Some notable artists affiliated with the Catholic Church include Giotto (1266–1337), Donatello (1386–1466), Fra Angelico (1395–1455), Raphael Sanzio (1483–1520), Salvador Dalí (1904–1989), and Moira Forsyth (1905–1991). However, when it comes to Catholic artists, two masters stand above all others: Michelangelo and Gian Lorenzo Bernini.

Michelangelo (1475–1564)

Born Michelangelo di Lodovico Buonarroti Simoni in Florence, Italy, "Michelangelo" was a true Renaissance man whose work spanned the fields of sculpting, painting, architecture, poetry, and engineering. He is not only considered to be one of greatest artists of all time, but is also a worthy rival of the multi-talented Leonardo da Vinci whose work is considered to be among the most well known in the world.

Michelangelo was responsible for sculptures such as the *Pietà* (1497) and *David* (1504), which were created prior to his thirtieth birthday, as well as *Moses* (1516). His portfolio also includes two of the most influential frescoes in Western Art, both found in the Sistine Chapel: the ceiling and *The Last Judgment*.

The Sistine Chapel project was one Michelangelo would have like to have turned down. It was too big in scale, fresco was not his favorite medium, and what Pope Julius II proposed initially was not nearly as grand. However, Michelangelo convinced the pope to give him a free hand and let him create the 5,000-square-foot masterpiece on the ceiling that includes nine stories from the Book of Genesis, the ancestors of Jesus, and images of the prophets.

 CATHOLIC QUOTE

A man paints with his brains and not with his hands.

—Michelangelo

The Last Judgment spans the entire wall behind the chapel altar and depicts the second coming of Christ, in which the souls of all humanity are judged and sent to their eternal dwelling place. The image is a majestic and haunting one designed to instill fear and awe of God's power to all who look upon it, but the overall composition rankled some people at the Vatican when they saw how many nude bodies were included in such a sacred place. There was talk that the painting should be removed, but ultimately the piece remained (though the majority of genitalia were covered by painted loincloths in the sixteenth century, many of which were removed in a major restoration in the 1990s).

Michelangelo's work with the Church continued, and in 1547, he agreed to oversee the construction of St. Peter's Basilica, which was begun by Donato Bramante and included intermediate designs from a number of well-known architects (including Raphael). Among Michelangelo's contributions to the massive project was the design of the dome, which was completed after his death by his student Giacomo della Porta in 1590. The dome has an interior diameter of 42.56 meters and measures 136.57 meters from its base to the top of the cross, and the lantern is 17 meters tall. The dome of St. Peter's eventually became the model for a number of domes throughout the western world, including St. Paul's in London, Les Invalides in Paris, and the U.S. Capitol building in Washington, DC.

Gian Lorenzo Bernini (1598–1680)

Gian Lorenzo Bernini was a worthy successor of Michelangelo who was not only a fellow Italian, but also a skilled sculptor and architect as well. One of his early patrons was Cardinal Scipione Borghese, who was a nephew of Pope Paul V. Bernini rose to prominence as a sculptor thanks to several important pieces he completed between 1619 and 1625: *Aeneas, Anchises, and Ascanius; The Rape of Proserpina; Apollo and Daphne;* and *David*. In 1629, he was appointed to be the chief architect on St. Peter's Basilica by Pope Urban VIII.

Bernini's first contribution to the basilica was the baldacchino, the four-pillared spiraled bronze canopy that rises above the tomb of Saint Peter at the center of the church. Designed after the columns from Solomon's Temple in the Old Testament, the baldacchino reaches 30 meters in height and is accented with gilded olive and laurel branches, statues on each corner, and crowned with an opulent gold sphere and cross. The bees found on the baldacchino are symbols of the Barberini family of Pope Urban VIII. A gold dove on the inside of the canopy denotes the Holy Spirit.

KEEP IT SIMPLE

Bernini's sculptures within St. Peter's Basilica include the statue of St. Augustine, the Altar Cross, the statue of Saint Longinus, and the tombs of Pope Urban VIII and Pope Alexander VII.

In 1656, Pope Alexander VII commissioned Bernini to design the piazza leading into St. Peter's Basilica. Bernini wanted the unstructured square to look as though it were opening its arms in an embrace, so he created two huge elliptical colonnades that extend the majesty of the basilica, showcase the beauty of the Vatican, and serve as an iconic piece of architecture symbolically reaching out to the whole world.

Over the years, Bernini made a number of additions to St. Peter's Basilica that exist to this day, including the renovation on the symbolic "throne" of St. Peter to match the opulence of the baldacchino. He also designed the papal stairway between St. Peter's Basilica and the Vatican Palace. Although the latter project was considerably less extravagant, it was an architectural nightmare considering the two odd shapes of the buildings.

Bernini, like other artists, later fell from favor as new artists came into vogue, but in the nineteenth century, he was once again regarded for his achievements and has become known as the preeminent baroque sculptor and architect of the seventeenth century.

Music

Music has been part of the Christian tradition since the night of the Last Supper when Jesus sang hymns with His friends prior to heading out to the Mount of Olives to await His fate. While it is unclear as to when music segued from its Judaic roots into more Christian-based tunes, we do know that St. Paul pushed the genre forward when he encouraged the Ephesians and Colossians to use the Psalms and other spiritual hymns in their church services. Typically, Catholic "music" is divided into four categories: chant, music for the Mass, carols, and hymns.

Gregorian Chant

The earliest and most revered is Gregorian chant (named for St. Pope Gregory the Great), which developed in the ninth and tenth centuries as an *a cappella* single-tune melody sung in monastery and convent chapels before being incorporated into liturgical celebrations throughout the Christian West.

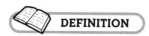 **DEFINITION**

> The term **a cappella**, literally meaning "from the chapel," refers to unaccompanied singing. It comes from the type of chant that was sung by the Sistine Chapel Choir—unaccompanied Gregorian chant.

Originally, the music was taught orally, before written notation came into prominence in the twelfth and thirteenth centuries. A rich treasury of chants were written through the centuries for both the Proper Texts of the Mass, which varied depending on the liturgical season or feast being celebrated, and the Ordinary Texts, which are consistent at every Mass. These texts were originally all in Latin, but in recent years, many of them have been translated into vernacular languages and are now sung either in Latin or the spoken language of the people.

Gregorian chant also includes the chants of the Liturgy of the Hours, which are primarily antiphons used to frame the singing of the Psalms, as well as chant tones for the Psalms themselves. Night Prayer, the final daily prayer in the Liturgy of the Hours, was closed with one of four Marian Antiphons, which were written in the eleventh century and continue to be sung today.

Mass: The Musical

Beginning in the fourteenth century, composers began creating polyphonic versions of the Ordinary of the Mass, which added harmonies to the plain tunes of Gregorian chant. These continued to be sung *a cappella,* but eventually more and more instrumentation was incorporated. Some of the later Masses that were written were so over the top, they were rarely used during an actual Mass.

The *Requiem Mass* evolved as a modified version of the ordinary Mass. A number of notable musicians contributed to this variation of liturgical music during the Baroque, Romantic, and Classical eras, including Johannes Brahms, Giuseppe Verdi, Wolfgang Amadeus Mozart, Ludwig van Beethoven, and Franz Joseph Haydn, who often turned to his rosary whenever he was composing or suffering from writer's block. Haydn was also known for beginning each manuscript of his compositions with "in nomine Domini" ("in the name of the Lord") and ending them with "Laus Deo" ("praise be to God").

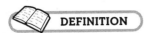 **DEFINITION**

A **Requiem Mass** is a Mass for the dead and is sung for the repose of the soul of the deceased.

Carols

Carols are festive songs that are religious; however, they are not always connected with the liturgy. They were often sung communally at harvest time, as well as the holidays, and while the tradition of the Christmas carol dates to the thirteenth century, they were not sung in church nor relegated to the holiday season until much later. Some of the most notable carols sung in the Catholic Church include the following:

- **"Lo How a Rose e're Blooming":** This German Christmas carol and Marian hymn comes from an unknown author in the sixteenth century.

- **"Angels from the Realms of Glory"**: Sung to a variety of tunes, the text was written by Scottish poet James Montgomery.

- **"Bring a Torch, Jeanette, Isabella"**: Originating in the sixteenth century from the Provence region of France, this carol is attributed to Marc-Antoine Charpentier.

- **"O Come, All Ye Faithful"** (**Adeste Fideles**): One of the most well-known carols has unknown origins, but it was translated into English by Father Frederick Oakeley in 1841.

- **"Infant Holy, Infant Lowly"**: Showing that carols come from a variety of cultures, this one comes from Poland.

- **"Silent Night"**: The world's most famous Christmas carol was written in a small village in Austria in 1818 by parish priest Father Joseph Mohr and his church organist, Franz Xaver Gruber.

- **"O Holy Night"**: This was composed in 1847 by Adolphe Adam using the text of a French poem "Midnight Christians" by Placide Cappeau.

- **"Angels We Have Heard on High"**: French in origin, this anonymous carol was translated into English by Roman Catholic Bishop James Chadwick in 1862.

- **"Gesù Bambino"**: This Italian carol was composed in 1917 by Pietro Yon, a former organist at the Vatican.

Hymns

The first mention of Christian hymns outside of the Bible occurred in AD 370 by St. Basil the Great, who notes the Greek Hymn "Hail Gladdening Light" in his writings. It is believed that Latin hymns appeared around the same time and were heavily influenced by the poetic writings of St. Ambrose of Milan. By the fourth century, the poet Prudentius became one of the most well-known hymn writers, followed by the early Celtic hymns affiliated with St. Patrick and St. Columba. Prudentius wrote one of the oldest hymns still sung today: "Of the Father's Love Begotten."

The Protestant Reformation had a big impact on Christian music, especially hymns. Some groups, such as the Zwinglians, Calvanists, and other radical reformers, felt that sacred music had no real place in the worship service and should be eliminated, while a contrasting Reformation approach caused a burst of creative energy that resulted in a wealth of hymns and congregational singing.

In Catholicism, hymns continue to play an important role in Church celebrations, whether calling the faithful to assembly, proclaiming the Word of God, or sending people forth with song. While the genre continues to grow through current composers, here are a few of some of the most well-known and best-loved Catholic hymns:

- **"Ave Maria":** Franz Schubert set the Latin text of the "Hail, Mary" to music as part of his Opus 52, seven songs based on Walter Scott's epic poem "Lady of the Lake."

- **"Holy God We Praise Thy Name":** Attributed to Father Ignaz Franz, this eighteenth-century German hymn is based on the text of the *Te Deum* from the Liturgy of the Hours.

- **"To Jesus Christ Our Sov'reign King":** Sung usually during the Feast of Christ the King, this relatively modern hymn was written by Monsignor Martin Hellreigel in 1941.

- **"Hail, Holy Queen Enthroned Above":** A poetic translation of the "Salve Regina" from the Liturgy of the Hours, it is one of the most popular hymns honoring the Blessed Virgin Mary.

- **"Jesus Christ Is Risen Today":** Based on a fourteenth-century Latin text by an unknown author, this hymn celebrates the resurrection of Jesus.

Literature

When we think of Catholic writers, it is tempting to think only of those whose works focus primarily on the faith, Church tradition, and prayer. But there are many Catholic authors who have used their God-given talents to inspire not only the sacred but the secular world as well.

Dante Alighieri (1265–1321)

Best known for the *Divine Comedy,* Dante Alighieri was born in 1265 to a family embroiled in the complicated political scene of Florence. His mother died early in his childhood, he was arranged to marry the daughter of a family friend, and he was in love with a woman who didn't love him back.

By 1290, Dante became involved in the study of philosophy, as well as the tumultuous world of Florentine politics. He held a number of important posts, but in 1302, he fell out of favor and was exiled from the city. His banishment enabled him to travel and gave birth to his most productive artistic period.

His *Divine Comedy* is an allegory of human life and what comes after. It is an epic poem told from his perspective as he is led through the various levels of Hell, Purgatory, and Heaven. More than being a classic piece of literature, it is a very Catholic poem, embodying the beliefs and symbols of Catholicism throughout the text. In the centuries that have followed, the *Divine Comedy* is considered to be a major contribution to literature and has influenced writers such as T. S. Eliot.

J. R. R. Tolkien (1892–1973)

The creator of Middle Earth, the shire of the Hobbits, and a dragon named Smaug, J. R. R. Tolkien was indeed the Lord of the Rings. Born in 1892 in Bloemfontein, South Africa, but raised in the Warwickshire countryside in England, "John" Tolkien's upbringing was pleasant despite the fact that his parents both died when he was quite young and his care was entrusted to a Catholic priest. He was an excellent scholar who initially lost out on a grant to study at Oxford due to the fact that he fell in love with his childhood sweetheart and wanted to marry her.

The priest forbade this union until Tolkien was 21 and the separation was a fortuitous one, as it enabled him to study the classics and English literature at Exeter College at Oxford a year later. When World War I broke out, Tolkien enlisted, seeing the effects of the "great war" up close and losing many of his close friends. Though he rarely talked about it, no doubt his combat experiences influenced his later works.

In 1917, he began work on the *Silmarillion*, a history of a fictional universe that Tolkien revised until his death in 1973. He also became involved in teaching and spent much of his time in classrooms and lecture halls. In 1930, he had the inspiration to write an original fairy tale called *The Hobbit*. His friend C. S. Lewis read the manuscript and encouraged Tolkien to publish it. Needless to say, *The Hobbit* became a huge success. Eventually, the publisher requested a sequel, but Tolkien was already hard at work on an epic story that would become his crowning achievement—*The Lord of the Rings*, which was published in 1954.

Although the fantasy genre of his books might be deceiving, Tolkien viewed *The Lord of the Rings* as a fundamentally Catholic work. His works are imbued with symbols and themes that come from his beloved Catholic faith, including the Eucharist, the Blessed Virgin Mary, sacrificial love, courage, and the everlasting struggle between good and evil. Tolkien died in 1973, but the books he wrote have remained well loved and are considered to be some of the finest examples of modern literature.

The Least You Need to Know

- The sacred arts consist of a number of visual art forms, as well as music and literature.
- Two of the masters who contributed visual art pieces associated with the Catholic Church are Michelangelo and Bernini.
- The earliest known "Catholic" music was Gregorian chant.
- Authors such as Dante Alighieri and J. R. R. Tolkien have incorporated their faith into their popular secular writings.

Catholic Practices

Catholicism is full of distinct practices that may seem strange and unfamiliar. In addition to its unique infrastructure, scriptural texts, liturgical celebrations, and prayers, there are a number of Catholic activities that can seem superstitious to the uninitiated.

If you've ever wondered why Catholics light candles, pray before "graven images," wear ashes, or avoid meat on Fridays during Lent, then this chapter is for you! Here you will learn what Catholics do, and more importantly, why they do it.

In this chapter, we will explore the everyday practices that take religion off the page and help Catholics experience their faith on a sensory level. You will find out the answers to questions like these: What is the big deal about blessings? What is really in holy water? What on earth is that *smell?* We will also go behind the scenes of the head-turning prayer ritual immortalized by Hollywood and misunderstood by the general public: the exorcism.

In This Chapter

* Sacramentals help Catholics experience their faith
* Light a candle to offer your intention to the Lord
* Do Catholics really worship statues?
* What are the Works of Mercy?
* What happens during an exorcism

Common Sacramentals

Sacramentals are a myriad of tangible and intangible items that Catholics use to take the faith to the next level. They are reminders of what the Catholic faith tradition is all about. However, those who see these things as something akin to "superstitious voodoo" misunderstand them. So let's take a moment to learn a little more about these items that embellish the official liturgies of the Church and weave the faith into a Catholic's daily life. Sacramentals can include the following:

- Blessings

- Candles

- Religious articles, such as rosaries, chaplets, scapulars, and so on

- Statues

- Holy water

- Relics

Bless You

Christians are no strangers to blessings. They are the sacramentals that enable us to receive God's grace and help us to be more like Him. Blessings are usually comprised of prayer, a Scripture reading, and a visible or tangible sign when given in a formal way by a priest or other ordained member of the clergy. But they also can be as simple as a prayer before a meal or making the Sign of the Cross on an individual.

Catholics often rely on a book of Catholic Household Blessings and Prayers to help them do the following:

- Pray for family members

- Invoke God's blessing on household sacramentals, such as the advent wreath, nativity scene, candles, and holiday meals

- Lead grace before and after meals

- Bless the home before or after a move and in times of trouble

When it comes to blessing more significant objects or people for a particular purposes, Catholics will often call a priest to lead them in the rite of blessing. There are prescribed Scripture readings and prayers for any variety of blessings, including the blessing of a new car, the blessing of a new home, the blessing of fields before planting time, the blessing of travelers and pilgrims, and the blessing of married couples on the anniversary of marriage. God's presence extends far beyond church buildings, and the practice of blessings is a reminder of that presence.

This Little Light of Mine

Candles give Catholics a warm glow (pun intended), and there is no shortage of them in the church. In Catholic sanctuaries, there is the sanctuary lamp that is always lit to denote Christ's presence, as well as altar candles, the Paschal Candle, which is lit at Easter and is part of the Baptism ritual, and a variety of votive candles placed in holders before statues of the saints. Candles are also used in various sacramental rites and in the home.

The custom of lighting candles dates back to the early days of Christianity. Not only do candles represent Christ's light shining in the darkness of the world, but they were also used to keep vigil at the tombs of the martyrs as a way to maintain solidarity with those who have gone before them. This is no different than cultures that burn incense in tribute to past generations as part of their prayer life or those who leave candles at a place of significance, such as Ground Zero in New York after 9/11 or Kensington Gardens after the death of Princess Diana in 1997. Catholics like to let their little lights shine to accompany a prayer or to remember a significant person or event.

> **CATHOLIC QUOTE**
>
> The putting on of vestments and lighting candles, it's a wonderful ritual that never changes from one Mass to another.
>
> —Liam Neeson

Usually, there is a small collection box near the candleholders for those who want to help the parish replenish the supply; however, it is a donation, not an obligation. Even if you have no money, you are invited to light a candle and offer up your petition to God directly or ask for intercession from the saint whose image stands before you.

Saints and Statues

Statues are to Catholicism as peanut butter is to jelly, but few people truly understand the significance of them. Statues are religious images placed wherever Catholics want a reminder of their faith. They are not only found in church buildings but are often located in Catholic homes, gardens, and classrooms and even on car dashboards.

The most obvious Catholic three-dimensional image is the *crucifix*. A crucifix is more than the bare cross found in other Christian churches. A crucifix is a cross with the body of Christ affixed to it as He might have appeared during His execution. It is a graphic image that some find a little jarring; however, Catholics believe it is important to "proclaim Christ crucified" (1 Corinthians 1:23) and feel that a bare cross is an incomplete picture.

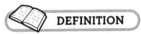 **DEFINITION**

A **crucifix** is a religious image that depicts Jesus' execution. It includes the cross, as well as the body of Christ upon it.

Catholics take great comfort in the crucifix. Its presence does the following:

- Helps Catholics adore Christ

- Reminds them of his Paschal sacrifice

- Reminds them of the seriousness of sin

- Comforts them in their sorrows

- Helps them bear suffering patiently

- Represents an historical reality that all Christians accept to be true—that Christ died on the cross for their sake and conquered death in His glorious resurrection

In addition to the crucifix, Catholic churches often have statues of Mary and Joseph, the saint for whom the building is dedicated, as well as other individuals of special significance. (For example, if there is a school on the campus, the church may include a statue of St. Thomas Aquinas— patron saint of scholars.) During the holidays, the church often erects a nativity scene complete with the Holy Family, Magi, shepherds, and the Angel of the Lord.

Regardless of what image is depicted in the concrete and plaster, Catholics do not venerate the figurines, only what they represent. This is not going against the second commandment, which forbids worshipping graven images at all. In actuality, God did not forbid the use of statues in religion, only the worship of them.

In fact, Scripture tells us that God was not against sacred images. After giving Moses the Ten Commandments, God commands him to make the Arc of the Covenant and to fashion two cherubs (angels) on either end of the mercy seat. "The cherubim shall spread out their wings above overshadowing the mercy seat with their wings." (Exodus 25:20) Ezekiel also mentions the nave of a temple that includes a patterned décor featuring the cherubim and palm trees. "Each cherub had two faces: a human face turned toward the palm tree on the one side, and the face of a young lion turned toward the palm tree on the other side. They were carved on the whole temple all around; from the floor to the area above the door, cherubim and palm trees were carved on the wall." (Ezekiel 41:18-20)

> **CATHOLIC QUOTE**
>
> Every block of stone has a statue inside of it and it is the task of the sculptor to discover it.
>
> —Michelangelo

It's sort of like putting pictures of family members on your mantle or hanging pictures on your walls at home; statues and images of holy people acknowledge that they are members of our Church family and remind us to look to them for guidance and inspiration on how to live a good and holy life.

Holy Water and Incense

Though it is closely associated with the sacrament of baptism and found in tiny basins near the doors of the church building, holy water is one of the most common and important sacramentals in the Catholic Church. It is filled with religious significance. Water is a central element of key miracles, such as the parting of the Red Sea and the Wedding at Cana. The ancient Israelites used it to purify people and places and to cleanse themselves prior to religious services. John the Baptist used it to wash away the sins of the repentant.

Holy water is just plain water that has been blessed by a priest or deacon to be used for sacred purposes. Catholics use holy water inside and outside of the church for the following:

- As a reminder of baptism

- To denote God's blessing on an object or person

- To protect them from evil

The belief that water can cleanse the soul comes from Psalm 51, which reads in part, "Wash me thoroughly from my inequity, and cleanse me from my sin … purge me with hyssop, and I shall be clean; wash me, and I shall be whiter than the snow." This idea has been incorporated in the Mass as an option during the Penitential Act in which the priest passes through the congregation and sprinkles holy water on the assembly to remind them of their baptism.

Holy water also reminds us of our baptismal vows in which we were set free from original sin. Whenever Catholics enter a church building, they dip their fingers in the holy water fonts and make the Sign of the Cross as a way to remind themselves of the promises made through baptism and confirmation: to reject Satan, all his works, and his empty promises and to profess the faith.

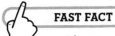

A baptismal font is the name of the larger basin where holy water is located and which is used for baptisms, while a stoup is the name of the smaller vessels located at the doors of the church.

Finally, Catholics use holy water as a sign of blessing and a protection from evil. When ordinary water is prayed over and given God's blessing, it can be a powerful tool in a Catholic's life. Holy water is used in virtually all blessings of the Church, whether it is a car, a rosary, or a cemetery plot that is being blessed. Catholics also often have small containers of holy water in the home to bless the building so that all who are in it will receive the protection of God.

Like holy water, incense is used to honor holy things and holy people. In the book of Exodus, God told Moses to build a golden altar for the purpose of burning incense, and it is a tradition that Christians most likely adopted from Judaism. Psalm 141 asks that our prayers may rise up to God just like incense rises up to heaven. In addition to the smoke, the sweet smell of incense is meant to raise our minds to thoughts of heaven.

Incense often adds a note of solemnity; it isn't used every day, but rather on Sundays or more important feast days. During Mass, incense may be used for the following:

- During the entrance procession

- At the beginning of Mass, to incense the altar

- At the procession and proclamation of the Gospel

- During the offertory

- At the elevation of the Sacred Host and chalice of Precious Blood after the consecration

The priest may also incense the crucifix, as well as the Paschal Candle. During funeral Masses, the priest may incense the casket at the final commendation as a sign of honor to the body of the deceased—which became the temple of the Holy Spirit at baptism—and as a sign of the faithful's prayers for the deceased rising to God.

Ashes to Ashes

Have you ever mistaken ashes for dirt on a Catholic's forehead on the first Wednesday of Lent? If so, you're not the first and you won't be the last. Catholics are used to it, so don't be embarrassed. They are accustomed to well-meaning friends who point out the smudge without fully understanding what significance it has.

Ash Wednesday ashes are made from burned palms used the previous year during Palm Sunday. They are designed to be a reminder of where we came from and to what we will eventually return, as well as a sign of repentance. In the Book of Genesis, humanity is created out of the dust of the earth, and God reminds us that we will return to dust after death until Christ raises our bodies at the end of time. Ashes also appear throughout the Old Testament and the days of the early Church as a sign of repentance for sin. On Ash Wednesday, we begin the Lenten season of repentance by reminding ourselves of our total reliance on God, without whom we are no more than dust.

KEEP IT SIMPLE

While there are a myriad of tongue-in-cheek responses to the "Hey, you have a smudge of something on your head" comment, the most basic Catholic responses include "Ash Wednesday reminds me that it is only through God that I have life" and "Ash Wednesday begins a Catholic's preparation for Holy Week and the Passion and resurrection of Jesus, without whom we have no life."

Fasting and Abstinence

Fasting is the voluntary act of restricting something that is good or pleasurable—in other words, denying one's self of excess. In Catholicism, this usually refers to the curbing of certain foods that we like and "giving things up" for Lent.

It is unclear as to how the practice of fasting began, but both the Old and New Testaments make mention of it. We know that Moses fasted for 40 days prior to receiving the Ten Commandments. We know that Jesus fasted in the wilderness prior to beginning His public ministry. We know that David fasted at the loss of Abner, the Ninevites fasted in hopes that God would spare their city, and Paul fasted during his conversion. Regardless of whether one was in mourning, preparing for a spiritual event, or atoning for their sins, fasting is a ritual that predates Catholicism but is an important component of the faith.

By restricting the foods they eat, Catholics believe they can control the passions of the body and devote their souls to prayer. The season of Lent is the most common time during which Catholics fast. Not only do they give something up—like desserts or television—as penance for past excessive behavior, but the Church also asks them to observe a common fast on Ash Wednesday and Good Friday and to avoid meat on those two days as well as all Fridays during the Lenten season.

This does not mean that Catholics starve themselves during those two days. In fact, the rules on fasting and abstinence are a lot less rigorous than they used to be. Catholics age 18 to 59 can enjoy one full meal each day of the fast and two smaller meals provided that the smaller meals combined are not equivalent to the full meal. They should also not eat anything between meals.

The rule concerning abstinence from meat on Ash Wednesday, Good Friday, and Fridays in Lent applies to anyone 16 and older, though it can be suspended for health reasons where applicable. And fish and shellfish are not considered meat, so they can be eaten on the days of abstinence.

Years ago, the rule on abstinence applied to all Fridays throughout the year and not just those that fell during Lent. What many Catholics do not realize is that this is still a recommendation of the Church and if they choose not to abstain from meat on non-Lenten Fridays, they are asked to substitute with another form of penance.

 KEEP IT SIMPLE

Although they sound the same, fasting and abstaining are two different ideas. Fasting restricts the quantity of food that people eat and when they consume it, while abstinence refers to the elimination of particular foods from people's diet for a period of time.

Works of Mercy

Jesus is not an easy person to buy a present for. We do not know His size, hair color, or whether or not He is a "summer" or "winter" person. Even if we found the perfect item, there's no way to get it to Him and because He is God and He created everything, it would be a bit like giving Him something He already owns anyway.

However, Jesus did leave us with a wish list of things that we could do for Him. In Matthew's Gospel, Jesus tells us when the Son of Man comes in glory, He will gather all of the nations together and those who have acted in charity will be placed at the right hand of the Father:

> "For I was hungry, and you gave me food, I was thirsty and you gave me drink, I was a stranger and you welcomed me, I was naked and you gave me clothing, I was sick and you took care of me. Then the righteous will answer him, 'Lord, when was it that we saw you hungry and gave you food, or thirsty and gave you something to drink? And when was it that we saw you a stranger and welcomed you, or naked and gave you clothing? And when was it that we saw you sick or in prison and visited you?' And the king will answer them, 'Truly I tell you, just as you did it to the least of these who are members of my family, you did it to me.'" (Matthew 25:35-40)

The Works of Mercy are our gift to Jesus. They are actions we perform out of kindness rather than obligation in order to extend God's grace to those in need. They are the ways in which Catholics live the social teaching of the Church and look out for their fellow man. The Corporal Works of Mercy compel us to care for one another's physical and material needs, while the Spiritual Works of Mercy command us to care for one another's soul.

The Corporal Works of Mercy:

1. Feed the hungry.

2. Give drink to the thirsty.

3. Clothe the naked.

4. Shelter the homeless.

5. Visit the sick.

6. Visit the imprisoned.

7. Bury the dead.

The Spiritual Works of Mercy:

1. Admonish the sinner.

2. Instruct the ignorant.

3. Counsel the doubtful.

4. Comfort the sorrowful.

5. Bear wrongs patiently.

6. Forgive all injuries.

7. Pray for the living and the dead.

Through the Works of Mercy, Catholics concretely practice the faith. They show a willingness to be like Christ and enter into chaos with the intent of restoring order and serving as a beacon for the Catholic lifestyle.

Exorcism

Out of all of the Catholic practices, the one that everyone tends to be curious about is the one that few really understand: the Rite of Exorcism.

In the Gospels, Jesus is credited with driving a demon out of a boy who had been possessed since childhood. The boy's father approached Christ to ask for his help:

> "'Teacher, I beg you to look at my son; he is my only child. Suddenly a spirit seizes him, and all at once he shrieks. It convulses him until he foams at the mouth; it mauls him and will scarcely leave him. I begged your disciples to cast it out, but they could not.' Jesus answered, 'You faithless and perverse generation, how much longer must I be here

with you and bear with you? Bring your son here.' While he was coming, the demon dashed him to the ground in convulsions. But Jesus rebuked the unclean spirit, healed the boy and gave him back to his father." (Luke 9:38-42)

There are actually two types of exorcisms in the Catholic Church: a simple exorcism that occurs at times like the Sacrament of Baptism designed to remove an individual from the power of Satan and bring them closer to God, and the one that has been immortalized by Hollywood in all of it gruesome glory. Though this type of exorcism is real, it is also very rare.

FAST FACT

Exorcists are priests who have been delegated by their bishop to receive special training to perform the rite. It's not a job most would campaign for. Most are surprised to learn they have been chosen for this role, but true to their vocation of service, they accept the call willingly.

Despite the over-the-top depictions, exorcisms are, at their core, a series of fervent prayers recited by a priest who has been delegated by the bishop to perform the rite.

When the family or close friends of an individual believed to be possessed by a supernatural spirit contact a priest, his first reaction must be one of skepticism. He takes time to learn about the case, review existing documentation, and consult with medical professionals to rule out any physical or psychological phenomena that might explain the person's behavior. Caution is, above all, the Church's policy regarding reported demonic activity.

Priests look for signs that allude to the presence of a demonic spirit in the individual. These can vary depending on the situation and the type of demon invasion but include the following:

- A loss of appetite (or lack of appetite)

- Lesions on the skin (for example, cuts, scratches, or something that appears to be bite marks)

- A cold feeling in the room that does not occur anywhere else in the house

- Unnatural body posturing

- Loss of control in the individual, which results in frenzy, rage, or attack

- A radical change in a person's voice

- Supernatural strength inconsistent with the individual's body type or age

- The sudden knowledge of another language that the individual has never spoken in the past

- A sudden and violent reaction toward religious items or objects

- The sudden opposition to church attendance, the name of Jesus, or Scripture

After reviewing the medical evidence and eyewitness accounts to determine that an exorcism is necessary, the priest arranges to perform the rite. Before arriving onsite, the priest attends confession and Mass in order to ask forgiveness of his own sins and the strength to perform this all-important duty.

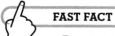

FAST FACT

Exorcism is not a sacrament; however, there are a lot of sacramentals used in the rite, including holy water, crucifixes, blessings, prayers, relics, and so on.

The rite itself is typically broken down into four stages:

1. **Pretense:** During this portion, the demon(s) is hiding within the individual and refuses to reveal itself.

2. **Breakpoint:** This is the moment when the demon(s) reveal its presence to the exorcist.

3. **Clash:** This refers to the moment when the priest and the demon(s) battle for the individual's soul.

4. **Expulsion:** This is the moment when the demon leaves the individual's soul.

The priest begins the ritual by tracing the Sign of the Cross on himself, the possessed person, and anyone else who happens to be in the room. He also sprinkles holy water on all in attendance. The presence of eyewitnesses is extremely important not only as support for the individual, but also for the priest so they can attest to the proceedings after the fact in case questions arise.

The priest then recites the Litany of the Saints, which rallies the troops and calls upon those believed to be in Heaven with God to pray for the soul of the possessed individual. What follows is a series of readings from the Psalms as well as the Gospels, along with a barrage of prayers designed to drive the demon(s) from the individual's soul.

No two cases of possession are exactly alike. Sometimes the individual may be restrained in order to prevent harm to himself or others. Some have physical reactions to the prayer being recited. At various points, the priest may place a crucifix or *relic* to the individual's forehead or sprinkle him with holy water as they do battle with the devil. It is an intense process and once it has begun, it must be concluded. (Sometimes the rite must be repeated when a particularly stubborn demon is involved.) The Catholic Church takes the presence of evil seriously, but at the same time knows that the power of God is more powerful than any demonic force.

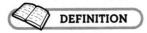

DEFINITION

> A **relic** is an object associated with a saint. It can be a body part or an object that once belonged to or was used by a saint.

The Least You Need to Know

- Catholics use blessings and sacramentals to experience their faith on a sensory level.
- A statue is not a graven image and Catholics do not worship them.
- The Works of Mercy are gifts we can give back to God.
- A relic is a venerated item associated with a saint.
- Exorcisms are real but they are extremely rare.

The Catholic Calendar

At every Mass, the Catholic Church commemorates the central mystery of Christian belief: Christ's paschal sacrifice. However, that's only part of the greatest story ever told. In order to offer the faithful a more complete picture, the Church developed the liturgical year in which the entire plan of salvation unfolds.

Over the course of the calendar year, Catholics learn about and celebrate the whole mystery of Christ: the Old Testament prophecies, incarnation, ministry, passion, death, resurrection, and ascension into Heaven, along with the promise that Jesus will come again. Each element of the liturgical calendar is designed to put Christ's sacred reality into the minds and hearts of the faithful where it transforms lives.

In this chapter, we will examine the seasons of salvation. We will turn the pages of the biblical basis for the celebrations associated with each, and we will chronicle the holy days and feast days, and the ordinary days in between.

In This Chapter

- The Church's liturgical calendar
- How Catholics celebrate the seasons
- Lent: the longest 40 days of the year
- There's nothing ordinary about Ordinary Time
- The Holy Days of Obligation

The Liturgical Year

The liturgical year is comprised of five "seasons" of celebration based on the life and mystery of Jesus Christ and the plan of salvation. It begins not in January like the traditional calendar, but in late November/early December with the first Sunday in Advent. The Church segues into the Christmas season followed by a brief period of Ordinary Time before the seven weeks of Lent and then the Easter Season. After the feast of Pentecost, Ordinary Time resumes and continues until the feast of Christ the King, which ends the Church's calendar year one week before the start of the next season of Advent.

In addition to covering the entire life of Christ (including events that happened before the New Testament), the liturgical year is interrupted by feast days of saints and of Mary as well as Holy Days of Obligation that Catholics observe quite faithfully in order to rejoice in the grace of God that has led mankind to redemption.

Advent and Christmas

Advent is the period of time before Christmas when Catholics are busy making preparations for one of the most celebrated days of the Christian year, December 25. While not exclusively a "Catholic thing," Advent literally means "coming," and during the four weeks prior to the feast of the Nativity, the Church is waiting and watching for the arrival of the Son of God in the form of Jesus Christ. Catholics wait until Christmas Eve to sing carols and decorate their churches with trees and poinsettias, with the days of Advent focused on intense watching, waiting, and preparing our hearts for the birth of the Messiah.

 CATHOLIC QUOTE

The Church year, which makes present and portrays anew the life of Christ, is mankind's greatest work of art; and God has acknowledged it and allows it year after year, always granting it new light, as though one were encountering it for the first time.

—Jochen Klepper

Throughout the Advent season, Catholics hear readings from the Old Testament in which prophets foretell the coming of the Messiah as well as excerpts from the epistles that urge the faithful to be prepared for the Second Coming. The Gospels are full of stories leading to the birth of Jesus, including the Annunciation, the Visitation, the birth of John the Baptist, and John's ministry in the desert where he called people to repentance.

There is also the custom of the Advent wreath. Though this is not something exclusive to the Catholic faith, it is important to offer an overview of the symbolism of the wreath and what it means to Christians everywhere. The circular shape of the Advent wreath signifies the infinite nature of God, the Father of eternal life. Interspersed around the wreath are four candles, which are lit over the course of the season (one candle is lit for week one, two Candles are lit for week two, and so on).

While there are different customs regarding the color of the candles in various parts of the world, the most common practice is to use three violet candles and one rose candle. Each candle represents 1,000 years, so they total the 4,000 years the world had been waiting for its Savior to arrive.

 CATHOLIC QUOTE

Christmas is fast approaching. And now that Christ has aroused our seasonal expectations, he'll soon fulfill them all!

—St. Augustine

Violet is the color the Church uses to denote a time of penance and sacrifice. The purple candles are lit on the first two and last Sundays of Advent. The rose candle, which is lit on the third Sunday, signifies a week of rejoicing that the wait for Jesus is almost over. During the liturgical year, the priest and deacons will don vestments in the colors that reflect the tone of the season.

According to tradition, the four candles on the Advent wreath represent more than a numerical timeline. The first candle, known as the Prophet's Candle, symbolizes hope and the second candle, called the Bethlehem Candle, recalls the journey Mary and Joseph made to the City of David. The third candle, the Shepherd's Candle, symbolizes the joy the world experienced when Jesus was born, and finally the Angel's Candle on the fourth Sunday of Advent reminds us of the angels' message of peace on earth and goodwill toward all mankind.

 CATHOLIC QUOTE

Nowhere has so great a miracle occurred as in that little stable in Bethlehem; here God and man become one.

—Thomas à Kempis

The Christmas season begins with the feast of the Nativity of our Lord on December 25 and continues through the feast of the Baptism of our Lord in early January. The earliest evidence we have of the holiday is approximately AD 330 when the celebration was centered not on the actual date of Christ's birth (which is unknown) but on the pagan rituals associated with the winter solstice. There is a unique connection to the practice of celebrating the shortest day of the year with the return of light and the symbolism of Christmas in which God gave light to the world in His Son.

However, for Catholics, Christmas is more than a celebration of a baby born in an uncomfortable manger. It is the commemoration of the whole *"Emmanuel* Mystery" that begins with Jesus' birth at Bethlehem and does not end until the Church commemorates the Baptism of Jesus in the Gospel reading several weeks later. There are high points in the Christmas season after Christmas Day itself: the feast of the Holy Family, the Solemnity of Mary, the Holy Mother of God, the Epiphany, and Jesus' Baptism. During this time, priests wear white or gold to celebrate this festive occasion and familiar Christmas carols are sung until January 6, the feast of the Epiphany.

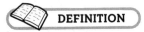

DEFINITION

Emmanuel means "God with us."

Ordinary Time

Ordinary Time refers to the Sundays and weekdays of the liturgical year that do not correspond to the Advent, Christmas, Lenten, or Easter seasons. There are 33 or 34 weeks of Ordinary Time broken up into two periods throughout the calendar year. The first period of Ordinary Time begins after the Baptism of the Lord on January 6 and concludes with the start of Lent on Ash Wednesday. Depending on where Easter falls in that particular year, this first period of Ordinary Time can be as short as four weeks or as long as nine.

The second part of Ordinary Time begins after Pentecost and continues until the first Sunday of Advent. During both periods of Ordinary Time, the priests and deacons wear green vestments. As Catholics continue to celebrate the resurrection of Jesus within the Mass, the readings between Epiphany and Lent center on the beginning of Jesus' public ministry. Those that are read after Easter are a semi-continuous narrative of the Synoptic Gospels and focus on the development of Christ's life and teachings. Despite the name "Ordinary Time" there is nothing ordinary about this period of the liturgical year, and it is no less important than the other celebrations throughout the year. The name comes from the fact that each of the Sundays of this season are numbered, or ordered, as time moves along, such as the Seventeenth Sunday in Ordinary Time.

Lent/Triduum

Have you ever heard the expression, "It's always darkest before the dawn"? This is the perfect analogy to describe the period of time between Ash Wednesday and Easter Sunday, known as Lent.

Like Advent, Lent is not exclusive to Catholicism; and like Advent, it is a period of preparation for one of the highlights of the Church year. However, unlike the four weeks of wide-eyed excitement associated with Advent, the seven weeks of Lent have a very different tone. It is a very somber time in which there is a focus on repentance, conversion, and sacrifice. Catholics are encouraged to fast, abstain from eating meat on Fridays, give up a favorite food, hobby, or pastime as a form of penitence, and perform charitable works all with the promise that at the end of these 40 days, they will be rewarded with a miracle even greater than the Incarnation—the Resurrection.

The earliest documentation relating to Lent dates back to the writings of Dionysius of Alexandria in the third century. During the Council of Nicaea, the idea of a 40-day Lenten season was tabled, but it's not clear when the actual practice began. We do know that the number 40 has a lot of Biblical significance. The Great Flood lasted 40 days and 40 nights. Moses was on Mount Sinai for 40 days. Jesus fasted for 40 days in the desert after His baptism, and during Lent, Catholics are called to offer 40 days of penitence to prepare themselves for the most sacred days of the Church year.

Ash Wednesday

Lent begins with Ash Wednesday, which is the day millions of Catholics attend Mass and receive a cross-shaped mark made from ashes on their foreheads as a sign of their mortality. In many cultures there is a "last blast bash" of sorts on the Tuesday before Lent. *Mardi Gras*, for example, means "Fat Tuesday" and people indulge in one last feast before making their Lenten sacrifices. You may also hear the term *Carnival*, which literally means "farewell to meat" and denotes a celebration just prior to the Lenten season.

During Lent, the church décor is usually very stark, and once again purple is the color of the season. The Confiteor, a prayer of confession, is often said and the Gloria is omitted from the Mass. The word Alleluia is notably absent as well. On the fifth Sunday of Lent, there is the option of covering all images in Church buildings in purple fabric, which gives a completely different look. Over the course of the season, the readings focus almost exclusively on conversion, having a change of heart, and repenting of one's sinfulness and are geared to help Catholics prepare for Holy Week celebrations.

Another tradition that occurs on Fridays during Lent, including Good Friday, is the Stations of the Cross—a commemoration of 14 events in Jesus' journey to His execution:

1. Jesus is condemned.

2. Jesus carries His cross.

3. Jesus falls.

4. Jesus meets His mother.

5. Simon helps Jesus carry the cross.

6. Veronica wipes the face of Jesus.

7. Jesus falls again.

8. Jesus counsels the women of Jerusalem.

9. Jesus falls a third time.

10. Jesus is stripped.

11. Jesus is nailed to the cross.

12. Jesus dies on the cross.

13. Jesus is removed from the cross.

14. Jesus is laid in the Tomb.

Holy Week

Holy Week begins with Palm Sunday, which commemorates the day Jesus made His triumphant entry into Jerusalem. In the Gospels, He is riding on a donkey as crowds gather around him waving palm branches and singing, "Hosanna to the Son of David! Blessed is he who comes in the name of the Lord! Hosanna in the Highest!" (Matthew 21:9)

The custom of this solemn feast has roots in the fourth century, when people marched through the Holy City in order to recreate the scene in which the Jews hailed Jesus' arrival. By the ninth century, the celebration had spread throughout the world, and today many churches continue the tradition of outdoor processions and the blessing of palm branches, which are distributed to the faithful.

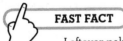

FAST FACT

Leftover palm branches are later burned and used for the ashes distributed on the next Ash Wednesday.

The feast starts on a high note and is set apart from the rest of Lent by the red décor on the altar and red vestments, but the festive mood shifts as the readings segue from songs of praise to a darker mood as the entire narrative of the Passion of Christ is proclaimed. It is a foreshadowing of the days ahead on the Church calendar, and although there is only one week to go until Easter, it sometimes feels like the longest week of the year.

The Triduum: Holy Thursday and Good Friday

Put simply, the Paschal Triduum refers to the three days of solemn prayer in the Church calendar that lead up to Easter Sunday. These are the holiest days of the year and constitute a separate liturgical season between Lent and Easter. The three days begin on Holy Thursday evening and continue through the evening of Easter Sunday. There are very special services connected with these three days, beginning with the Mass of the Lord's Supper on Holy Thursday.

This Mass is usually the only one celebrated by a parish on that day and is the last Mass said prior to the Easter Vigil. There are a lot of interesting nuances about this Mass that do not happen in other celebrations. On Holy Thursday, a parish receives the oils that are blessed by the bishop at the annual Chrism Mass. In many parishes, there is also the custom of the washing of the feet, in which the parish priest recreates the scene in John 13:3–5 when Jesus who "had come from God and knew he was going to God, got up from the table, took off his outer robe and tied a towel around himself. Then he poured water into a basin and began to wash the disciples' feet and wipe them with the towel that was wrapped around him." At the end of the Mass, the Eucharist is processed around the church to an Altar of Repose in a space separate from the main church, where prayer continues until midnight. With the altar stripped of its adornments and the empty tabernacle standing open, the whole church feels as if it is in mourning.

On Good Friday, the entire focus is on the crucifixion. All eyes turn to Calvary as Catholics gather for a commemoration of the Lord's Passion typically around 3 P.M. This is the reported time at which Jesus died on the cross, but the scheduling of the event is at the discretion of the parish. There is no Mass celebrated that day. Rather, the service consists of:

- The Liturgy of the Word and the reading of the Passion according to St. John
- Solemn intercessory prayers
- Veneration of the Cross
- The distribution of pre-consecrated hosts

Traditionally, there are no instruments used in this celebration (though this varies from parish to parish) and all music comes in the form of unaccompanied chant.

The Triduum: The Easter Vigil

The Easter Vigil takes place on Holy Saturday. It must begin after nightfall and be completed before the break of day on Easter. This is hands down one of the longest Masses in the Church year, but it is also the most beautiful. It is divided into four parts:

1. The Service of Light
2. The Liturgy of the Word

3. The Liturgy of Baptism

4. The Liturgy of the Eucharist

On Holy Saturday, the parishioners meet outside the church building where a new fire is lit and blessed. The new Paschal (or Easter) Candle is blessed and lit and is processed throughout the Church. There is a very different atmosphere inside the building. All of the holy water fonts are drained, the lights are out, and the tabernacle is empty. Everyone is given a small candle, which is lit from the Easter candle, and the congregation processes into the church until the whole building is full of light. The Easter song of the Catholic Church, called the Exultet, follows the procession.

There are nine readings that can be read during the Liturgy of the Word (seven from the Old Testament and two from the New Testament). While most parishes do not read all nine of them, at least three of the Old Testament readings must be read (including Exodus 14, which pertains to the crossing of the Red Sea). Unlike traditional Masses, the Gloria is sung prior to the reading of the epistle and the Alleluia is sung prior to the Gospel acclamation, making its first appearance since before Lent.

FAST FACT

There is a big misconception that Catholics are not allowed to receive the Sacraments of Baptism or Matrimony during the Lenten season. While these sacraments are forbidden on Good Friday and Holy Saturday (with the obvious exception of the Easter Vigil for Baptism), it is up to the individual priest or parish. Most do not promote these sacraments during Lent, and of course any celebration during this time has to be solemn, but they can happen.

After the Gospel reading, the Easter water is blessed and those candidates who have been preparing for the Sacrament of Baptism through the RCIA program are brought forward to receive the first two Sacraments of Initiation. The Liturgy of the Eucharist follows, and the entire congregation takes part in the service, including those who are receiving the Eucharist for the first time as new members of the Catholic faith. There are special prayers inserted, but for the most part, the format is similar to Masses celebrated throughout the year. The Concluding Rites follow and the congregation is told to "go in peace" and rejoice in the morning that will follow.

Easter

The Easter season is the high-water mark of the Church year. For 50 days, Catholics celebrate the Resurrection of Jesus, the 40 days in which he appeared to people throughout Judea and Galilee, and his ascension into Heaven. After the somberness of Lent, Catholics feel a great sense of relief when they see the church adorned with the white and gold colors of the season and the flowers bedecking the altar, and they hear the glorious refrains of "Alleluia" once more. After the homily on Easter Sunday, the priest invites the congregation to a renewal of their baptismal vows. The holy water fonts are filled with the water that was blessed the night before.

CATHOLIC QUOTE

Do not abandon yourselves to despair. We are the Easter people and hallelujah is our song.

—Pope St. John Paul II

Easter Sunday is followed by the Octave of Easter, the eight days stretching to the following Sunday, which helps continue the celebration and make each day feel like a Sunday. The Easter season concludes with the feast of Pentecost, when priests and deacons wear red vestments. This is the celebration of the descent of the Holy Spirit onto the apostles and by extension the entire Body of Christ.

Holy Days of Obligation

In addition to weekly Mass attendance on Saturday evening or Sunday, Catholics are expected to attend Mass on special feast days throughout the year. The Roman Rite of the Catholic Church has 10 Holy Days of Obligation, though in many countries the bishops' conference has reduced the number by transferring the obligation of certain feasts to the nearest Sunday. This may make it seem like there are fewer obligatory occasions.

New Year's Day, January 1, is the Solemnity of Mary, the Holy Mother of God. This is the occasion when Catholics are reminded of the role Mary played in God's divine plan and how she became the mother of His incarnation.

The Epiphany of Our Lord Jesus Christ on January 6 is one of the oldest Christian feasts. Originally, it highlighted four different events including the Baptism of the Lord, the changing of the water into wine at Cana, and the Nativity of Christ, in addition to the appearance of the star in the East and the visit of the Magi to the Christ Child. Today, it is associated primarily with the visit of the Magi, but the overall message remains: God's revelation to man through His son, Jesus.

March 19 is the Solemnity of St. Joseph, when Catholics celebrate the paternal role Joseph played in the raising of Jesus. In recent years there has been a push to include Joseph as an integral part of the Holy Family rather than an accessory character. After all, he was called by God as well to serve as His foster father, to love His mother, and to raise Him in the traditions and customs of the culture.

FAST FACT

Although all Catholics are encouraged to attend Mass on Ash Wednesday and Holy Thursday as well as Good Friday services, you may be surprised to learn that none of these three are Holy Days of Obligation.

Though the actual date changes from year to year, Ascension Thursday occurs 40 days after Easter. It is, as you might suspect, the celebration of the Lord's return to the Father after commissioning the apostles to carry on His ministry. In some places, the celebration of the ascension is transferred to the nearest Sunday.

When the Church returns to Ordinary Time after Pentecost, there are still some special celebrations in the first weeks of that season. The Sunday after Pentecost is Trinity Sunday, which is a day of obligation because it falls on Sunday, and the Thursday after Trinity Sunday is the feast of Corpus Christi or the Body and Blood of Christ. This Holy Day commemorates the presence of Christ's body and blood in the Eucharist. The celebration of Corpus Christi is often transferred to the following Sunday.

The feast of Saints Peter and Paul occurs on June 29. It is the liturgical feast in honor of the martyrdom of two of the most preeminent figures in Church history. While it is a Holy Day of Obligation as far as the Holy See is concerned, the individual bishops conferences have the right to waive the obligation.

FAST FACT

Variations in the observance of Holy Days of Obligation are as numerous as there are countries. Although there are 10 recognized in the *Catechism of the Catholic Church*, different countries do things differently. For example, the United States (with the exception of Hawaii) celebrates 8 of the 10 obligatory feasts, although some of these are transferred to Sunday. Canada only commemorates two: Christmas and Mary, the Mother of God. Hong Kong only has one: Christmas.

The Assumption of Mary occurs on August 15 and is the Mass in which Catholics celebrate Mary being taken body and soul into Heaven at the end of her life. This is the second of three Holy Days of Obligation that center completely on the Blessed Mother.

November 1 is All Saints Day. It celebrates all of those who have died in Christ, whether they have been officially recognized as canonized saints or not. While not a Holy Day of Obligation, the day after All Saints Day, November 2, is All Souls Day, a time to remember in a special way those who have died during the past year.

The Immaculate Conception is celebrated on December 8, near the middle of the Advent season. While so much about this time centers on Jesus' amazing conception, as we learned in Chapter 15, this feast day commemorates Mary's origin and how she was the perfect vessel who was born without the stain of Original Sin. This day takes on special significance in the United States because it is the patronal feast day of the country.

As you might expect, Christmas is the last Holy Day of Obligation in the calendar year. It always occurs on December 25 and focuses on the birth of Jesus in Bethlehem. Aside from Easter (which is a Holy Day of Obligation because it occurs on a Sunday) it is one of the biggest feast days of the Church calendar.

In the United States, Christmas and the Immaculate Conception of Mary are always Holy Days of Obligation, no matter what day of the week they fall on. The feast of Mary, the Mother of God, the Assumption of Mary, and All Saints Day are Holy Days of Obligation unless they fall on Saturday or Monday, when the obligation to attend Mass is lifted because of the day's proximity to Sunday. The ascension is transferred to Sunday in many dioceses, but for those dioceses in which it is celebrated on a Thursday, it is a Holy Day of Obligation. The Epiphany and Corpus Christi are always transferred to Sunday, and the feasts of St. Joseph and St. Peter and Paul are not days of obligation in the United States.

The Least You Need to Know

- The Catholic liturgical calendar is comprised of five seasons: Advent, Christmas, Lent, Easter, and Ordinary Time.
- Lent is the period of time between Ash Wednesday and Holy Saturday.
- Holy Week festivities include Palm Sunday and the Triduum of Holy Thursday, Good Friday, and the Easter Vigil.
- Easter is the most important season of the Church calendar.
- There are 10 Holy Days of Obligation in the Catholic Church, but individual observance of them is directed by the bishops' council in each country.

Being Catholic in a Digital Age

As the spiritual leader of over 1 billion people worldwide, the pope knows how important it is to spread the Church's message through channels in which Catholics can hear it, appreciate it, and make it part of their daily lives.

For the Church, the Information Age did not begin with Steve Jobs, Bill Gates, and other computer gurus. It began with the apostles, who traveled far and wide spreading the gospel orally at first and then through written correspondence. As technology improved and advanced, the Church turned to books, film, radio, television, and the internet to promote its platform, and it is often not only an early adopter of new media, but also one of its strongest supporters (believe it or not).

In this chapter, you will learn how the Church uses digital media communication to spread the gospel message and help the apostolic mission continue to flourish.

In This Chapter

* The Catholic Church in the Information Age
* The pope taking a selfie?
* What is the New Evangelization?
* Technology's patron saints

Knowledge Is Power

The Catholic Church is no stranger to advancements in communication. In fact, the Church spearheaded one of the first: the Council of Nicaea. The Council of Nicaea (and subsequent Ecumenical Councils) was essentially a public relations strategy session designed to streamline doctrine, answer key theological questions, and hammer out a mission statement that would be easy for the Christian community to memorize and understand. Though few people would call the Council "God's PR team," it was a meeting geared toward clarifying the Church's understanding of its God-given message and deciding how they would get that message out to the people.

Once the Nicene Creed was written and the books of the Bible compiled, handwritten copies of Scripture became available, provided one was wealthy enough to afford it (and patient enough to wait a year or more for the scribe to complete the task). However, in 1450, Johann Gutenberg invented two things that would revolutionize written communication and pave the way for every innovation that came afterward: moveable type and the printing press.

KEEP IT SIMPLE

Gutenberg's invention not only made mass production of written texts possible, but without his genius, we never would have had typewriters, word processors, computers, or the tablet technology we rely on today.

To be fair, Gutenberg's invention would prove to be bad news and good news for the Church. Initially, the Church was less than pleased with Gutenberg's technology. While it put printed pages on the fast track to publication, helped streamline spelling, and offered folks everywhere the opportunity to read the Bible and other great works of literature, it also meant the Church could not control what "forbidden" texts came off the presses. (Forbidden texts included translations of the Bible that weren't in Latin, among other manuscripts.)

Prior to Gutenberg, it was easy for the Catholic Church to make sure religious texts were true to Church doctrine prior to being published, but after this technology, it was impossible to keep up. When the Protestant Reformation movement got underway in 1517, Martin Luther believed that Christians should be allowed to read the Bible in their own language, and the printing press not only helped spread his ideas, but it also enabled this change to occur. Many see the printing press as the device that ended the Church's control over northern Europe, but also one that opened the door for folks to expand their world and learn about the news, developments, and breakthroughs that simply were not possible only a century before.

Eventually, the Catholic Church embraced the technology that they once saw as a threat to their establishment. The printing press enabled the Church to publish its own literary works, as well as newspapers designed to put a Catholic spin on current events. While these early periodicals and texts were not published at the speed of light like they are today, it happened a lot faster than the faithful were used to and it connected people to the Church in exciting, "modern" ways.

As media technologies became more innovative, the Church continued to advance its communications campaign, and by the end of the twentieth century, the Church had used every available medium to improve its visibility and spread its message to the masses, including print, broadcast, video, and online outlets.

The Pope Plugs In

When the pope talks, people tend to listen. Catholics are very interested in their leader's opinion on social, political, and spiritual issues, and over the years, they have kept up with the Vatican in a variety of ways. Not only does the Vatican have its own television station, radio station, and newspaper to keep the public informed on things that affect the faithful, but they have also embraced the 24/7 news cycle, the dawn of the internet, as well as social media opportunities.

In fact, the following are some of the Catholic media firsts when it comes to the pope:

- **First pope to appear on film:** Leo XIII in 1896

- **First pope to broadcast on the radio:** Pius XI c. 1931

- **First pope to be the star of a full-length movie:** Pius XII in 1942

- **First pope to appear on television:** Pius XII in the late 1940s

- **First pope to invite cameras into the Vatican to film a day in his life:** St. John XXIII in 1961

Historically, popes have always been keen to adopt new technology when they think it can help the Church, however the two who have been the most media savvy have been Pope St. John Paul II who became the first pope to use the internet in 2001 and Pope Benedict XVI who was the first pope to use social media in 2012.

John Paul Superstar

When Pope St. John Paul II was elected to the papacy in October 1978, he was an instant hit with the media. The former actor was the total package, with plenty of stage presence, charisma, and that certain indefinable something. No matter where he went, his appearances possessed the pomp and circumstance of a coronation and the energy of a rock concert and were covered in both print and broadcast media.

He was the perfect pontiff for the dawn of the cable era, which saw the rise of the 24/7 news networks, such as CNN. Wilton Wynn, the former Rome bureau chief at *Time* magazine, said that although Pope St. John Paul II was not the first pope to use the media to his advantage, "this man is the first who fully understands that the Church has a great opportunity here to reach the entire world by using the mass media."

The former pontiff's media accomplishments are impressive. In 1987, an estimated 1 billion people tuned in as 23 satellites linked the pope to 16 countries and he led them in a "Prayer for World Peace." He also took the stage in Hollywood, where he held a satellite conversation with thousands of young Catholics in four cities. He appeared in a music video, recorded the rosary, wrote best-selling books, answered reporters' questions, and offered candid photo opportunities to journalists. And on Christmas 1995, he launched the Vatican's website, beginning a whole new era in communication for the Catholic Church by connecting it to the World Wide Web.

The site (www.vatican.va) includes information about the papacy, Church history, document transcripts (in a variety of languages), contact information for the Holy Father, tourist information, and virtual tours of some of the Vatican's best-known treasures. Though few people would call the late pontiff a "computer geek," Pope John Paul II believed strongly in the Church's online presence and constantly looked for ways to push it forward. This was a far cry from the 1500s, when the Church saw new advancements in communication as a threat rather than as a complement to its mission.

On November 22, 2001, he made cyberspace history when he became the first pope to email an official apostolic letter to the Churches of Oceania. The following spring, he observed the 36th World Communications Day by inviting the faithful to use the internet to spread Christ's message. He noted the obvious pitfalls associated with the medium, but he preferred to see global communications as an opportunity rather than an obstacle:

> "While the internet can never replace that profound experience of God, which only the living liturgical and sacramental life of the Church can offer, it can certainly provide a unique supplement and support in both preparing for the coming encounter with Christ in community and sustaining the new believer in the journey of faith, which then begins."

Benedict Backs Social Media

After being elected to the papacy in 2005, Pope (Emeritus) Benedict XVI continued to embrace new media technology and explored new opportunities for communication among Catholics and the world around them. During his pontificate, he called the media a network of communication, communion, and cooperation and encouraged Catholics everywhere to use their gadgets and gizmos to explore their faith, to communicate their faith to others, and to connect with the worldwide community. He addressed this in his message for the 43rd World Communications Day in 2009:

"I ask you to introduce into the culture of this new environment of communications and information technology the values on which you have built your lives … Be sure to announce the Gospel to your contemporaries with enthusiasm. You know their fears and their hopes, their aspirations and their disappointments: the greatest gift you can give to them is to share with them the "Good News" of a God who became man, who suffered, died and rose again to save all people …"

Pope Benedict XVI later told Church leaders in his message for the 47th World Communications Day in 2013 that if they hoped to reach the next generation of Catholics, embracing social media was not optional. He understood that the digital environment was part of the faithful's daily experience, especially the younger generation and it was important to meet them in this forum in order to build a stronger relationship with them.

CATHOLIC QUOTE

Rarely affirm, seldom deny, always distinguish.

—St. Thomas Aquinas

New Media and the Year of Faith

Near the end of 2011, Pope Benedict announced that from October 2012 to November 2013, the Church would engage in a Year of Faith during which Catholics would be called to renew their relationship with Christ and to share that faith with others. With a significant number of Catholics connected via social media sites and other online portals, it was a sure bet that new media would play a key role in this effort.

The announcement came at the perfect time. Social media had hit its stride. A significant amount of Catholics connected through social media sites, such as Twitter, Facebook, and LinkedIn; 8 percent of Catholics had at least one Catholicism app downloaded on their mobile devices; and YouTube exploded with Catholic content channels, including the Vatican's own channel, EWTN, Catholic News Service, the Catholic TV Network, Young Catholic Minutes, and a variety of channels launched by local dioceses throughout the world.

It was the perfect opportunity to see how Catholics would use these platforms to get the gospel message across, and as usual, the Vatican led the way. In December 2012, Pope Benedict XVI became the first pontiff to send a personal "Tweet." Using the Twitter handle @Pontifex, his first message read: "Dear friends, I am pleased to get in touch with you through Twitter. Thank you for your generous response. I bless all of you from my heart."

The response ranged from the surprised to the skeptical, but for the most part, Catholics were happy to see that their leader was in touch with the current rage and was willing to speak to them on their level. There were gaffes along the way, of course. A few minutes after his first Tweet, the pope asked the faithful, "How can we celebrate the Year of Faith better in our daily lives?" He answered his own question a few minutes later, prompting a few followers to chuckle that perhaps the Holy Father didn't understand the interactive nature of social media.

FAST FACT

There are a number of social media pages that bear the pope's name, but most of these are fan sites. (Some pages will admit this, while others do not.) As of this writing, there is no official Facebook page for the papacy, so be aware that your "like" is not linking you to the successor of St. Peter.

Despite his "newbie" status, the pope got the hang of Twitter and used the forum to connect with the people. Although he championed the use of social media, Pope Benedict XVI warned Catholics not to let virtual socializing lead to an obsession. Though it was important to embrace new innovations and use them to responsibly promote Christ's message to the world, he cautioned Catholics to strike a balance between research and reflection. He said that when information is widely available, it is important to make time for those quiet moments in which one can distinguish what is vital and what is insignificant. He believed that in the silence, people could discover the connections between things that on face value do not seem related and then form an opinion based on what we discover, as he said in his message for the 46th World Communications Day in 2012:

> "For this to happen, it is necessary to develop an appropriate environment, a kind of 'eco-system' that maintains a just equilibrium between silence, words, images and sounds."

The Year of Faith was not about changing the message of the past, but giving people a new way to hear it so that they could recommit themselves to Christ; center their family on the teachings of the gospel; and make a difference at the local, diocesan, and global level. National bishops' conferences provided resources to the faithful in their regions and encouraged Catholics to connect with their parishes to find out how they could become more involved in these efforts.

CATHOLIC QUOTE

"Like it or not, I think Facebook is the new parish hall."

—Mary DeTurris Poust, Catholic journalist

In the end, the success of the Year of Faith was not dependent on how many new members came into the Church, but rather the individual impact that it had on Catholics and non-Catholics considering the Church everywhere. Cardinal Daniel DiNardo of the Archdiocese of Galveston-Houston said the Year of Faith "will not be judged as successful by the conversion of the world," but it will be judged as successful by those of us who have grown closer to the Lord."

There's an App for That

On January 23, 2013, as part of the Year of Faith, Pope Benedict XVI launched the first "Pope App," managed by the Pontifical Council for Social Communications. Using content from the Vatican's news organizations, the mobile application offers news and speeches from the Holy See in addition to images and video appearances. Users can also stream papal events live and receive alerts to upcoming events. Users can also access live webcams scattered throughout the Vatican, including the following:

- A view of the dome of St. Peter's Basilica

- A view of the tomb of Pope St. John Paul II

- A view of the papal retreat Castel Gandolfo

Within two months, the free app became the most downloaded news app for iPhone in the United States, Canada, Spain, Venezuela, Peru, Poland, Chile, Mexico, Portugal, and Argentina, according to CNA.

Catholic bloggers see the Church's use of new media like apps as something encouraging that not only connects Catholics to the faith, but also promotes open dialogue and may be the most powerful technology available to reach out to Catholics and non-Catholics alike.

Vacancy at the Vatican

Few papal announcements have made such a media impact as the one Pope Benedict XVI made on February 11, 2013, when he revealed that he would step down from the papacy at the end of that month. It was the kind of story that set social media abuzz with hashtags such as #pontifexit and caused pundits to speculate on the reasons behind his sudden retirement.

Understandably, it was a big deal. It was the first time in 600 years that a pope had made the decision to step down from the throne of Peter rather than die on the job, and the announcement caused a lot of Catholics to wonder, "Can he do that?"

Yes, he could. Vatican spokesperson Rev. Federico Lombardi, SJ, assured the press that the decision was not prompted by failing health or a fatal diagnosis and that the pope would live out his days known as Pope Emeritus, be addressed as "your holiness," and live in a small apartment in a refurbished convent on the Vatican grounds.

Reactions poured in from around the world, some on social media and others in a more traditional manner. World leaders wished the pontiff well and religious figures applauded his brave decision to step down when he felt that he could no longer perform the duties the job entailed.

Pope Benedict XVI's last day in office was February 28, 2013. There was no formal ceremony, but merely a final tweet to the faithful before he departed. His resignation meant that a new pope would be elected from the 115 cardinals eligible to participate in the conclave. This would be the first papal election to be followed not only on television and online, but also discussed widely through social media. Even though there was nothing to see until the white smoke rose from the Sistine Chapel, there was no shortage of insiders weighing in via social media with their thoughts of who should fill the shoes of St. Peter.

Francis Fuels the Media Fire

Although there was no real frontrunner for the job, the cardinals made their decision quickly. On March 13, 2013, after two days and five ballots, the white smoke appeared and an hour later Argentinean Jesuit Jorge Mario Bergoglio was presented to the world as Pope Francis. Word of his election spread like wildfire over social media outlets and spawned hashtags such as #whitesmoke, #habemuspapum, and #papa among others. One Catholic group in the United States had developed a Pope Alarm app that sent a text message or email when the white smoke appeared, although so many people signed on for the app that it ended up being one of the slower forms of communication that day. In addition to live news coverage of the conclave, pundits and bloggers scrambled to find any and all information about this virtually unknown person who was now the Vicar of Christ.

 CATHOLIC QUOTE

In the London betting houses I was in 44th place. Look at that. The one who bet on me won a lot, of course!

—Pope Francis

Pope Francis was an immediate hit with Catholics and non-Catholics alike. Naming himself after St. Francis of Assisi, the new pope was someone who believed in living simply, performing charitable acts of mercy, and being a bit of a social reformer as well. In Buenos Aires, he eschewed the archbishop's palace for a simple apartment, cooked his own meals, and relied on public transportation rather than owning a car or engaging the services of a chauffer.

Upon taking office, it was obvious that Pope Francis had every intention of continuing his unconventional but humble lifestyle in the Vatican. Stories swirled about the following when it came to him:

- Returning to his hotel after the papal conclave to pay his bill and collect his luggage himself rather than sending an assistant to do it for him.

- Eschewing the opulent papal apartments for a smaller residence that kept him connected to the people.

- Cold-calling people who had written him.

- Insisting that the Vatican needs to reflect the poor rather than those who are wealthy.

- Granting an interview to an atheist.

- Slipping out of the Vatican at night dressed as a simple priest in order to give alms to the poor (This is a rumor that Vatican officials will not confirm.)

Make no mistake, despite these unique news reports, Pope Francis is not radically changing the way the Church has done things for 2,000 years. He has no plans to allow women to be ordained. He's ruled out gay marriage, based on the book of Genesis and consistent Catholic moral theology, and his stance on human rights is loud and clear, but his actions show that the Church does not need to talk constantly about these issues, especially when there is real work to be done. He marvels that a drop in the stock market is front-page news while someone dying in the street is not. He expresses empathy for women considering abortion when faced with an unplanned pregnancy even as he adheres to the belief that all life is precious. And of course, he believes that it's not up to him to judge the heart of anyone living a good life and who is seeking Christ.

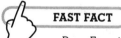 **FAST FACT**

Pope Francis is considerably more blue-collar than his academic predecessors. Early in life, Pope Francis completed stints as a nightclub bouncer, janitor, chemical technician, and literature teacher before following his vocation to the priesthood.

After his election, it was obvious that Pope Francis was ready to connect with his people. He assumed the papal Twitter handle @Pontifex and regularly tweets in English, Latin, German, Polish, Spanish, French, Portuguese, Italian, and Arabic. He has been known to pose for selfies with pilgrims he encounters. He's said that he considers the internet a unique gift and believes that the web is a tool that not only inspires unity among the faithful, but as the global community grows ever smaller, it gives new meaning to the term, "Who is my neighbor?" He addressed this in his message for the 48th World Communications Day in 2014:

"A culture of encounter demands that we be ready not only to give, but also to receive. Media can help us greatly in this, especially nowadays, when the networks of human communication have made unprecedented advances. The internet, in particular, offers immense possibilities for encounter and solidarity. This is something truly good, a gift from God."

The New Evangelization

Pope Francis and the new image he has portrayed of Catholicism could make him the poster child of a major movement in the Church recent years: the New Evangelization.

Generally speaking, the term *evangelization* is used to describe the act of spreading a system of beliefs or a religious message to someone who has not heard it yet. The intention of this act is to convert someone to this particular practice, and though it is associated with Christian movements, it is not limited to Christianity.

The apostles were the early evangelists associated with the Church, and it was their job to travel far and wide in hopes of establishing churches throughout the world. Their mission was carried on through the bishops, priests, and deacons who came after them, as well as the missionaries who traveled the world and introduced people to Christ for the first time.

In 2010, Pope Benedict XVI announced that it was time for the Church to make a concerted effort not only to continue its evangelization efforts with those who had never heard of Christ, but also to reach out to those who have fallen away from the Church and needed to reconnect with the gospel message. He called it the *New Evangelization.*

Unlike evangelization, the New Evangelization is aimed at those who have already heard the message—they have some general idea of who Jesus is and what Christianity is—but are not active disciples. Perhaps they never were formal members of a church, or they gradually fell away from active participation in a church out of indifference or apathy or laziness, or they deliberately turned their back on what they thought Christianity is about.

The New Evangelization seeks to re-propose the message of Jesus to those who have already heard the message with new ardor and new methods (such as digital media). An important part of the New Evangelization is that it is aimed not just at individuals—though personal discipleship and conversation is an important aspect—but also at culture.

Western culture historically was very much formed by Christianity, especially the moral teachings of the Church, but contemporary culture has separated itself from Christianity and is no longer friendly to dialogue with the Church. The New Evangelization proposes that Christianity still has much to speak to culture and should enter into dialogue with modern society. So part of the New Evangelization is about dialogue with business, media, academia, and politics, especially in Western Europe and North America, historically Christian areas that have been highly secularized in recent generations.

Resources Everywhere

With the Vatican promoting social media with a big thumbs-up (or "Like," if you prefer), there is no shortage of resources for Catholics to connect with one another online or read about current issues that are important to the Church. Here is a smattering of online resources for Catholics to get you started!

Vatican-Sponsored Apps

In May 2013, Pope Francis used the keys of St. Peter—the papal symbol depicting the crossed keys of Heaven—to launch Missio, a brand-new smartphone app developed by Little i Apps in conjunction with the Pontifical Mission Societies. Like the Pope App, Missio is free and available on iTunes and Google Play.

FAST FACT

Missio is available in eight different languages, including English, Spanish, Italian, German, French, Portuguese, Chinese, and Arabic.

Unlike the pope's Twitter account, Missio is designed to offer world news from a Catholic perspective. Like the Pope App, users have access to the pope's daily homilies, videos, and photos and according to an article in the *New York Daily News*, Missio is designed to serve as "a supplement to the Church's daily work on the ground in missions across the world."

Father Andrew Small, the U.S. director of Pontifical Mission Societies, was present as Pope Francis unlocked the app. He told the Holy Father that this app had the ability to put the gospel in the pocket of every person in the world with access to the technology.

Other Vatican-sponsored apps include Vatican.va, the app version of the official Vatican website, Vatican Web Radio, and the Pope App, mentioned earlier.

Catholic News Apps

The following are some current apps where you can find the latest Catholic news:

- **Catholic News Live:** The number-one Catholic news app, this offers a variety of stories from hundreds of websites. New stories are added every five minutes.

- **The Catholic Herald:** Lauded as one of the sharpest and most highly respected Catholic newspapers on the market, these weekly reports are essential reading.

- **National Catholic Register:** A service of EWTN, the National Catholic Register offers some of the finest Catholic journalism in the palm of your hand.

- **Catholic News Feed:** This brings some of the latest Catholic news from top Catholic news organizations in one convenient app.

Liturgical and Prayer Apps

The following apps provide Catholic prayers and information about Catholicism:

- **iMissal:** This app is the number-one Catholic app and has been granted an imprimatur from the Catholic Church. It contains all daily/Sunday readings, prayers, lives of the Saints, and daily Scripture reflections.

- **iRosary:** Built for the busy Catholic's lifestyle, iRosary is user friendly, customizable, and resembles a traditional rosary.

- **iBreviary:** This free app contains the complete Liturgy of the Hours, as well as prayers for Mass, in multiple languages.

- **Inner Monk:** This free app developed by the Benedictine monks of St. Meinrad Archabbey has short daily prayers at morning and evening. It is particularly designed for youth.

- **The Mass Explained Vol. 1 (iPad2 or newer):** This pricey but wonderful educational resource offers a rich and profound understanding of the Mass. (Volume 2 is coming soon.)

- **Laudate (Free iOS and Android):** This Catholic mash-up app offers daily readings, Saint of the Day, Chaplet of Divine Mercy, podcasts for daily meditation, and much more.

Online Resources

If you're looking for something beyond an app, check out the following websites:

- **Catholicity (catholicity.com):** This site offers prayers, rosary, saint stories, a Catholic encyclopedia, daily Mass readings, a voting guide, and much more!

- **Catholic Education Resource Center (catholiceducation.org):** This is an online resource library for Catholic faith and culture.

- **American Catholic (americancatholic.org):** From the Franciscans at St. Anthony Messenger Press, the daily features of this site include Saint of the Day, minute meditations, Catholic questions, and top Catholic news.

- **New Advent (newadvent.org):** One of the largest Catholic internet resources in the world, this contains daily news updates, the complete Catholic Encyclopedia, and the writings of the Church Fathers online.

- **Word on Fire (wordonfire.org):** Founded by Chicago priest Fr. Robert Barron, this site spans a variety of new and traditional media to connect Catholicism with culture.

Catholic YouTube Channels

YouTube is also a great resource with different Catholic channels, such as the following:

- **Catholic Answers:** This has a variety of media platforms with the goal of explaining and defending the Catholic faith.

- **EWTN:** Also a national TV and radio network, this media outlet founded by Mother Angelica is perhaps the most widely distributed Catholic media source in the United States.

- **Catholic News Service:** This is the official news agency for the U.S. Conference of Catholic Bishops whose mission is to report fully, fairly, and freely on the involvement of the Church in the world today.

- **The Catholic TV Network:** Based in the Archdiocese of Boston, this is an internet television network focusing on authentic Catholic programing.

 CATHOLIC QUOTE

Instead of being just a church that welcomes and receives by keeping the doors open, let us try also to be a church that finds new roads, that is able to step outside itself and go to those who do not attend Mass, to those who have quit or are indifferent.

—Pope Francis

Patron Saints of Technology

Not surprisingly, there are patron saints to cover any and all media. Have you ever wondered who could possibly be the patron saint of periodicals, the press, and public relations? Here's your chance to find out.

St. Clare of Assisi (1194–1253)

Not only was St. Clare of Assisi one of the first followers of St. Francis of Assisi and the founder of the Poor Clares, a female religious order based on the Franciscan tradition, Clare was also the first person to experience "televised" Mass.

No, she was not a time traveler, but when she was too ill to attend Mass, the Holy Spirit brought the Mass to her by projecting the image on her wall so she could participate in the sacrament from her bed. In 1958, at a time when new-fangled sets were finding their place in homes everywhere, Pope Pius XII named St. Clare of Assisi the patron saint of television.

St. Isidore of Seville (c. 560–636)

Known as the "schoolmaster of the Middle Ages," St. Isidore of Seville believed that knowledge truly was power and created a culture of education in his home country of Spain. He wrote an encyclopedia that became a textbook that was used for 900 years. In addition, he insisted that seminaries be installed in every diocese, wrote rules for religious orders, and penned numerous books, including one that chronicled the history of the world.

His role as the first "search engine" makes St. Isidore of Seville the patron saint of the internet.

St. Bernardine of Siena (1380–1444)

St. Bernardine was the go-to person whenever something needed to be done. He was a mover and a shaker who was not only the greatest preacher in the region, but also had the ability to relax war-torn cities, fight paganism that he could not abide by, and stay in touch with the mood of the people.

After entering the Franciscan Order and being ordained at the age of 22, St. Bernardine used his skills as a preacher and developed the IHS symbol (referencing the first three Greek letters of the name of Jesus) to combat the pagan symbolism of the day. His efforts to promote Christianity and create a "brand" symbol that everyone could get behind helped St. Bernardine of Siena become the patron saint of public relations.

St. Francis de Sales (1567–1622)

St. Francis de Sales was similar to a lot of spiritual writers who were told to "get a real job." His father pushed him into the legal profession and after securing his doctorate, he returned home to tell his folks that he needed to follow his call to become a priest.

At the age of 35, St. Francis de Sales was named the bishop of Geneva. In his career, he wrote two well-known books, the *Introduction to the Devout Life* and *A Treatise on the Love of God,* as well as plenty of pamphlets. He also kept up an impressive correspondence. For these reasons, he is considered the patron saint of the Catholic press.

St. Maximilian Kolbe (1894–1941)

Though he is best known for volunteering to die in place of a stranger at Auschwitz concentration camp, St. Maximilian Kolbe is the patron saint of the twentieth century, families, drug addicts, and journalists.

The last category is largely due to the fact that the Imaculata Friars (the order he joined) possessed the most cutting-edge printing equipment of the day and published not only devotional tracts, but a daily newspaper (with a 230,000 circulation) and monthly magazine (with a circulation of over 1 million) as well. He was recognized as a martyr and canonized a Catholic saint in 1982.

The Least You Need to Know

- The Catholic Church has been promoting communication since the first century.
- The Church promotes the use of social media and sees its potential to connect Catholics to their faith.
- The first pope to use the internet was Pope St. John Paul II.
- Through social media, the Catholic Church is aiming for the New Evangelization, or sharing the Church's message with those who have already heard it but are not active disciples.

A Conversation with a Priest

It's not always easy to "make your defense to anyone who demands from you an accounting of the hope that is within you." (1 Peter 3:15) However, through his vocation, a priest does exactly that and strives to help his congregation do the same.

On any given day, a priest may celebrate Mass, listen to confessions, visit the sick, council parishioners, teach a class, and so on. No two days are exactly alike, but the questions he fields have a lot of similarities. Cradle Catholics, converts, and the curious alike often have the same concerns and hope that a priest can shed a little light on them.

For this appendix, I talked to Father Eric Augenstein, Vocations Director for the Archdiocese of Indianapolis, and asked about the common queries he faces on any given day, his reflections on the Church's past, and where he sees Catholicism in the future.

Apologetics

A priest often finds himself defending the faith, especially when the Church is in the news. As you might imagine, a priest is no stranger to a vast number of questions ranging from the argumentative to the awkward and everything in between. Within the first year after his ordination, he has not only heard every confession one can imagine (and a few that one can't!), but he has also answered for everything the Church has ever done throughout its 2,000-year history. Here are just a few of the inquiries a priest responds to on a regular basis.

What is the biggest misconception about the Catholic faith?

Fr. Eric: The greatest misconception about Catholicism that I hear from non-Catholics is that we worship Mary and place her on the same level as God. While we certainly show great honor to Mary as the Mother of God and the model disciple, she is a human being, created by God, and definitely not an equal with God.

What is the most common question you are asked as a priest?

Fr. Eric: Especially now, in my work as a vocations director, the most common question I am asked is how can someone know what God wants them to do. Or, more generally, how can we listen to God's voice and know that it is God? In response, I often share my own experience of listening for God's voice and hearing His call to serve as a priest. The call first came through another person—one of my high school teachers—who recognized in me qualities that he thought indicated a possible priestly vocation. But where I really heard God's call was in prayer, regular prayer over a long period of time, as I grew in relationship with Jesus Christ.

The way I was able to discern what was God's voice—and not my own voice, the voices of other people, or the pressures of society—was that God's voice leads to peace and joy, not fear or anxiety. When I spent time in prayer in the presence of the Blessed Sacrament in the chapel at the college I attended and contemplated the possibility of being a priest, my heart was filled with an overwhelming sense of peace and joy. God speaks to the heart, and the best way to hear God's voice is to be attentive to what brings peace and joy and love to your heart.

Conspiracy Theories

There is no shortage of rumors that the Catholic Church is sitting on secrets, has destroyed evidence that could change the course of human history, and has single-handedly orchestrated the biggest cover-up ever recorded. When popular books, movies, or documentaries sensationalize these conspiracies, it often falls to a priest to remind folks what is fiction and what the Church believes to be fact.

Have movies such as *The Da Vinci Code, The Exorcist, Angels and Demons,* and others helped or hurt the reputation of the Church?

Fr. Eric: I have always thought that the best movies lead to conversation, no matter what the subject matter. When movies have as a major theme religion in general, or the Catholic Church in particular, the conversations people have after seeing these movies are critical. If the Church is unwilling to dialogue or talk about them, it can hurt our reputation and possibly perpetuate misconceptions about Catholicism. But if we're open to conversation, we can tell our story and listen to other people's perspectives as well.

When the movie version of *The Da Vinci Code* came out shortly after I was ordained a priest, we held a discussion night at the parish that was extremely well attended and was even covered by the local media! The conversations that resulted helped many people understand the history and teachings of the Catholic Church better, including ways *The Da Vinci Code* distorted that history—and those conversations were made possible by a book of fiction and an action-packed movie based on that book.

Big question: Has the Church gone to great lengths to hide the fact that Jesus was married and had a child prior to his death?

Fr. Eric: No. Everyone loves a conspiracy theory—and they can make great movies and novels! But when it comes down to historical evidence, there is absolutely no indication that Jesus was married and had a child or children prior to His death. If that had been true, imagine what great honor and respect would have been shown to His family at the time—and yet there is no record of this.

The early Church was anything but organized—it took several generations for the ragtag group of disciples and their descendants to develop a structure and a regular means of communication, both of which would have been necessary to "hide" such a significant thing as a wife and child of the Son of God. There's simply no evidence to support such a theory, and the most recent "discovery" of the "Jesus wife" papyrus has been shown to be more fraud than truth.

Did the Church really burn several texts in an effort to censor scriptural material from the faithful?

Fr. Eric: No. The process of discerning what texts are divinely inspired and what texts are human inventions is not an easy one. But to be included in Scripture, texts had to meet certain criteria: they had to be early and connected to someone who actually knew Jesus Christ while he was on Earth; they had to conform to the "Rule of Faith," the universally understood beliefs of the followers of Jesus Christ; and they had to agree with each other on matters of faith and morals, because one divinely inspired text cannot contradict another divinely inspired text (God can't contradict Himself).

Of all of the texts written since Jesus walked on earth, an extraordinarily small minority meets these criteria and can thus be considered Christian Scripture. In recent years, a number of writings about Jesus have been rediscovered—the only existing copies had been lost for many centuries and are now being studied with great interest. We imagine that the early Church Fathers would have been familiar with many of these texts, but did not include them in the collection of Christian Scripture for good reasons, because they did not meet the criteria for discerning whether they were divinely inspired. For example, they were often written by people or communities that were on the fringes of Christianity and held beliefs that are not consistent with the common faith tradition. So they can't be considered Scripture—they are not the Word of God speaking to the people of God. Some of them might contain pieces of the Word of God, but not in their entirety.

It's possible that the Church at times may have destroyed some of these texts in an effort to preserve the recognized teachings of Jesus Christ, but that's very different from "hiding Scripture" for the purpose of withholding truth or being deceptive. Out of great love and concern for the authentic truth of the gospel, the Church has safeguarded the texts of Scripture that we believe come to us directly from God, not as an invention of human beings.

Peeking into the Past

Fr. Eric, in your opinion, what are the top ten events that historically define the Catholic Church?

1. **The Debate over the Date of Easter (195):** In the early Church, some Christians celebrated Easter on the actual anniversary of Jesus' resurrection, regardless of the day of the week it fell on, while others always celebrated Easter on Sunday. Pope Victor I weighed in on the debate in favor of the Sunday celebration, and that decision became the prevalent practice. It's the first example of the influence of the bishop of Rome, the pope, over the entire Church.

2. **The Edict of Milan (313):** Publicly professing and practicing the Christian faith was illegal in the Roman Empire, and Christians suffered on-and-off persecutions for the first three centuries of the Church. Constantine's Edict of Milan legalized Christianity in the Roman Empire and thus opened the door for the spread of the Church throughout the known world.

3. **The Rule of St. Benedict (529):** During a time of decline in the Roman Empire, St. Benedict became the father of a new Christian movement—monasticism. The monasteries that followed his Rule became some of the most influential communities in preserving and promoting the faith up to this day.

4. **The Sack of Constantinople (1204):** One of the saddest days in the history of Christianity. While on their way to the Holy Land, soldiers participating in the Fourth Crusade captured, looted, and vandalized the city of Constantinople, the center of the Orthodox Christian Church. It was a battle of Christian versus Christian and solidified the break between the Eastern and Western Churches that had formally begun a century and a half earlier.

5. **St. Francis of Assisi and the Mendicant Friars (1205):** St. Francis of Assisi revolutionized religious life in the Church by founding a group of wandering, begging friars who spread the faith throughout Europe, as opposed to the monastic communities, which were isolated from the world in their monastic enclosures. His solidarity with the poor and with God's creation continues to be inspirational today.

6. **The Black Death (1347–1350):** An estimated one third of the population of Europe died in a three-year period, one of the most devastating periods in human history. Priests and religious either fled infected towns for fear of contracting the plague or helped care for the victims and then died of the disease themselves—so Europe was left in desperate need of new priests and religious after the Black Death passed. In the rush to bring new clergy and religious into ministry, standards were lowered and training was scarce, leading to many of the abuses in the Church that sparked the Protestant Reformation.

7. **St. Francis Xavier and Evangelization in the Far East (1541):** The sixteenth century saw the first major movement of the Church beyond Europe, and perhaps no one was more successful as a Christian missionary than St. Francis Xavier. His mission of evangelization took him to China, India, and Japan, where he personally baptized over 40,000 people.

8. **The Ecumenical Council of Trent (1545–1563):** The Council of Trent was the Catholic Church's answer to the Protestant Reformation, solidifying doctrine and taking steps to ensure unity of liturgical practice and belief. The Council produced a Catechism and a Missal (both in Latin) that would be in use for 400 years.

9. **Pope Leo XIII's *Encyclical Rerum Novarum* (1891):** Written in the midst of worldwide industrialization, this first of many *Social Encyclicals* of the popes called for a just wage and articulated the rights and duties of both workers and employers. The unified body of Catholic social teaching has its origin in this document.

10. **The Second Vatican Ecumenical Council (1962–1965):** Unlike previous Ecumenical Councils, which had been convened to determine the teachings of the Church, the Second Vatican Council was a Pastoral Council, bringing the Church into the modern world and articulating the relationship between the Church and society. It marked a change in attitude more than a change in belief.

Setting the Stage for the Future

The past 50 years have also seen several historic events that have set the stage for the future of the Catholic Church. In your opinion, which ones make the top five list?

1. **Meeting of Pope Paul VI and Patriarch Athenagoras I, Ecumenical Patriarch of Constantinople (1964):** Held in Jerusalem, this encounter marked the first meeting of a pope and an ecumenical patriarch since the formal split between the Catholic Church and the Orthodox Churches in 1054. Ecumenical dialogue between East and West has been strengthened in the past 50 years.

2. **World Youth Day (begun in 1984):** Held every two or three years in cities around the world, Pope St. John Paul II began these gatherings of young people, which are part spiritual pilgrimage, part catechesis, and part mega-concert. The largest gathering of humanity in one place was at Manila in the Philippines for World Youth Day 1995, when an estimated 5 million people gathered for the closing Mass.

3. **Publication of the Catechism of the Catholic Church (1992):** The first universal Catechism since the Council of Trent in the sixteenth century, this Catechism grew out of the Second Vatican Council and presents a unified body of Catholic beliefs. Having

been translated into countless languages, people throughout the world can now learn what the Catholic Church is all about.

4. **Joint Declaration on the Doctrine of Justification (1999):** Signed by the Vatican and the Lutheran World Federation, this document acknowledged that Catholics and most Lutherans believe the same thing about justification, one of the central dividing points of the Protestant Reformation. Such an agreement marked one of the most important steps in ecumenical dialogue between the Catholic Church and a major Protestant community.

5. **Election of the First Pope from the Americas (2013):** The largest growth of the Catholic Church over the past century has been in South America, Africa, and Asia. The election of Pope Francis from Argentina marks the rise of global Catholicism and the decline of Western Europe as the center of the Church.

Current Events

Pope Francis may not be the first pope to be named *Time* magazine's Person of the Year, but he is the first to land on the cover of *Rolling Stone,* and his popularity rivals that of Pope St. John Paul II. Some people think he is the best thing to happen to the Catholic Church in ages, and even priests have commented, "Is he too good to be true?" I asked Fr. Eric his opinion on Pope Francis and the state of the Catholic Church throughout the world.

What is your take on the unprecedented popularity of Pope Francis?

Fr. Eric: The Church and the world have been blessed over the past century with some extraordinary popes, holy and wise men who have shepherded the Church well. Each one has brought his own gifts to the Chair of St. Peter—Pope St. John XXIII brought an openness to the movements of the Holy Spirit, Pope St. John Paul II brought a missionary zeal and an ability to connect with young and old around the world, Pope Benedict XVI brought the heart of a teacher and a witness to humility. Pope Francis has brought to the papacy a love of the poor—those on the fringes of society—and an authenticity that challenges others to follow his example.

It's not fair to compare popes to each other and to try to rank them in order of effectiveness. I truly believe that the Holy Spirit provides the right pope for the Church and the world at the right time. In inspiring the College of Cardinals to elect Pope Francis, I think the Holy Spirit was guiding us to consider how the Church at this moment in our history needs to go outside of itself to be a visible presence of love and mercy in the world.

One reason Pope Francis has been so popular and universally praised is that the world is in desperate need of the very things he has focused on, both before and after being elected pope—the Church and the world desperately need love and mercy and healing and hope and humility.

Pope Francis has been a witness to all of these things, and he is challenging all of us to follow his example.

Will there be revolutionary changes with Pope Francis in office?

Fr. Eric: I think the call for revolutionary changes in the Catholic Church is more a product of the media than of Catholics in the pews or in the sanctuaries. Around the time of the 2013 papal election, Cardinal Timothy Dolan, the Archbishop of New York, remarked that the Church is about change, big time—a change of heart, a conversion within each person away from love of self and toward love of God and neighbor. That's the kind of change that Pope Francis is calling us toward, not a change of structures or doctrine or moral teaching.

Now, there may be some visible changes that are necessary for the Church to fulfill her mission of helping people grow in relationship with God and in love of neighbor—perhaps some changes to the structure of the offices in the Vatican or the way bishops seek consultation and assistance in setting priorities for ministries. But it's a change of heart that is the focus of Pope Francis' papal ministry.

Some people may be disappointed when they realize this, or they may be resistant to this message because change of heart isn't easy and can be a messy affair. But if true change of heart happens, then we will see revolutionary changes in the way people treat one another, in the ways we work for justice and peace in the world, in the way we distribute resources, and in the way we set our daily priorities as Catholics and as human beings.

Pope Francis has suggested that there needs to be a better theology for women in the Church. What could that look like?

Fr. Eric: In his comments on the role of women in the Church, Pope Francis said that women are more important than bishops and priests, just like Mary was more important than the apostles. But just as Mary's role was different than the role of the apostles, so the role of women in the Church is different than the role of bishops and priests—and that's the part that we need to do a better job figuring out.

What Pope St. John Paul II called *the feminine genius* is seen in Scripture in the women who were faithful to Jesus during His suffering, when most of the men had fled in fear; in the women who were the first witnesses to the resurrection of Jesus Christ and the first to spread that good news; and in the women of the early Church who provided for the needs of the community out of their own resources. Today, this "feminine genius" is seen in those who care for the suffering when no one else wants to, who hand the faith to future generations, and who are a source of community and fellowship for those on the path of discipleship.

All of those ministries are central to the mission of the Church, and it is often women who are best equipped to lead the way and chart the path. In addition, I imagine that a major way women can be given a more active role in the Church is through leadership in decision-making positions on the diocesan and parish level, in addition to the Vatican. When important decisions need to be made and priorities for ministry set, the people around the table should reflect the entirety of the Church: ordained, consecrated religious, married, single, lay, men, women, rich, poor, from multiple ethnic groups and backgrounds. And we as a Church can do a better job of gathering everyone together.

How do you feel about the Church's promotion of new media?

Fr. Eric: Priests are really no different from the general population when it comes to technology—some embrace it willingly and utilize it fully, while others stay as far away as they can from the latest gadgets. But for most of us, we try to strike a balance—effective use of technology and digital media as tools of communication and evangelization, while not allowing them to take the place of building personal relationships. When St. Paul traveled throughout the ancient world spreading the message of Jesus Christ, he went to where the people were—the marketplaces and public gathering spaces in the cities.

Today, we clergy recognize that many people are found in the digital marketplace, and so we want to be there, too. We go where the people are. But along the way, we are cautious about technology and social media eclipsing the heart of Christianity—which is all about personal relationships. And for every priest with a Facebook account and a blog, there is another priest who only communicates through handwritten notes. And that's okay!

Calling the Faithful

The New Evangelization efforts have done a lot to encourage the Church to invite new members to join and to welcome back those who have fallen away. This is a departure from the standard method of connecting Catholics and non-Catholics to the faith, but it is a movement people are embracing. I asked Fr. Eric about this effort and how it has transformed the way the Church looks at evangelization.

Why is there such a need for evangelization right now?

Fr. Eric: Because of a number of different historical factors, Catholics in recent centuries have been pretty insulated. In the United States, Catholics were often a distrusted minority, and so for several generations they interacted almost exclusively with other Catholics, usually from their same country of origin—hence the enclaves in different parts of the country of Irish Catholics, German Catholics, Polish Catholics, and so on. Catholics had their own schools, their own health care institutions, their own social clubs, their own service organizations, and their own neighborhoods.

Over the past 50 years, things have changed, and Catholics have begun to get more involved with people and communities outside the Church. As this process has continued, the Catholic Church has seen the need to reach out beyond its own numbers to share the gospel message, both with individuals and with the culture as a whole. It's not really a new thing for Catholics to evangelize—think of the early apostles, the great missionaries like St. Patrick in Ireland in the fourth century and St. Boniface in Germany in the seventh century, or the Jesuit and Franciscan missionaries in Asia and the Americas in the fifteenth and sixteenth centuries. But especially for Catholics in the United States and Western Europe, it has been a while since we have focused on evangelization—so it seems like something new, which it is, since the New Evangelization is a different model of evangelization that is geared toward those who have heard about Jesus before but have fallen away from an active faith life.

How can ordinary Catholics evangelize and encourage others to explore the Catholic faith?

Fr. Eric: The first step in evangelization is to grow in your own relationship with God, to become an intentional disciple of Jesus Christ who strives to grow daily in faith, hope, and love. Then, simply be a good example and witness to the people around you. We evangelize most effectively by our actions and our attitude. A dour, unhappy hypocrite does not attract. But a joyful, loving, merciful person does, and people will start to wonder, "What makes that person so happy, so ful-filled, so generous?" And then we can tell them about our relationship with Jesus Christ in the Church that is the foundation of our lives.

What do you want people to know about Catholicism?

Fr. Eric: More than anything else, Catholicism is not an institution—it is a relationship, or, as Pope Francis has said, a love story. Catholicism helps us recognize God's love for us, celebrate that love, and learn how to love in turn.

Glossary

a cappella   A term for unaccompanied singing, literally meaning "from the chapel."

abortion   The termination of a pregnancy through a medical procedure.

annulment   A decree recognizing a marriage that was previously sanctified by the Catholic Church as invalid.

apocalyptic   Derived from the Greek word *apocalypsis,* meaning "revelation"; describes a type of literature that includes visions of the end of the world.

apocrypha   The seven books of the Catholic Bible that are not considered official canon by the Jewish tradition or by other Christian denominations.

apostolic   Of or based on the teachings of the original 12 followers of Jesus Christ.

beatification   The term used to denote that a venerated servant of God has used his or her intercessory power to secure a miracle for someone on earth.

begotten   To give rise or to create. In the matter of the Holy Trinity, it explains the existence of God the Son outside our understanding of creation.

canon   An official law of the Church or a list that meets certain criteria. It comes from the Greek word *kanon,* meaning "rule" or "measuring stick."

catechumen   An unbaptized adult who is studying the Catholic faith with the intention of joining the Church.

catholic   A derivation from the Greek word *Katholikos,* meaning "universal" or "concerning the whole."

common good   That which benefits the interests of everyone involved.

conclave   A secret meeting during which the College of Cardinals elects a new pope. It comes from the Latin term *cum clavis* meaning "with a key."

conscience   The awareness of and attentiveness to the voice of God guiding our actions toward the good, the true, and the beautiful.

contrition   The longing inside one's self to turn away from sin and improve one's life for the better.

covenant   An agreement between God and His people.

creed   A formal statement of Church beliefs, doctrine, or ideology.

crucifix   A religious image that depicts Jesus' execution. It includes both the cross and the body of Christ upon it.

deuterocanonical   Refers to the seven books that were the second group of books to be recognized as authentic Scripture by the Catholic Church.

diocese   The regional Catholic structure led by a bishop, archbishop, or cardinal that oversees a number of parishes within a specific geographical region.

discernment   The process by which one discovers how God is calling him or her to follow Him.

domestic church   The faith environment within the home.

Emmanuel   A Hebrew word that means "God with us."

ex cathedra   From the Latin, meaning "from the chair." It is used as a technical term when referring to a special case in which the pope exercises his authority to speak infallibly on a matter of faith or morals.

excommunication   The exclusion of a Catholic from the sacraments of the Church.

faith   The complete knowledge and trust in something that lacks empirical proof.

free will   The God-given ability to act on one's own behalf without being influenced by someone else.

godparent   One who promises to assist the parents of a newly baptized child in raising the child according to the laws of the Catholic Church.

gospel   From the Greek word *evangelion,* meaning "good news," this is a unique literary form that tells the story of Jesus Christ for the purpose of leading people to faith.

grace   God's free and unmerited help.

Holy Trinity   The idea of a single God that inhabits three separate but equal parts.

Immaculate Conception   The conception of Mary without the stain of Original Sin on her soul.

litany   A repetitive series of petitions used in formal services or private prayer.

Kyrie   A Greek word that means "Lord." In the Mass, the Kyrie is a chanted call asking for mercy from Christ.

Magnificat   Mary's song of praise found in the Gospel of Luke; often called "Mary's Hymn."

Messiah   A Hebrew word meaning anointed one. Christ is the Greek translation of Messiah.

Missal   A book that contains the texts and directions for celebrating Mass in the Catholic Church.

mystagogy   The ongoing study of the mysteries of the Catholic faith.

novena   A vocal prayer (sometimes invoking a saint) that is prayed over an extended period of time and is usually connected to a specific intention.

Original Sin   Man's natural inclination to reject the will of God in favor of his or her own selfish desires and personal satisfaction.

Paschal Mystery   Refers to all of the events surrounding the suffering, death, and resurrection of Jesus and its meaning for humanity.

parable   A story with a moral lesson, used often in the Gospels.

parish   The name for the local Church structure where Catholics attend Mass and participate in the sacraments, and also the group of people who gather there.

Pentecost   In the Jewish tradition, the word refers to the festival of Weeks, but it is celebrated by Christians as the day the Holy Spirit came to the apostles.

positio   A documented account of the life, work, and writings of an individual being considered for eventual canonization.

prophet   A messenger who proclaims the will of God.

relic   An object associated with a saint. It can be a bone or other part of the body, or an object that once belonged to or was used by a saint.

Requiem Mass   A Mass for the dead that is sung for the repose of the soul of the deceased.

retreat   A withdrawal from daily life in order to renew and rejuvenate. From a religious perspective it is an opportunity to help one improve one's relationship with God.

rite   A tradition that regulates the liturgy, discipline, and governance of particular churches.

Roman Curia   The administrative body of the Holy See that through the pope governs the Catholic Church.

sacrament   Derived from the Latin word *sacramentum,* meaning a holy and visible sign that represents the intangible in order to refine ones faith.

sacramental   A sacred sign or action featured in a blessing. These can include holy water, candles, incense, and oil.

saint   Any deceased individual who is believed to be residing in Heaven.

Sanctus   A Latin word that means holy. In the Mass, it is the name of the chant praising God as the people did when He made his entry into Jerusalem.

Satan   Derived from a Hebrew term meaning "adversary."

server   A young person (boy or girl) who assists the priest at Mass.

sin   Any thought, word, or deed that causes man to disrupt the natural order of things as God has arranged them.

soul   The part of a human being that is immortal and is the presence of God within us. It is unique to each individual, has its origin at the moment of the person's conception, and continues to live on after death.

subsidiarity   The principle that all matters should be handled at the lowest level of authority possible for a good solution, rather than the highest.

Synoptic   A Greek term that means "to look similar." In describing the first three Gospels, it recognizes that they share a similar outline, structure, and stories.

Torah   The first five books of the Bible considered the law of the Jewish people. It is also called the Pentateuch (literally "five books").

transubstantiation   A theological term used to explain the presence of Christ in the bread and wine during a Catholic communion service.

triune God   A term for a single God with three separate yet equal parts.

Viaticum   A Latin word meaning "food for the journey." It refers to the last Eucharist one receives before death.

vocation   A call from God into a field for which one is particularly well suited. In a spiritual sense, it is not a career or a profession, but can overlap with these areas as well.

Yahweh   The name God revealed to Moses from the burning bush. In Hebrew, its translation means "I Am Who I Am."

Quick Reference

The Apostles' Creed (Chapter 1)

I believe in God,

the Father almighty,

Creator of heaven and earth,

And in Jesus Christ, his only Son, our Lord,

who was conceived by the Holy spirit,

born of the Virgin Mary,

suffered under Pontius Pilate,

was crucified, died and was buried;

he descended into hell;

on the third day he rose again from the dead;

he ascended into heaven,

and is seated at the right hand of God the Father Almighty;

from there he will come to judge the living and the dead.

I believe in the Holy Spirit,

the holy catholic Church,

the communion of saints,

the forgiveness of sins,

the resurrection of the body,

and life everlasting. Amen.

The Nicene Creed (Chapter 1)

I believe in one God,

the father almighty,

maker of heaven and earth,

of all things visible and invisible.

I believe in one Lord Jesus Christ,

the only Begotten Son of God,

born of the Father before all ages.

God from God, Light from Light,

true God from true God,

begotten, not made, consubstantial with the Father;

through him all things were made.

For us men and for our salvation

He came down from heaven,

and by the Holy Spirit was incarnate of the Virgin Mary,

and became man.

For our sake he was crucified under Pontius Pilate,

He suffered death and was buried,

and rose again on the third day

in accordance with the Scriptures.

He ascended into heaven

and is seated at the right hand of the Father.

He will come again in glory

to judge the living and the dead

and his kingdom will have no end.

I believe in the Holy Spirit, the Lord, the giver of Life,

who proceeds from the Father and the Son,

who with the father and the Son is adored and glorified,

who has spoken through the prophets.

I believe in one holy catholic and apostolic Church,

I confess one baptism for the forgiveness of sins

and I look forward to the resurrection of the dead

and the life of the world to come. Amen.

Our Father (Chapter 14)

Our Father, Who art in heaven, hallowed be Thy name; Thy kingdom come, Thy will be done on earth as it is in heaven. Give us this day our daily bread, and forgive us our trespasses, as we forgive those who trespass against us; and lead us not into temptation, but deliver us from evil. Amen.

Glory Be (Chapter 14)

Glory Be to the Father, and to the Son, and to the Holy Spirit. As it was in the beginning, is now, and ever shall be, world without end. Amen.

Prayer Blessing Before Meals (Chapter 14)

Bless us, O Lord, and these Thy gifts, which we are about to receive from Thy bounty through Christ our Lord. Amen.

Grace After Meals (Chapter 14)

We give You thanks, Almighty God, for these and all thy gifts, Who live and reign forever. Amen.

Guardian Angel Prayer (Chapter 14)

Angel of God, my guardian dear, to whom God's love commits me here, ever this day be at my side, to light and guard, to rule and guide. Amen.

Prayer to the Holy Spirit (Chapter 14)

Come, Holy Spirit, fill the hearts of your faithful and kindle in them the fire of your love.

Verse: Send forth your Spirit and they shall be created.

Response: And you shall renew the face of the earth.

O God, by the light of the Holy Spirit you have taught the hearts of your faithful. In the same Spirit help us to relish what is right and always rejoice in your consolation. We ask this through Christ our Lord. Amen.

Prayer to St. Michael (Chapter 14)

St. Michael the Archangel, defend us in battle. Be our safeguard against the wickedness and snares of the devil. May God rebuke him, we humbly pray, and do thou, O prince of the heavenly host, by the power of God cast into hell Satan and all the evil spirits who prowl through the world seeking the ruin of souls. Amen.

Prayer for the Deceased (Chapter 14)

Eternal rest grant unto him/her, O Lord, and let perpetual light shine upon him/her. May he/she rest in peace. Amen.

Prayer of St. Francis (Chapter 14)

Lord, make me an instrument of your peace. Where there is hatred, let me sow love; where there is injury, pardon; where there is doubt, faith; where there is despair, hope; where there is darkness, light; where there is sadness, joy. O Divine Master, grant that I may seek not so much to be consoled, as to console; to be understood, as to understand; to be loved, as to love. For it is in giving that we receive, in pardoning that we are pardoned, and in dying that we are born to eternal life.

The Divine Praises (Chapter 14)

Blessed be God.

Blessed be His Holy Name.

Blessed be Jesus Christ, true God and true man.

Blessed be the Name of Jesus.

Blessed be His Most Sacred Heart.

Blessed be His Most Precious Blood.

Blessed be Jesus in the Most Holy Sacrament of the Altar.

Blessed be the Holy Spirit, the Paraclete.

Blessed be the great Mother of God, Mary Most Holy.

Blessed be her Holy and Immaculate Conception.

Blessed be her Glorious Assumption.

Blessed be the name of Mary, Virgin and Mother.

Blessed be Saint Joseph, her most chaste spouse.

Blessed be God in His angels and in His saints.

Act of Hope

Good Jesus, in You alone I place all my hope. You are my salvation and my strength, the source of all good. Through Your mercy, through Your Passion and Death, I hope to obtain the pardon of my sins, the grace of final perseverance and happy eternity.

Act of Love

Jesus, my God, I love You with my whole heart and above all things, because You are the one supreme Good and infinitely perfect Being. You have given Your life for me, a poor sinner, and in your mercy You have offered Yourself as food for my soul.

My God, I love You. Inflame my heart to love You more.

Act of Faith

Jesus I firmly believe that You are present within me as God and Man, to enrich my soul with graces and to fill my heart with the happiness of the blessed. I believe that you are Christ, Son of the living God!

Act of Contrition (Chapter 7)

Oh my God, I am heartily sorry for having offended Thee, and I detest all of my sins because of Thy just punishments, but most of all for having offended Thee, my God who are all-good and deserving of all my love. I firmly resolve with the help of Thy grace, to sin no more and to avoid the near occasion of sin. Amen.

Hail Mary (Chapter 15)

Hail Mary, full of grace! The Lord is with thee; blessed art thou among women, and blessed is the fruit of thy womb, Jesus. Holy Mary, Mother of God, pray for us sinners now and at the hour of our death. Amen.

Memorare (Chapter 15)

Remember, O most gracious Virgin Mary, that never was it known that anyone who fled to thy protection, implored thy help, or sought thine intercession was left unaided.

Inspired by this confidence, I fly unto thee, O Virgin of virgins, my mother; to thee do I come, before thee I stand, sinful and sorrowful. O Mother of the Word Incarnate, despise not my petitions, but in thy mercy hear and answer me. Amen.

Hail, Holy Queen (Chapter 15)

Hail, Holy Queen, Mother of mercy, our life, our sweetness, and our hope! To thee do we cry, poor banished children of Eve! To thee do we send up our sighs, mourning and weeping in this valley of tears!

Turn then, most gracious advocate, thine eyes of mercy towards us; and after this our exile, show unto us the blessed fruit of thy womb, Jesus!

O clement, O loving, O sweet Virgin Mary!

The Ten Commandments (Chapter 10)

1. I am the Lord your God: you shall not have other gods before me.
2. You shall not take the name of the Lord your God in vain.
3. Remember to keep holy the Sabbath day.
4. Honor your father and mother.
5. You shall not kill.
6. You shall not commit adultery.
7. You shall not steal.
8. You shall not bear false witness against your neighbor.
9. You shall not covet your neighbor's wife.
10. You shall not covet your neighbor's goods.

(Adapted from Exodus 20:2–17 and Deuteronomy 5:6–21)

The Beatitudes (Chapter 11)

- "Blessed are the poor in spirit, for theirs is the kingdom of heaven.

- "Blessed are those who mourn, for they will be comforted.

- "Blessed are the meek, for they will inherit the earth.

- "Blessed are those who hunger and thirst for righteousness, for they will be filled.

- "Blessed are the merciful, for they will receive mercy.

- "Blessed are the pure in heart, for they will see God.

- "Blessed are the peacemakers, for they will be called children of God.

- "Blessed are those who are persecuted for righteousness' sake, for theirs is the kingdom of heaven.

- "Blessed are you when people revile you and persecute you and utter all kinds of evil against you falsely on my account. Rejoice and be glad, for your reward is great in heaven." (Matthew 5:3–12)

The Seven Sacraments of the Catholic Church (Chapter 5)

1. Baptism

2. Eucharist

3. Confirmation

4. Penance and Reconciliation

5. Holy Orders

6. Holy Matrimony

7. Anointing of the Sick

The Gifts of the Holy Spirit (Chapter 6)

1. Wisdom

2. Understanding

3. Counsel

4. Fortitude

5. Knowledge

6. Piety

7. Fear of the Lord

Cardinal Virtues (Chapter 11)

1. Prudence

2. Justice

3. Fortitude

4. Temperance

Theological Virtues (Chapter 11)

1. Faith

2. Hope

3. Charity (Love)

Seven Deadly Sins (Chapter 11)

1. Lust

2. Sloth

3. Gluttony

4. Greed

5. Pride

6. Envy

7. Anger

Mysteries of the Rosary (Chapter 15)

The Joyful Mysteries

1. The Annunciation

2. The Visitation

3. The Nativity

4. The Presentation in the Temple

5. The Finding in the Temple

The Luminous Mysteries

1. The Baptism of Jesus

2. The Miracle at the Wedding of Cana

3. The Proclamation of the Kingdom of God

4. The Transfiguration

5. The Institution of the Eucharist

The Sorrowful Mysteries

1. The Agony in the Garden

2. The Scouring at the Pillar

3. Jesus Is Crowned with Thorns

4. Jesus Carries His Cross

5. The Crucifixion

The Glorious Mysteries

1. The Resurrection

2. The Ascension

3. The Descent of the Holy Spirit

4. The Assumption of the Blessed Virgin Mary

5. The Crowning of the Blessed Virgin Mary

The Corporal Works of Mercy (Chapter 21)

1. Feed the hungry

2. Give drink to the thirsty

3. Clothe the naked

4. Shelter the homeless

5. Visit the sick

6. Visit the imprisoned

7. Bury the dead

The Spiritual Works of Mercy (Chapter 21)

1. Admonish the sinner

2. Instruct the ignorant

3. Counsel the doubtful

4. Comfort the sorrowful

5. Bear wrongs patiently

6. Forgive all injuries

7. Pray for the living and the dead

Traditional Stations of the Cross (Chapter 22)

1. Jesus is condemned.

2. Jesus carries His cross.

3. Jesus falls.

4. Jesus meets His mother.

5. Simon helps Jesus carry the cross.

6. Veronica wipes the face of Jesus.

7. Jesus falls again.

8. Jesus counsels the women of Jerusalem.

9. Jesus falls a third time.

10. Jesus is stripped.

11. Jesus is nailed to the cross.

12. Jesus dies on the cross.

13. Jesus is removed from the cross.

14. Jesus is laid in the tomb.

Scriptural Stations of the Cross

1. Jesus in the Garden of Gethsemane.

2. Jesus, betrayed by Judas, is arrested.

3. Jesus is condemned by the Sanhedrin.

4. Jesus is denied by Peter.

5. Jesus is judged by Pilate.

6. Jesus is scourged and crowned with thorns.

7. Jesus bears the cross.

8. Jesus is helped by Simon the Cyrenian to carry the cross.

9. Jesus meets the women of Jerusalem.

10. Jesus is crucified.

11. Jesus promises His kingdom to the good thief.

12. Jesus speaks to His mother and disciple.

13. Jesus dies on the cross.

14. Jesus is placed in the tomb.

Common Catholic Abbreviations

In your exploration of the Catholic faith, you may come across some abbreviations that are confusing. Though we have avoided using a lot of them in this book for purposes of clarity, here are a few you may run into and what they mean:

JMJ: Jesus, Mary, and Joseph

BVM: Blessed Virgin Mary

AMDG: *Ad Majorem Dei Gloriam,* Latin expression meaning "For the Greater Glory of God."

WYD: World Youth Day

NCYC: National Catholic Youth Council

FOCUS: Fellowship of Catholic University Students

USCCB: United States Council of Catholic Bishops

IHS: In Greek, the name "Jesus" is translated "ihsous," so this symbol represents the first three letters of His name.

XP (on top of each other, also known as the ✳): This symbol, known as Constantine's Cross, is another monogram, using the Greek spelling of the word "Christos."

CCC: Catechism of the Catholic Church

AD: *Anno Domini* (Latin for "Year of our Lord")

BC: Before Christ

VF: A title found after a priest's name to denote that he is a *Vicar Forane*, or a dean of his diocese.

VE: a title found after a priest's name, which stands for the Latin *Verbo Encarnado* meaning Institute of the Incarnate Word.

VG: Stands for Vicar General.

STD: Found after a priest's name. It stands for the Latin term *Sacrae Theologiae Doctor* or "Doctor of Sacred Theology."

HH: Found before the pope's name to denote "His Holiness."

INRI: These letters are often found above the body of Jesus on the crucifix and stand for the Latin term *Iesus Nazarenus Rex Iudaeorum* which means "Jesus of Nazareth King of the Jews."

IC XC: Another Greek monogram for Jesus. This one stands for the complete term "Jesus Christ."

Abbreviations for Common Catholic Religious Orders

SJ: Society of Jesus

OFM: Order of Friars Minor (Franciscans)

OSB: Order of St. Benedict

OP: Order of Preachers (Dominicans)

CSsR: Congregation of the Most Holy Redeemer

MC: Missionaries of Charity

OCSO: Order of Cistercians of the Strict Observance

CSC: Congregation of Holy Cross (Holy Cross Fathers)

FSC: Brothers of the Christian Schools (Christian Brothers or Lasallians)

OCD: Order of Discalced Carmelites

OSA: Order of St. Augustine (Augustinians)

OMI: Oblates of Mary Immaculate (Missionary Oblates)

(Source: http://www.fisheaters.com/religiousorderabbreviations.html)

Popes of the Catholic Church

1. St. Peter (AD 33–67)

2. St. Linus (67–76)

3. St. Anacletus I (76–88)

4. St. Clement I (88–97)

5. St. Evaristus (97–105)

6. St. Alexander I (105–115)

7. St. Sixtus I (115–125)

8. St. Telesphorus (125–136)

9. St. Hyginus (136–140)

10. St. Pius I (140–155)

11. St. Anicetus (155–166)

12. St. Soter (166–175)

13. St. Eleuterius (175–189)

14. St. Victor I (189–199)

15. St. Zephyrinus (199–217)

16. St. Callistus I (217–222)

17. St. Urban I (222–230)

18. St. Pontian (230–235)

19. St. Anterus (235–236)

20. St. Fabian (236–250)

21. St. Cornelius (251–253)

22. St. Lucius I (235–254)

23. St. Stephen I (254–257)

24. St. Sixtus II (257–258)

25. St. Dionysius (259–268)

26. St. Felix I (269–274)

27. St. Eutychian (275–283)

28. St. Caius (283–296)

29. St. Marcellinus (296–304)

30. St. Marcellus I (304–309)

31. St. Eusevius (309–311)

32. St. Melchiades (311–314)

33. St. Sylvester I (314–335)

34. St. Marcus (336)

35. St. Julius I (337–352)

36. Liberius (352–366)

37. St. Damasus I (366–384)

38. St. Siricius (384–399)

39. St. Anastasius I (399–401)

40. St. Innocent I (401–417)

41. St. Zosimus (417–418)

42. St. Boniface I (418–422)

43. St. Celestine I (422–432)

44. St. Sixtus III (432–440)

45. St. Leo (440–461)

46. St. Hilarius (461–468)

47. St. Simplicius (468–483)

48. St. Felix II (483–492)

49. St. Gelasius I (492–496)

50. Anastasius II (496–498)

51. St. Symmachus (498–514)

52. St. Hormisdas (514–523)

53. St. John I (523–526)

54. St. Felix III (526–530)

55. Boniface II (530–532)

56. John II (533–535)

57. St. Agapitus I (535–536)

58. St. Silverius (536–537)

59. Vigilius (537–555)

60. Pelagius I (556–561)

61. John III (561–574)

62. Benedict I (575–579)

63. Pelagius II (579–590)

64. St. Gregory I (590–604)

65. Sabinianus (604–606)

66. Boniface III (607)

67. St. Boniface IV (608–615)

68. St. Deusdedit (615–618)

69. St. Boniface V (619–625)

70. Honorius I (625–638)

71. Severinus (638–640)

72. John IV (640–642)

73. Theodore I (642–649)

74. St. Martin I (649–655)

75. St. Eugene I (655–657)

76. St. Vitalian (657–672)

77. Adeodatus (672–676)

78. Donus (676–678)

79. St. Agatho (678–681)

80. St. Leo II (682–683)

81. St. Benedict II (684–685)

82. John V (685–686)

83. Conon (686–687)

84. St. Sergius I (687–701)

85. John VI (701–705)

86. John VII (705–707)

87. Sisinnius (708)

88. Constantine (708–715)

89. St. Gregory II (715–731)

90. St. Gregory III (731–741)

91. St. Zacharias (741–752)

92. Stephen II (752–757)

93. St. Paul I (757–767)

94. Stephen III (768–772)

95. Adrian I (772–795)

96. St. Leo III (795–816)

97. Stephen IV (816–817)

98. St. Paschal I (817–824)

99. Eugene II (824–827)

100. Valentine (827)

101. Gregory IV (827–844)

102. Sergius II (844–847)

103. Leo IV (847–855)

104. Benedict III (855–858)

105. St. Nicholas I (858–867)

106. Adrian (867–872)

107. John VIII (872–882)

108. Marinus I (882–884)

109. St. Adrian III (884–885)

110. Stephen V (885–891)

111. Formosus (891–896)

112. Boniface VI (896)

113. Stephen VI (896–897)

114. Romanus (897)

115. Theodore II (897)

116. John IX (898–900)

117. Benedict IV (900–903)

118. Leo V (903)

119. Sergius (904–911)

120. Anastasius III (911–913)

121. Lando (913–914)

122. John X (914–928)

123. Leo VI (928)

124. Stephen VII (928–931)

125. John XI (931–936)

126. Leo VII (936–939)

127. Stephen VIII (939–942)

128. Marinus II (942–946)

129. Agaptus II (946–955)

130. John XII (955–964)

131. Leo VIII (964–965)

132. Benedict V (965)

133. John XIII (965–972)

134. Benedict VI (973–974)

135. Benedict VII (974–983)

136. John XIV (983–984)

137. John XV (985–996)

138. Gregory V (996–999)

139. Sylvester II (999–1003)

140. John XVII (1003)

141. John XVIII (1003–1009)

142. Sergius IV (1009–1012)

143. Benedict VIII (1012–1024)

144. John XIX (1024–1032)

145. Benedict IX (1032–1045)

146. Sylvester III (1045)

147. Benedict IX (1045) (Second)

148. Gregory VI (1045–1046)

149. Clement (1046–1047)

150. Benedict IX (1047–1048) (Third)

151. Damasus II (1048)

152. St. Leo IX (1049–1054)

153. Victor II (1055–1057)

154. Stephen IX (1057–1058)

155. Nicholas II (1059–1061)

156. Alexander II (1061–1073)

157. St. Gregory VII (1073–1085)

158. Bl. Victor III (1087)

159. Bl. Urban II (1088–1089)

160. Paschal II (1099–1118)

161. Gelasius II (1118–1119)

162. Callistus II (1119–1124)

163. Honorius II (1124–1130)

164. Innocent II (1130–1143)

165. Celestine II (1143–1144)

166. Lucius (1144–1145)

167. Bl. Eugene III (1145–1153)

168. Anastatius IV (1153–1154)

169. Adrian IV (1154–1159)

170. Alexander III (1159–1181)

171. Lucius III (1181–1185)

172. Urban III (1185–1187)

173. Gregory VIII (1187)

174. Clement III (1187–1191)

175. Celestine III (1191–1198)

176. Innocent III (1198–1216)

177. Honorius III (1216–1227)

178. Gregory IX (1227–1241)

179. Celestine IV (1241)

180. Innocent IV (1243–1254)

181. Alexander IV (1254–1261)

182. Urban IV (1261–1264)

183. Clement IV (1265–1268)

184. Bl. Gregory X (1271–1276)

185. Bl. Innocent V (1276)

186. Adrian V (1276)

187. John XXI (1276–1277)

188. Nicholas III (1277–1280)

189. Martin IV (1281–1285)

190. Honorius IV (1285–1287)

191. Nicholas IV (1288–1291)

192. St. Celestine V (1294)

193. Boniface VIII (1294–1303)

194. Benedict XI (1303–1304)

195. Clement V (1305–1314)

196. John XXII (1316–1334)

197. Benedict XII (1334–1342)

198. Clement VI (1342–1352)

199. Innocent VI (1352–1362)

200. Bl. Urban V (1362–1370)

201. Gregory XI (1370–1378)

202. Urban VI (1378–1389)

203. Boniface IX (1398–1404)

204. Innocent VII (1404–1406)

205. Gregory XII (1406–1415) (Resigned during the Western Schism to permit a proper election of a successor.)

206. Martin V (1417–1431)

207. Eugene IV (1431–1447)

208. Nicholas V (1447–1455)

209. Callistus III (1455–1458)

210. Pius II (1458–1464)

211. Paul II (1464–1471)

212. Sixtus IV (1471–1484)

213. Innocent VIII (1484–1492)

214. Alexander VI (1492–1503)

215. Pius III (1503)

216. Julius II (1503–1513)

217. Leo X (1513–1521)

218. Adrian VI (1522–1523)

219. Clement VII (1523–1534)

220. Paul III (1534–1549)

221. Julius III (1550–1555)

222. Marcellus II (1555)

223. Paul IV (1555–1559)

224. Pius IV (1559–1565)

225. St. Pius V (1566–1572)

226. Gregory XIII (1572–1585)

227. Sixtus V (1585–1590)

228. Urban VII (1590)

229. Gregory XIV (1590–1591)

230. Innocent IX (1591)

231. Clement VIII (1592–1605)

232. Leo XI (1605)

233. Paul V (1605–1621)

234. Gregory XVI (1621–1623)

235. Urban VII (1623–1644)

236. Innocent X (1644–1655)

237. Alexander VII (1655–1667)

238. Clement IX (1667–1669)

239. Clement X (1670–1676)

240. Bl. Innocent XI (1676–1689)

241. Alexander VIII (1689–1691)

242. Innocent XII (1691–1700)

243. Clement XI (1700–1721)

244. Innocent XIII (1721–1724)

245. Benedict XIII (1724–1730)

246. Clement XII (1730–1740)

247. Benedict XIV (1740–1758)

248. Clement XIII (1758–1769)

249. Clement XIV (1769–1774)

250. Pius VI (1775–1799)

251. Pius VII (1800–1823)

252. Leo XII (1823–1829)

253. Pius VIII (1829–1830)

254. Gregory XVI (1831–1846)

255. Pius IX (1846–1878)

256. Leo XIII (1878–1903)

257. St Pius X (1903–1914)

258. Benedict XV (1914–1922)

259. Pius XI (1922–1939)

260. Pius XII (1939–1958)

261. St. John XXIII (1958–1963)

262. Paul VI (1963–1978)

263. John Paul I (1978)

264. St. John Paul II (1978–2005)

265. Benedict XVI (2005–2013)

266. Francis (2013–Present)

Glossary of Saints

Catholic saints are a diverse group of men and women from throughout the world and from all walks of life. Whether they were young, old, rich, poor, married, or lived a celibate life, they all strove to love God in the most perfect way possible. Some saints are more well known than others, but in this appendix we allow you to get to know some of their stories a little better.

St. Anne

Though the Bible never mentions her by name and what Catholics believe about her is largely steeped in legend and tradition rather than historical fact, St. Anne is the wife of St. Joachim, the mother of the Blessed Virgin Mary, and Jesus' biological grandmother.

The oldest mention of St. Anne by name is found in the Gospel of James, a document that is not part of the Canonical Scriptures and is not considered official doctrine of the Catholic Church. However, it is the first narrative that offers insight into the childless Jewish couple and their struggles to conceive. According to the author, after years of infertility and at the pinnacle of their despair, an angel appears to Anne and Joachim and tells them they will have a child one day.

Delighted with the news, Anne immediately dedicates her unborn daughter's life to God in the same way Hannah dedicates Samuel to God in 1 Kings. Anne has no way of knowing that the child she is to carry is an extraordinary individual tapped to be God's pristine vessel and the one who will carry His Son into the world.

Though St. Anne's name may be inaccurate and her biography largely unreliable, what is important to the Church is the fact that Mary did have parents—parents who loved her and nurtured her in the ways of their faith. Whoever they were, they were people who led by example and taught their daughter to respond positively to God when He calls. Anne and Joachim instilled a sense of courage and faith in Mary, and their example serves as a model for parents everywhere. Her feast day is July 26, along with her husband, St. Joachim.

St. Mary Magdalene

She is one of the most important women in the New Testament (after Mary, the mother of Jesus), yet little is known or understood about this enigmatic figure who traveled with Jesus, was present at the crucifixion, and became the first witness to the resurrected Christ.

What is known about the Magdalene is that Jesus chased seven demons from her, but contrary to popular myth, there is no biblical evidence that she was a prostitute or adulteress. This rumor came about when some Church leaders tried to ease confusion caused by the presence of so many "Mary"s in the New Testament and thereby saddled Mary Magdalene with her unfortunate reputation. She is clearly someone of historical importance as she is mentioned by name 12 times in the Gospels (more than any of the apostles). And despite the speculation that she may have been more than a mere follower of Jesus, the Church maintains that she was a prominent leader for women in the Christian movement, much as St. Peter was for men. Her feast day is July 22.

St. Nicholas (AD 270–343)

Known as the model for a popular figure of Christmas, St. Nicholas of Myra was born at Patara in Lycia (Asia Minor) on March 15, 270. He became the bishop of Myra and was renowned for his piety, zeal, generosity, and many miracles.

He was the child of pious parents who left him well off when they died. As a young man, he pledged to use his inheritance to help others and he dedicated his life to works of charity. Stories abound about Nicholas's generosity, and one of the most famous concerns a citizen of Patara who had no money to provide dowries for his three daughters.

Just as the man was about to send the girls into the streets to become prostitutes, Nicholas learned of his plight and under the cover of darkness threw a bag of gold into the open window of the man's house. (Other versions of the legend say the gold landed in a stocking that was hanging by the fireplace.) He did this two more times as each of the daughters reached marrying age. On the last event, the man realized who was financing his daughters' futures and he was overcome with gratitude for the holy man.

In 325, Nicholas appeared at the first Council of Nicaea (at the behest of Emperor Constantine) and was one of the bishops chosen to sign the Nicene Creed. (One story recounts that Nicholas was so angry at Arius, who was the leader of those who did not believe Jesus was God, that he got up during the debates, walked across the room, and punched Arius in the face!) He died on December 6, 343, and his relics are enshrined at the Basilica of St. Nicholas in Bari, Italy. His feast is December 6 and he is the patron saint of children, sailors, bakers, and pawnbrokers.

St. Agnes (d. 304)

St. Agnes was a Roman teenager who suffered martyrdom for her devotion to Christ. As a young girl she became enamored with her religion and promised never to lose her purity and never to worship pagan gods.

Agnes was a beautiful girl who drew the attention of many potential suitors, including the governor's son, but she turned them all away and insisted that Jesus was the only spouse she could ever want. When the governor's son realized that Agnes was a Christian, he turned her in to his father. The governor tried everything he could think of to encourage her to turn from her religious ways. He promised her many gifts if she would recant her beliefs, but she refused. He then shackled her in chains and dragged her through the streets, to no avail. He forced her to go to a place of sin, but an angel protected her from harm. Finally, with no other recourse and being unwilling to free her, the governor sentenced her to death.

Agnes was not upset with his edict. In fact, she was delighted at the idea that she would soon see her true bridegroom, Jesus Christ. The locals all thought it was a shame that such a beautiful girl would come to such a fate, and they begged her to save herself even if it meant casting Christ aside. Still, she would not give in. She willingly accepted death by beheading in AD 304. Her feast day is January 21.

St. Lucy (d. 304)

Although little is known about this courageous young woman who became a martyr in the early fourth century, the legend of her bravery spread quickly. Within 200 years after her death, the whole Church recognized her fearlessness and dedication to the faith.

The legend associated with St. Lucy is that at a very young age, she promised her life in service to God. Her mother, who suffered from chronic illness, arranged a marriage for her daughter with a pagan, but Lucy refused the proposal.

She did offer to pray for her mother in hopes that God would hear her intentions and grant her mother a speedy recovery. Lucy went to the tomb of St. Agatha, where she prayed for her mother. While she was there she had a vision of the saint, who told Lucy that her mother would indeed recover, but that she herself would die a martyr. Lucy went home the next day, and her mother was miraculously healed.

Her mother was so thankful that she was finally willing to listen to her daughter's plans for a religious vocation, but unfortunately the pagan she was to marry didn't share their elation. He turned her in to the governor as a known Christian. The governor attempted to force Lucy into prostitution, but when the guards came to take her away, they discovered that her body was too heavy to move. (Legend also says that Lucy's eyes were gouged out as part of the torture she endured, leading to her patronage of those suffering from diseases of the eye, but no one knows for sure.)

Ultimately Lucy was killed for her beliefs, and no matter what the truth is behind her story, she was a courageous Christian who was willing to die for her faith and is considered a role model for our lives. Her feast day is December 13.

St. Cyril (827–869) and St. Methodius (826–885)

Saints Cyril and Methodius were ninth-century Byzantine brothers born in Macedonia. They lost their father when Cyril was only 14, and the two fell under the protection of one of the chief ministers of the Byzantine Empire named Theoktistos. The two received an education, and not long after completing their studies, both brothers were ordained priests.

Together, Cyril and Methodius were sent as missionaries to various regions in Eastern Europe, including Moravia, Bohemia, Poland, Russia, and what is now the Czech Republic. They learned the local Slavonic languages and developed an alphabet that was eventually named after St. Cyril—and the Cyrillic alphabet is still in use today for a number of Slavonic and Eastern languages. They also convinced Church leaders to allow the liturgy to be celebrated in the local Slavonic languages, and translated the Bible into these languages.

Saints Cyril and Methodius are considered two of the greatest missionaries in the history of Christianity. Known as the "apostles of the Slavs," they continue to be venerated throughout the Orthodox Church as men who were "equal to the apostles." In 1880, Pope Leo X approved their feast for use in the Roman Catholic Church, and in 1990, Pope John Paul II further validated the brothers by naming them co-patron saints of Europe alongside St. Benedict of Nursia. Their feast day is February 14.

St. Thomas Aquinas (c. 1225–1274)

He is the patron saint of universities and of students and one of the most influential writers in the Church. St. Thomas Aquinas was the son of a count who was placed under the care of the Benedictines of Monte Cassino when he was only 5 years old.

When Thomas felt the call to religion, nothing and nobody was going to stand in his way, including his family. He joined the Dominicans of Naples in 1243 and never looked back. He studied in Cologne and was a pupil of St. Albert the Great. He was a brilliant student who became a brilliant teacher, a prolific author, and a decorated scholar. He is the preeminent theologian in the Catholic Church and championed a rebirth of philosophical and theological study known as Scholasticism.

Despite his academic accolades, Thomas was not a fan of adulation. He downplayed his friendship with King Louis IX and Urban IV. When Clement IV offered to appoint him as the archbishop of Naples, he declined the offer. Though he wrote 20 volumes of theology, he left his master-piece, the *Summa Theologica* unfinished when he died on his way to the Second Council of Lyons. Near the end of his life, he had a vision after which he considered all his theological writings to be nothing more than straw in the wind compared to the glory of God that he had seen. St. Thomas was canonized in 1323 and named a Doctor of the Church by Pope Pius V. His feast day is January 28.

St. Joan of Arc (1412–1431)

Born on January 6, 1412, to pious peasant parents, Joan of Arc was special right from the very start. As a young child, she heard the voices of St. Michael, St. Catherine, and St. Margaret. At first, the messages whispered to the girl were general and personal in nature. However, in 1428, the trio told the teen to approach the king of France and help him reclaim his kingdom from the English.

Although she was not yet an adult, the 17-year-old was given a small army, which she led effectively in the siege of Orleans in 1429. She led several other campaigns, including one that resulted in King Charles VII being able to enter Rheims and to be crowned with his star soldier at his side.

Joan hoped to return to her family after her success, but the king wanted her to continue her military service. She agreed, but in May of 1430, the Burgundians captured Joan while she was attempting to relieve Compiègne. When King Charles and the French did nothing to save her, she was sold to the English and was imprisoned for several months. She was eventually accorded a trial, presided over by Peter Cauchon, the bishop of Beauvais. He hoped that if he helped con-vict the girl, the English would promote him to archbishop.

The tribunal did not end well for Joan. Being young and inexperienced worked against her, and she made several damaging statements on the stand. When she refused to retract her statement that the saints had told her to reclaim France for its king, she was labeled a heretic, sorceress, and adulteress and was sentenced to death by being burned at the stake. She was only 19 years old. Thirty years later, she was officially exonerated of any wrongdoing, and in 1920, the Church canonized the young girl who bravely went into battle in service of the Lord. Her feast day is May 30.

St. Ignatius Loyola (1491–1556)

St. Ignatius Loyola was born on October 23, 1491, to a local Basque family in Loyola, Spain. He was the youngest of 13 children, and as a child he became a page before enlisting in the Spanish army to fight the French. In 1521, Ignatius was wounded in battle, bringing his career as a soldier to an unceremonious end.

During his recovery period, Ignatius began reading about Christ and the lives of the saints. Inspired by their stories, he thought he could do what they did. After all, the world was a battlefield, and what better way for a military man to live out his days than as a soldier for Christ?

Ignatius studied at the University of Paris, where he met others who wanted to serve in the Christ brigade alongside him. Together they called themselves the Companions of Jesus, but they were quickly nicknamed the "Jesuits." The community later became known as the Society of Jesus. Over the years, 38 members of the Society have been beatified and 38 have been canonized Catholic saints. Today, the Jesuits remain one of the most well-known religious orders in the world. They are respected for their humility, their dedication to the poor, and their commitment to educating people throughout the world.

Ignatius also became one of the greatest Christian teachers of spirituality. He promoted a way of praying with Scripture using the imagination and developed a 30-day retreat to guide those who wanted to deepen their relationship with God. The Spiritual Exercises of St. Ignatius have since been adapted into a wide variety of retreats, meditations, and daily spiritual practices.

St. Ignatius died on July 31, 1556, at the age of 65 in Rome. His feast day is July 31 and he is the patron saint of Catholic soldiers.

St. Francis Xavier (1506–1552)

Considered the greatest missionary since St. Paul, St. Francis Xavier was born on his family's estate near Pamplona, Spain, on April 7, 1506. As a student at the University of Paris, he was the quintessential overachiever who won all of the big prizes. He was a great athlete, a champion runner, a class leader, and a serious scholar.

It was at the university that he met St. Ignatius Loyola, who became Francis's lifelong friend and mentor. Ignatius asked Francis what good it would do him to win every award at school if he lost his very soul in the process. Francis considered this query and then opted to become a missionary in order to win the world over for the Lord.

In 1534, Francis and seven others (including Ignatius) founded the Society of Jesus in Montmartre. After Paris, he followed Ignatius to Venice where he was ordained a priest in 1537. A stint in Rome occurred a year later and in 1540, the Vatican recognized the Society of Jesus as an order.

Francis spent his entire life traveling the world. Some of the areas in which he ministered include India, New Guinea, Japan, the Philippines, and Mozambique. He lived among the natives and was credited for the fact that some of these regions were committed to Christianity for centuries.

Francis endured countless struggles in his journeys. There were language barriers (contrary to the rumor that he was proficient in a number of foreign tongues), a lack of monetary resources, plenty of resistance, and uncooperative officials in the areas he served. Nevertheless, Francis Xavier was successful in his mission, personally baptizing tens of thousands of people during his travels.

In 1552, Francis headed for China. He landed on the island of Sancian with the last leg of his journey in sight, but he died before he could reach his final destination. The zeal he had for his work became the hallmark of his legacy and Pope Gregory XV canonized him in 1622. He was later named the patron saint of all foreign missions. His feast day is December 3.

St. Vincent de Paul (c. 1580–1660)

He is the patron saint of charitable societies, and during his lifetime he performed more acts of charity than can be chronicled here.

St. Vincent de Paul was born into a poor family in the village of Pouy in Gascony, France, around 1580. He was educated by the Franciscan Fathers and enjoyed his schooling so much that within four years, he was chosen by a local gentleman to be the private instructor for his children. This arrangement enabled Vincent to continue his own studies and earn money so he was no longer a burden to his parents. He ultimately studied theology at the University of Toulouse, and was ordained a priest in 1600.

A few years later, Vincent was en route to Narbonne from Marseilles when African pirates captured his ship. He was taken as a slave to Tunis and remained there for two years until he was able to escape. He eventually returned to France and his work as a private tutor, but in 1617 he began to preach about missionary work, and in 1625 he started laying the foundations for his future Congregation of the Mission.

"Give" became Vincent's byword. He earned money and gave it all away. He fed the children who clung to him. He cared for the elderly. He welcomed all classes with open arms. Although those he served lauded him, he always remained humble about his work and stayed connected to God. He died in Paris at the age of 80. His feast day is September 27.

St. Martin de Porres (1579–1639)

Born in Lima, Peru, on December 9, 1579, St. Martin de Porres was the son of a Spanish knight and a free black woman from Panama. At the age of 15 he joined the Dominican friary, and over the years he served as a barber, an agricultural worker, an almoner, and a health care worker.

Initially, his multi-ethnicity was a problem for Martin. He suffered from many insults, some of which came from his own fellow friars. But eventually, his kindness and generosity won everyone over and people turned to him for prayers and comfort when they were worried, sick, or hungry. Martin cared for everyone who came to him, and he went so far as to turn private homes into hospitals and orphanages while begging in the streets for the supplies he needed to operate his facilities.

He had a burning desire to go on a foreign mission in hopes that he would become a martyr, but that was not meant to be. Instead, he used his body as a martyr, subjecting himself to numerous penances and sacrifices. Martin was a close friend of St. Rose of Lima. He died on November 3, 1639, and was canonized in 1962. His feast day is November 3.

St. Rose of Lima (1586–1617)

Though she was born Isabel Flores y de Oliva on April 20, 1586, in the Viceroyalty of Peru, she was such a beautiful baby girl that she was called "Rose" right from the very start.

As she grew, Rose became even lovelier. Convinced that her daughter was the most beautiful girl in the world, Rose's mother put a crown of flowers on her head in order to show her off to her friends. Rose hated the attention, and she didn't want to be admired for something as superficial as her looks. In an effort to give herself the "ugly treatment," Rose chopped off her locks and irritated her face with pepper so that it would blister.

Rose loved her parents and for the most part obeyed them, but they didn't see eye to eye where her future was concerned. Her mother and father longed for her to marry, but Rose was not interested in being a bride to anyone but Christ. Her family didn't understand, and they were even more concerned about her habit of fasting and abstaining from meat. When they heard that she had taken a personal vow of virginity, they knew there was no point in trying to get their daughter to come around. They gave her private quarters in the family home and allowed her to work in the community, caring for the sick and the hungry, giving them lodging in her quarters, and selling her flowers and handicrafts as a way to help support the family.

Though Rose had a religious calling, her father was not in favor of her entering the convent. She settled for joining the Third Order of St. Dominic, wearing the habit of the order and donning a headpiece which contained a heavy metallic crown complete with silver protrusions to mimic the crown of thorns that Jesus wore during His execution. She vacillated between periods of ecstasy and despair for 11 years before her death on August 24, 1617. It is said that Rose predicted the date of her death, and her memorial was attended by all of the public officials from the area. She was canonized in 1671 and became the first Catholic saint of the Americas. Her feast day is celebrated on August 23.

St. John Baptist de la Salle (1651–1719)

Born on April 30, 1651, in Rheims, France, John Baptist de la Salle was the oldest of 10 children who studied in Paris and became known for his work with the poor.

After his ordination in 1678, de la Salle became very involved with education. It was almost an accident that it happened in the first place. He lived at a time when there was a great divide between the haves and the have-nots, and he knew that education was the only way to bridge that gap and give the poor a chance to climb out of their circumstances. He founded a new religious order, the Institute of the Brothers of the Christian Schools, and established three teachers colleges in France in order to train quality educators for the schools he would found.

De la Salle was a champion of formal classroom education as opposed to private tutoring. He also believed in teaching in the local vernacular rather than the more customary Latin and including secular subjects in addition to religious training. He encouraged parents to be involved in their children's education, and proposed that a quality education should be available to all rather than something only enjoyed by the privileged. This did not make him popular with those who believed in fee-based education.

De la Salle was a pioneer in educational training and a founder of modern pedagogy. He died on April 7, 1719, and was canonized on May 24, 1900. His feast day is April 7 and he is considered the patron saint of teachers.

St. Kateri Tekakwitha (1656–1680)

Born near what is now the town of Auriesville, New York, St. Kateri Tekakwitha is truly an American saint. She was the daughter of a Mohawk warrior and lost her mother to smallpox when she was 4 years old. The disease affected Kateri as well, disfiguring her face, and with her father away much of the time, her extended family members adopted her after her mother died.

When Kateri was a teenager, Christian missionaries arrived and shared the gospel message. Kateri had never heard anything like it. She was called to conversion and was baptized at the age of 20, to the chagrin of her tribe. She suffered greatly for her faith, but never turned her back on it.

Feeling like an outcast, she left the area and moved to what is now Canada where she lived in a colony for Christian Indians. She dedicated her life to prayer, penitential acts, and caring for those who were elderly and sick. She remained a virgin all her life and inspired those around her. The Christian missionaries called her the "Lily of the Mohawks" and marveled at her dedication to the Blessed Sacrament. Though she died in 1680, devotion to her greatly enhanced the number of Native American ministries in Catholic churches throughout North America. She was canonized in 2012 and her feast day is July 14. She is known (along with St. Francis of Assisi) as the patron saint of ecology.

St. John Bosco (1815–1888)

The patron saint of the Catholic Youth Organization was born Giovanni Melchior Bosco on August 16, 1815, in Piedmont, Italy. John Bosco was the third son of a poor couple who lived in a small cabin at a time of dire circumstances and great famine in the region. By the time he was 2 years old, his father had died, leaving his mother to care for three growing boys on her own.

Blessed with a ready wit, a good memory, and a thirst for knowledge, Bosco experienced a number of dreams as a child, in which he understood that he was to lead others through kindness and gentleness rather than through strength and might. He also felt called to the religious life, but this seemed impossible considering that he had no formal education and the seminary was primarily geared toward men of means or privilege.

Bosco left home at the age of 12 and lived in the streets, where he begged for food and did odd jobs to get by. A local priest, who recognized the boy's tenacity, took him in and offered to educate him. He joined the seminary in 1835 and was ordained a priest six years later.

Bosco took to the religious life naturally. In addition to visiting the imprisoned, feeding the hungry, and so on, he pledged to pay forward the kindness once shown to him as a young man by reaching out to the urchins he met and steering them away from a life of crime and poverty. He opened an oratory, instructing children in the street. Within a year, he had 400 students and was in need of a facility to hold everyone. It became the first Salesian home, named for St. Francis de Sales.

When he procured a building, Bosco realized that, in addition to classes, he could offer engaging activities for these children as well. Of course, not everyone was enthusiastic about his mission, but it prevailed despite the naysayers. By the time he died on January 31, 1888, his work had grown to include 250 Salesian homes with 130,000 students. More than 6,000 priests emerged from the institutions and approximately 1,200 continued the Salesian Society's work. He was canonized in 1934 and his feast day is January 31.

St. Dominic Savio (1842–1857)

Born on April 2, 1842, near Piedmont, Italy, Dominic Savio was a typical boy with an atypical love of God. When he was 4 years old, he wandered away from his mother's eye. When she went looking for him, she found her son tucked into a corner with his head bowed, praying every prayer he knew by heart. He became an altar boy at the age of 5, received his first communion at the age of 7 (it was customary at that time to wait until one was 12), and seemed committed to go to confession often; to sanctify all Sundays and feast days in a special way; to be friends with Jesus, Mary, and Joseph; and to die rather than commit an act of sin.

When he turned 12, Dominic became a pupil of St. John Bosco and attended one of his Salesian oratories. He was an active student who took his lessons very seriously. He was quick to question points that required extra clarification, and he chose his friends very carefully. When some boys brought an indecent magazine to school, he wasted no time in chastising them. He told the offenders that God did not give them eyes to look upon such things and that if they couldn't see the wrong in what they were doing, it was even worse because they were clearly used to it.

When another group of boys got into a fight, Dominic stood between them, held out a crucifix, and reminded them that Jesus died forgiving everyone and that it was an insult to Him to not forgive their enemies. He then told them that if they wanted to beat someone up, to start with him. The fight quickly ended and the other boys promised to go to confession.

One day when he was 15, Dominic began to feel ill. He was sent home to recuperate, but his condition worsened. (Evidence suggests he had an undiagnosed case of pleurisy.) He received the sacraments and told everyone he did not fear death, but was overjoyed at the prospect of going to Heaven. At one point he tried to sit up, and he told his father he could see wonderful things. He died shortly thereafter on March 9, 1857.

After his canonization on June 12, 1954, Dominic became known as the patron saint of the falsely accused. This is based on a story in which one of his teachers charged him with some nefarious deed in class. Dominic took the public punishment silently, even though he knew he was innocent, and he refused to implicate the real culprits. When the truth came out, Dominic was asked why he didn't come clean about the incident. He told his teacher he was imitating Christ, who remained silent during his trial and execution. His feast day is March 9.

St. Mary MacKillop (1842–1909)

Born in Fitzroy, Victoria, Australia, on January 15, 1842, Mary MacKillop was the oldest of eight children. She was educated at home by her father as well as in private schools, but in 1851, Alexander MacKillop left his family (and his mortgaged farm) behind to travel to Scotland. He was gone for 17 months.

Alexander was a loving man, but not a very successful one. He often kept the family together thanks in part to the meager wages his children brought home. As a result, Mary started to work at the age of 14, first as a clerk and then later as a teacher. She also took a job as a governess at her aunt and uncle's house. She had a servant's heart right from the beginning and knew that she wanted to work with the poor whenever she could. While at her relatives' home, she met a local priest who a few years later asked her and her sisters to help him establish a school in the area.

The girls agreed and began to educate 50 children. It was at this time that MacKillop dedicated her life to God and began wearing black. In 1867, she became the first sister and mother superior of a new religious congregation, the Sisters of St. Joseph of the Sacred Heart, and moved into the convent at Adelaide. It was the first religious order founded by an Australian, and it focused on poverty and a reliance on divine providence for one's needs. The sisters adopted a plain brown habit and became known as the "Brown Joeys."

MacKillop's order grew and was responsible for the establishment of several schools and welfare institutions in the area in an effort to reach out to the rural poor. Her career was not without its struggles. When she uncovered evidence of a scandal, it was MacKillop who was banished rather than the priest at the center of the charges. (She was later exonerated.)

After this ordeal, Mary rallied to continue her work and became very successful at helping the order grow. During the later years of her life, she suffered from numerous health problems, including rheumatism and the effects of a stroke. She died on August 8, 1909 and was canonized on October 17, 2010. She was the first Catholic saint from Australia. Her feast day is August 8.

St. André Bessette (1845–1937)

When Alfred Bessette showed up on the doorstep of the Holy Cross brothers in 1870 with nothing more than a note from his pastor saying, "I am sending you a saint," they thought he was kidding. They could not imagine what the 25-year-old had to offer their order. He was physically frail and illiterate and had struggled to hold down a job over the years.

Still, he seemed sincere enough. He was desperate to find a place to fit in and he was a prayerful person devoted to God as well as to St. Joseph, and he had a willingness to serve. However, it wasn't long before the brothers realized he was just too weak to be of much use. At one point they actually asked "Brother André" to leave, but he didn't want to go. Bessette appealed to a visiting bishop who assured him that he would remain and take his vows.

After making his vows, he was sent to Notre Dame College in Montreal, Canada, where he was put in charge of answering the door, greeting guests, and delivering the mail. In 1904, he approached the bishop about building a chapel to St. Joseph on a mountainside near the college, but the bishop refused to go into debt on the venture. Brother André decided to build it anyway, using about $200 in nickels and dimes he had collected over the years.

He couldn't build much of a chapel with that, but that didn't stop Brother André. He constructed a small wooden shelter that he continued adding to as he collected more money. Eventually this modest chapel grew to become a place where pilgrims came to experience healing and renewal.

Brother André was in the process of building a basilica on the site, but the Great Depression stopped its construction, and his health was failing. He told the workers to put a statue of St. Joseph in the unfinished building and was carried to see the statue in its new home before his death on January 6, 1937. He was canonized on October 17, 2010, and his feast day is January 6 in the United States and January 7 in Canada.

St. Christopher Magallanes (1869–1927)

Born on July 30, 1869, to a farming family in Totatiche, Jalisco, Mexico, Magallanes worked as a shepherd as a young man before entering the seminary at the age of 19.

After his ordination at the age of 30, he spent time as a parish priest and established a number of schools, a newspaper, and vocational centers such as carpentry shops and created an electric plant to power the mills of the area. He was also very passionate about evangelizing to indigenous people of the region and helping them shore up their relations with the community through agriculture cooperatives.

When the local government closed all the seminaries in the area, Magallanes rallied the seminarians and began his own. It was suppressed. He began another but it, too, was suppressed. Another followed, and another, but they were all closed. When he was out of options, the seminarians held their classes in private homes.

Magallanes made no secret that he was opposed to armed rebellion and he was incorrectly charged with backing the Cristero guerrilla revolt. When he was headed to Mass one day at a local homestead, he was taken into custody and locked in prison. While incarcerated, he gave the last of his personal effects to the two men who would ultimately be responsible for his death. He even went so far as to forgive them for their actions ahead of time. Magallanes never faced trial for the false accuasation and instead was martyred along with St. Agustín Caloca on May 25, 1927. He was canonized on May 21, 2000, and his feast day is the May 25.

St. Josephine Bakhita (1869–1947)

Born in the Sudan in 1869, the "African flower" knew all too well the horrors associated with kidnapping and slavery, but thanks to God's grace, she overcame her early struggles, joined the Daughters of Charity, and became known as Mother Moretta ("our Black Mother").

Sold in the markets of El Obeid and Khartoum, Josephine was given the name Bakhita (meaning "fortunate") by her captors. She suffered all of the pain and humiliation one associates with slavery until an Italian consul, Callisto Legnani, purchased her. In his household, she was treated with kindness and love even though she missed her family and her old life in the Sudan.

When Legnani was forced to leave Africa for Genoa, Italy, he took the young woman with him and left her in the care of his friend Augusto Michieli and his wife, who were expecting a child. When their daughter was born, Bakhita became her caregiver and friend. Business interests forced Michieli and his wife to move to Suakin on the Red Sea and on the advice of their family attorney, the couple left Bakhita and their daughter with the Canossian Daughters of Charity in Venice.

It was here that Bakhita learned about God and became a Catholic. She was given her new name of Josephine on January 9, 1890, and when her employer returned from Africa to reclaim her daughter and servant, Bakhita opted to stay with the sisters rather than return to her life as a domestic.

On December 8, 1896, Bakhita became a member of the Canossian Sisters. She spent the next 50 years living in their community where she was engaged in various service works, including cooking, sewing, embroidery, and answering the door. Her gentleness and simplicity won the hearts of everyone who came in contact with her and the sisters in her community considered her an exquisite witness to the faith.

As the years wore on, she experienced long bouts of sickness, but despite her ailments she continued to be a servant of God. Mother Bakhita died on February 8, 1947. Word of her sanctity spread and she was canonized on October 1, 2000. Her feast day is February 8.

Bl. Luigi Beltrame Quattrocchi (1880–1951) and Bl. Maria Corsini Beltrame Quattrocchi (1884–1965)

Saint stories are filled with pious religious men and women who cast away their worldly goods in an effort to live good and holy lives. This makes the story of the Quattrocchis extremely unique. In 2001, they became the first married laypeople to be beatified together.

In his homily at the beatification ceremony, then Pope John Paul II described the Quattrocchis as models of the domestic church. They were not only dedicated to the Sacrament of Holy Matrimony and raising their children in the faith, but they did not hesitate to be examples of Christ in their daily lives.

Luigi was an established attorney who met Maria in her family home and was instantly smitten. The couple was married on November 25, 1905, in the Basilica of Saint Mary Major in Rome. While Luigi concentrated on his successful law career, Maria dedicated her life to the home, her marriage, her writing, and a multitude of charitable works in addition to serving as a professor of education.

The couple had four children, three of whom were born easily; but Maria's final pregnancy was a difficult one and her doctor recommended terminating the pregnancy out of concern for Maria's health and safety. The couple refused, even though there was only a 5 percent chance of survival from her condition at the time. The two cast their lots with Providence and in the end both daughter and mother were safe.

Not only did the Quattrocchis make Christ the center of their personal lives, but they also reflected His generosity toward others. Both were very active during World War II. They donated food to the hungry, opened their home to refugees, and volunteered with the Red Cross.

They knew the ups and downs of life and marriage, but believed they could grow closer to Christ as a couple than they would separately. Luigi died in November 1951 and 14 years later Maria joined him in Heaven. Their feast day is November 25, their wedding anniversary, and their remains are interred at the Shrine of Divine Love in Rome.

St. Maria Goretti (1890–1902)

This patron saint of youth, young women, purity, and victims of rape was born in Ancona, Italy, on October 16, 1890. Maria Goretti was the daughter of a farmer who died of malaria when she was a little girl, leaving her mother to feed and care for the children of their household.

It wasn't an easy life. Maria often had to help with the chores and the operation of the farm, but she did so without complaint. She was known as an obedient, happy girl with a good heart and devotion to her mother.

However, when she was 11 years old, Maria experienced a horror that no child should ever face. An 18-year-old neighbor boy approached her and tried to rape her, but Maria told him that she would rather die than submit to his advances. He took her statement to heart and stabbed her repeatedly. She was taken to the hospital and forgave her attacker before her death, but he was unrepentant of his crime.

The young man was sentenced to 30 years in prison and while in jail, he dreamed that he was in a garden when Maria approached him and handed him some flowers. He woke up transformed. He repented the act he committed against Maria and vowed to live a reformed life. He was released from prison after 27 years and went immediately to Maria's mother to beg forgiveness for killing her daughter. She decided that if her daughter could forgive him, so could she.

Maria Goretti is considered a Catholic martyr for dying while fending off her attacker. In 1950, Pope Pius XII canonized her. Her feast day is July 6.

Bl. Pier Giorgio Frassati (1901–1925)

Pier Giorgio Frassati was a pious child who was committed to prayerful meditation and the community he lived in, as indicated by his role as a social activist and charitable servant.

Born on April 6, 1901, into a wealthy family in Turin, Italy, Frassati was far from a spoiled rich boy. His father went to great extremes to not overindulge his children with riches. It really didn't matter as Frassati was more likely to donate his money to the needy rather than spend it on himself.

As a young man, he became involved with a number of Catholic organizations, and he was not one to sit on the sidelines. No matter what group he joined, he was an active participant and gave his all to the group's mission. He was also a Third Order Dominican. He believed that charity alone was not enough to right the ills of the world and that social reform was needed. He actively participated in rallies with other young people for the causes that mattered to him, particularly fighting fascism. When his activism resulted in arrest, Frassati refused special treatment, despite his family's position in the community. He preferred to take his place alongside the other demonstrators and served his time like everyone else.

When Frassati died of polio on July 4, 1925, his family expected the Turin elite and regional political figures to pay their respects, in addition to family members and close personal friends. What they were not prepared for was the outpouring of support they received from thousands of mourners who lined the city streets as the funeral cortège passed. It did not take long for the community of Turin to campaign to the archbishop for a cause for canonization to be opened in honor of this young man who meant so much to so many. The cause for his canonization was opened in 1932 and he was beatified on May 20, 1990 by then Pope John Paul II. His feast day is July 4.

St. Faustina Kowalska (1905–1938)

Helena Kowalska was born on August 25, 1905, in Poland. She was the third of her parents' 10 children, and at the age of 19 she entered the Congregation of the Sisters of Our Lady of Mercy, a religious order whose ministry concentrated on the care and education of troubled women.

After receiving the habit of religion and taking the name Sister Faustina of the Blessed Sacrament, she received a message from Christ in which she was asked to become an ambassador for God's mercy and to live a life of sacrifice and service. Christ also told her to create the Divine Mercy image and that a celebration of God's mercy should be held on the first Sunday after Easter.

Unsure as to what was happening, and unable to paint, she told her confessor about this experience, and naturally he thought she was mentally disturbed. A doctor was called in to perform some tests and when Faustina was declared of sound mind, her priest began to believe that something extraordinary might be happening to her and he began preaching on Divine Mercy, per Jesus' request. The priest ordered that an artist create the image Jesus spoke about and he encouraged Faustina to keep a diary of her conversations with Jesus and the revelations he gave her.

Faustina spent her days offering up her sufferings to the Lord, praying for others, and performing charitable works of mercy. She was cheerful and humble and took the work Jesus gave her very seriously.

In 1935, she wrote the Chaplet of Divine Mercy, a series of prayers roughly a third the length of the rosary but prayed using the same set of beads. She had a vision that Christ wanted her to establish a new religious order devoted to Divine Mercy. There was resistance to this idea from her superiors, but Jesus insisted and she obeyed the Lord.

The following year, Faustina fell ill with tuberculosis. She spent the last two years of her life in Krakow, Poland, praying her chaplet, suffering in the service of God, and keeping her diary. By this time the feast of Divine Mercy was gathering momentum, and one of her last contributions was to pen the instructions for the Novena of Divine Mercy, which Jesus gave her on Good Friday, 1937. Faustina died on October 5, 1938, and was buried two days later. Her remains are located at the Basilica of Divine Mercy in Kraków, Poland. Pope St. John Paul II had a great attachment to St. Faustina and the Divine Mercy devotion and in the year 2000 officially designated the Sunday after Easter as Divine Mercy Sunday. Her feast day is October 5.

Index

Q–R

CHECK OUT THESE BEST-SELLERS

More than 450 titles available at booksellers and online retailers everywhere!

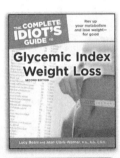

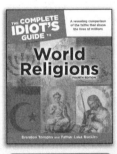

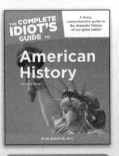
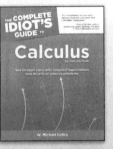

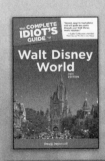